UNSETTLED

UNSETTLED

LORD SELKIRK'S SCOTTISH COLONISTS
AND THE BATTLE
FOR CANADA'S WEST, 1813-1816

ROBERT LOWER

LIBRARY AND ARCHIVES CANADA CATALOGUING
IN PUBLICATION

Title: Unsettled : Lord Selkirk's Scottish colonists and
the battle for Canada's west, 1813-1816 / Robert Lower.

Other titles: Lord Selkirk's Scottish colonists and the
battle for Canada's west, 1813-1816

Names: Lower, Robert, 1946- author.

Identifiers: Canadiana (print) 20220484368 | Canadiana
(ebook) 20220484430

ISBN 978-1-77041-718-2 (softcover)
ISBN 978-1-77852-1-652 (ePub)
ISBN 978-1-77852-166-9 (PDF)
ISBN 978-1-77852-167-6 (Kindle)

Subjects: LCSH: Red River Settlement—History. |
LCSH: Scots—Manitoba—History—19th century. |
LCSH: Pioneers—Red River Settlement—History. |
LCSH: Frontier and pioneer life—Manitoba—Juvenile
literature. | LCSH: Seven Oaks, Battle of, Man., 1816.
| LCSH: Manitoba—History—19th century. | LCSH:
Selkirk, Thomas Douglas, Earl of, 1771-1820. | CSH:
First Nations—Manitoba—History.

Classification: LCC FC3372 .L69 2023 | DDC
971.27/01—dc23]

Published by ECW Press
665 Gerrard Street East
Toronto, Ontario, Canada M4M 1Y2
416-694-3348 / info@ecwpress.com

Cover design: Michel Vrana
Cover image: Peter Rindisbacher, Library and Archives Canada,
e008299458
Map designs: Michaelin Lower
Author photo: Elise Swerhone

This book is funded in part by the Government of Canada. *Ce livre est financé en partie par le gouvernement du Canada.* We
acknowledge the support of the Canada Council for the Arts. *Nous remercions le Conseil des arts du Canada de son soutien.*
We acknowledge the funding support of the Ontario Arts Council (OAC), an agency of the Government of Ontario.
We also acknowledge the support of the Government of Ontario through the Ontario Book Publishing Tax Credit, and
through Ontario Creates.

ONTARIO ARTS COUNCIL
CONSEIL DES ARTS DE L'ONTARIO
an Ontario government agency
un organisme du gouvernement de l'Ontario

Canada Council   Conseil des arts
for the Arts   du Canada

Canadä

PRINTED AND BOUND IN CANADA   PRINTING: FRIESENS   5 4 3 2 1

MIX
Paper from
responsible sources
FSC
www.fsc.org   FSC® C016245

For my mother, Jean (Livingstone) Lower,
who gave me her love for history,
especially our own.

൚

And for my daughter, Michaelin,
who will carry it on.

TABLE OF CONTENTS

LIST OF MAPS

AUTHOR'S NOTE

This is a work of nonfiction, and as such I stand behind any and all statements and quotations. But it is not a history in any formal or academic sense. In the interest of smooth reading, I have kept citations to a minimum. Any quote without a citation comes straight from the Selkirk Papers, on microfilm in the Archives of Manitoba.

Because pre-Victorian sentence structure and vocabulary can be challenging, I have made alterations to spelling and punctuation in quotes where I believe it improves readability without altering meaning. When I have paraphrased, I've stayed as faithful to the documents as I can.

The Selkirk Papers are the chief archival source used for this book. Though I was always aware of the many other players involved, the point of view is unavoidably that of the Red River Settlers, the Selkirk Settlers. This is how they saw it, how my great-great-grandfather, a young millwright from Islay, must have seen it. Other points of view exist and I have indicated them in places where contention persists. Caveat lector.

Though my story is told through the eyes of the Scots who lived it, I am fully sensible of the social, cultural, economic and physical crimes that the descendants of these settlers, right up to my own generation, have perpetrated on the original inhabitants of the Canadian prairies, and as one of those descendants I accept my share of responsibility for that.

As a son of the prairies, it would be hypocritical to say I wish that my forebears had never come. But I am heartily sorry, in the name of those forebears, for the suffering and injustices inflicted on First Nations, Inuit and Métis peoples. And for my own part I am sorry — I apologize — for the great part of my life that I spent accepting those same legal and social crimes as the inevitable, if regrettable, result of historical processes. They were not inevitable; we, the settlers, could have done so much better, but we frankly didn't care. In our (including my own) unquestioning belief in European entitlement, we were blind and deaf. I hope now that a corner has been turned and that "we" have truly begun to care. Redress of grievances, recompense, and rehabilitation and recovery of stature and self-determination among Indigenous cultures must be a national priority.

The subjects of our story are Highland Scots, 250-plus men, women and children fleeing brutal displacement by another crime of humans against humans, the Highland Clearances. Hindsight tells us that they were the vanguard of the coming invasion, but they did not know that, nor intend it. They knew only that they were being offered a way out of poverty and oppression. They had become refugees in their own country and like refugees everywhere, they looked to distant lands for safe haven. That is the story I set out to tell, with all due respect, I hope, for those who were already here.

A NOTE ON NAMES.

I have tried to identify First Nations by the names they use for themselves today, sometimes coupling them with the settler terms, many of which are still in common usage. For the Métis, I have used the name by which they referred to themselves at the time: Bois-Brûlés, or just Brûlés. The term and spelling "Métis" came into common use in the years following the period covered by this book, and denotes a qualitative change in the way these unique people came to see themselves.

As for individuals' names, it's a free-for-all and anybody's guess which spelling is "correct." You're on your own except where I've made it clear why I am using a specific spelling.

Finally, Scots names: McDonalds, McDonells, Macdonells, McLeans, McLeods, McBeaths, McBeths, McKays and McRaes, not to mention the Alexanders, Archibalds, Anguses, Jameses, Jonathons and Williams. The names can be dizzying in their similarity and repetition. It behooves the reader to pay close attention.

Blame the Scots. I certainly do.

This book was researched and written in the place where most of its events took place, in Winnipeg, near the forks of the Red and Assiniboine Rivers, on the original lands of Anishinaabeg, Cree, Oji-Cree, Dakota and Dene peoples and on the Homeland of the Métis Nation. I hope it will play a small part in infusing real people and real life into this too-often-mechanical acknowledgement. This truly was and remains Their Native Land.

ROBERT LOWER

AUGUST 2022

INTRODUCTION

CITY ON THE RED.

I was born and have spent most of my life in Winnipeg, as did my father before me.

My city sits right at the centre of southern Canada, astride the confluence of the Red and Assiniboine Rivers, called locally The Forks, a continental crossroads and meeting place for peoples in every age since it emerged from the glacial meltwater, some 8,000 years ago.

Winnipeg is famous for its cold winters, its vibrant arts and music scene, its elm trees, Winnie the Pooh,[1] the invention of the remote car starter (give that man a knighthood) — and its history.

The Winnipeg General Strike of 1919 shook the world, convincing every bloated capitalist and cozy politician in the British Empire and America that the Bolshevik Revolution had arrived on their doorstep. They used the army to crush it.

The Métis Resistance ("Red River Rebellion") of 1870 was the first concerted backlash from Indigenous peoples against the wholesale western expansion and land grab by Settler Canada. Upon its suppression

---

1   Inspired by "Winnipeg," a bear at the London Zoo presented by a Winnipeg regiment in the Great War.

(also by an army), Winnipeg became the distribution and rail hub for that expansion and grew at such a rate that boosters thought it might rival Chicago. Virtually every immigrant of the hundreds of thousands who answered the call to transform Indigenous buffalo range into a vast wheat-producing machine came through Winnipeg. Many went no further, including my family.

History continues: As Canadians move forward with the difficult but necessary business of reconciliation between the settler population and the Indigenous cultures they (we) displaced and damaged almost to destruction, Winnipeg's large concentration of First Nations, families, along with its status as the Homeland of the Métis Nation, put it right at the heart of that process. If reconciliation is to succeed at all, it must succeed here.

THE PROMISED LAND.

Before any of these, before there was a Winnipeg or a land rush or an entity called the Métis Nation, there was the Red River Settlement — a puny patch of ground occupied by a hopeful band of Scots refugees, never more than 150 at one time, looking only for a place to sow crops and sink roots. One of them was my great-great-grandfather, and that's what brought me to this story.

As a child I was familiar with the Selkirk Settlers, as these uprooted Highlanders are called, and that an unspecified relative was one of them, but no story went along with that. Winnipeg and area abounded with their names — on streets, neighbourhoods, parks, schools and even a whole city, Selkirk. In school we heard about the Scottish Lord Selkirk and his attempts to help farmers of the Highlands, displaced by callous landlords. We knew the name Miles Macdonell and something called the Pemmican War (disappointingly for little boys, not really a war at all), which grew out of the bitter rivalry between two fur-trade giants, the Hudson's Bay Company and the North West Company. But in the end, these were just facts, a series of incidents that had no power to fire the imagination — with one notable exception.

Over the three years covered by this book, one event has remained alive and current through the generations: a clash now known simply as the Battle of Seven Oaks, but for over a century called by some, including the school system, the Seven Oaks Massacre, and by others La Grenouillière or its English translation, Frog Plain, referring to a campsite some distance from the battleground. This gunfight, which resulted in twenty-two deaths, has understandably stood out, both for its singular violence and for the division over its meaning. For my Scots forebears, it was a massacre of innocents who had done nothing wrong by uncivilized "half-breeds" (as they were called for far too long) out of some unfathomable primordial hatred. For Métis people, descendants of the other side of the field, it was a glorious victory over invaders who wanted to enslave them and destroy their way of life. For many on both sides of that divide, those opinions still prevail.[2] Small wonder, then, that for most people curious about the Red River Settlement, Seven Oaks is what they find and where they stop.

To be clear, Seven Oaks was no part of why I wrote this book. I wrote this book because I discovered the story that had been missing from those dry historical accounts. And that story makes Seven Oaks a far more interesting and complex event than its reduction to a fight between good guys and bad guys could ever convey.

Some years ago I happened to see my great-great-grandfather's name, Samuel Lamont, on a bronze plaque in a Winnipeg park listing those first settlers of 1813. Having a name to go with that vague old family story, I went online. I discovered that Sam, a recently minted millwright, was twenty-two years old in 1813 and that as "a well-regarded mechanic who knows his business," he had been hired to build a grist mill for the nascent colony. I went to the archives, to dig a little deeper.

The Selkirk Papers comprise 20,000 pages, of which about 3,000 are the letters, reports and journals written on the spot between 1812

---

2   In 1891, a group of Scottish Winnipeggers erected a cairn on the site of the gunfight
     to commemorate the event and rededicate themselves to the condemnation of
     those who had "massacred" their countrymen. In June of 2016, 125 years later, I
     witnessed a gathering of Métis Winnipeggers around that same cairn to celebrate
     their "victory" of two centuries before.

and 1817 by the participants themselves. That's where I would find any reference to my ancestor. I dipped into the first journal at the point where Sam's group were making their way up the complicated river system between Hudson Bay and Lake Winnipeg. It instantly took my breath away — the immediacy and spontaneity of this optimistic record, written as the journey unfolded without benefit of hindsight or reflection. It felt like standing at the edge of a precipice, staring into a fog-filled canyon. "Good heavens," I thought, "these people have *no idea* what they are getting into." I knew, though, and was hooked; I stepped over the edge and into the future with them.

I came to realize that previous researchers, however good their reporting on the events of these years, had, through choice or technical difficulty, missed or ignored the drama — the pulsing life — in these pages. It is in the daily details, and above all the personalities, that the real story emerges.

With a handful of exceptions the settlers themselves, including my great-great-grandaddy, the millwright from Islay, do not speak in these documents, though they are often spoken about. The journals and letters are written by the men appointed by Lord Selkirk to conduct "his" settlers to "his" lands and there to oversee "his" colony. Called Officers or Gentlemen, none of these men had ever been to western North America or seen the vast prairie at its heart. The settlers believed they were going to an unsettled, even unoccupied, tract of land belonging to his lordship, and therefore open to cultivation and settlement. In fact, a surprisingly large number of people already regarded The Forks as their home or territory. Most had never heard of Lord Selkirk and the rest regarded him as an enemy, so the Highlanders' reception ranged from open-hearted welcome by First Nations bands to dangerous hostility (as agents of the hated Hudson's Bay Company) from the North West Company. It would be up to their officers to navigate this compli-cated landscape and find that sweet spot of mutual acceptance and accommodation that any meeting of nations requires. To this challenge they proved singularly unsuited. One decision at a time, a few Gaelic farmers from a remote Highland strath (valley) would be led to make history in the worst possible way.

This is the story of how that unfolded. It is also something more, because this is where it all began. This is where a century and a half of commerce between Indigenous plains people and Europeans began to turn from a trading relationship into an imperial acquisition, an extension of Britain, pushing aside and dispossessing the original peoples. In this story are the seeds of that one-sided catastrophe and hints at how it all might have been done differently.

TIMELINE

The broad outline of these years is well established, and it may well assist readers in keeping events and actors straight to provide a thumbnail summary here, a timeline of the principal events of these three desperate years. If you are already familiar with it, or if you would rather discover it as you read, you may want to skip the next eleven paragraphs. For the rest, here is a capsule account of the events covered in this book, so you may know just where you are (see Maps 1 and 5).

1810: Lord Selkirk, who has already sponsored settlement schemes in Prince Edward Island and Upper Canada, decides his next colonization exercise will be in the extremely remote valley of the Red River, in what is now southern Manitoba, Canada, a place the earl himself has never seen. To that end he has bought a large stake in the vast fur-trading empire of the Hudson's Bay Company (HBC), whose charter gives them a monopoly on trade and colonization.

1811: Lord Selkirk acquires the colonization rights to a significant piece of territory, including the valley of the Red River. He sends an advance party under Captain Miles McDonell to prepare the site. In 1812, he sends a few adventurous farmers to test the waters.

1813: The first full contingent of migrants, almost one hundred Highland men, women and children, is dispatched from Scotland to York Factory, the Hudson's Bay Company post at the mouth of the Nelson River, thence to be ferried by open boats to their destination, 1,200 kilometres inland. A typhus outbreak on the ship leads to their being put ashore at the lesser post of Churchill, 250 kilometres north of York Factory. They will have to pass the winter here, in crude hovels hastily built against the arctic freeze, dependent on HBC supplies to survive.

1814, JANUARY: Miles McDonell, fearing shortage of winter food, issues the Pemmican Proclamation, an edict forbidding others to take meat in the form of pemmican out of the district. Since the North West Company (NWCo), mortal rival of the Hudson's Bay Company and therefore of Selkirk's colony, depends on pemmican to feed its Bois-Brûlé (mixed heritage) traders, the edict creates outrage. Though he doesn't know it, McDonell has just set off what will be called the Pemmican War.

1814, APRIL: From their Churchill refuge, fifty Scots stalwarts of both genders choose to walk across the still-frozen taiga to York Factory to be there for the spring thaw. After a hard twelve-day walk, they make it, and presently board the boats that will take them to their new homes at Red River.

1814, MID-JUNE: They reach their destination. They are instantly rapturous at its possibilities and barely aware of the animosity emanating from the North West Company, who want no part of a farming settlement straddling their fur-trade route and disrupting trade, not to mention eating their pemmican. They view it as an HBC plot, one they are determined to destroy.

1815: When the winter of 1814–15 proves even harder than expected, the colonists grow impatient with the short rations and arbitrary rules imposed by McDonell and his officers. The NWCo take advantage of the rift to offer free passage to Upper Canada for any wishing to leave. Resentment ignites into open revolt, and by mid-June well over half the colonists have deserted to the NWCo and left The Forks.

1815, JUNE: The Nor'Westers now turn their armed wrath on the few who remain, provoking exchanges of musket fire. Three men are wounded, one fatally. Miles McDonell surrenders himself to the enemy in an attempt to save the colony, but this changes nothing. Leaderless and facing continued threats, the remaining settlers and servants (employees) flee to the safety of HBC posts at the north end of Lake Winnipeg, and reconsider their future.

1815, AUGUST: An HBC adventurer named Colin Robertson comes to their rescue, rallying them and leading them back to The Forks, where in mid-summer there are too few Nor'Westers to oppose them. Robertson's experience in the country and his charismatic leadership succeed in restoring the confidence of these loyalists, and when a new governor, Robert Semple, and another contingent of eighty-four migrants arrive that fall, the colony is back in business.

1816: The Nor'Westers are still determined to stop them in their tracks, and through the winter and early spring of 1816, they convince their Bois-Brûlé hunters and traders that their food supply and way of life are at stake unless they gather once more at The Forks in June for an all-out attack. Colin Robertson builds Fort Douglas to withstand whatever force might present itself. He and Governor Semple disagree, Semple believing that his title of governor and his superior breeding should be enough to discourage a few men he dismisses as illiterate buffalo hunters. Robertson, whose respect for the Brûlés' fighting ability, independence and determination is both greater and in accord with reality, becomes more and more frustrated, finally giving up and leaving the colony in the hopes that on their own, the colonial officers can unite to oppose the coming attack.

1816, JUNE 19: Just one week after he leaves, the attacking force arrives on the scene, every bit as formidable as Robertson predicted. Still confident that his authority will prevail, Semple decides to face them, and here our story begins.

PART I

THE EARL

CHAPTER 1

SEVEN OAKS

JUNE 19, 1816

FORT DOUGLAS, RED RIVER SETTLEMENT.

It is June to perfection, a glorious day in Lord Selkirk's Red River Settlement. Most of the people have gathered in and around Fort Douglas. It is a fort in name only — its defensive wall only covers three sides of the cluster of crude buildings that house the colony's governor and officers, the stables, the collective stores and the three cannons that are key to its strength. The rest of the palisade is still just a scatter of logs.

Fifty settlers and employed men work to finish the fort. With their families, they total more than a hundred. Only a few have risked going out to their farm plots to tend their young crops. Reports abound of an approaching force of armed and mounted plainsmen, agents of the North West Company, whose aim is the final destruction of this colony. While the settlers have muskets and cannons, they are not warriors. They need this fort.

Sometime between four and five o'clock the alarm is raised by the lookout: a force of sixty or more armed men on horseback is passing to the northwest, heading toward a point on the Red River well north of Fort Douglas.

Governor Robert Semple peers through a telescope. No mistaking it — these folks are kitted out for a fight.

Conscious of the fort's vulnerability and worried for absent colonists, the governor calls for twenty men to arm themselves and follow him to confront this group. Others clamour to go, but he declines; he is certain that his authority as governor can cow "a gang of half-caste ruffians." Twenty-six men leave the fort and strike north on foot. The remainder, under Semple's deputy Alex Macdonell, stare anxiously after the rapidly disappearing governor with his posse of farmers, labourers and clerks.

Minutes pass. An excruciating hour. Suddenly, a crackle of distant muskets crescendos, then tails into ragged fire for a long minute, then dwindles to single shots, then nothing. The only sound among the watching settlers is their own breathing.

More waiting. At last, out of the woods come several men, one wounded, moving as fast as they can into the fort's protection. We confronted the group, they tell the others, but things went sideways. The settlers hadn't stood a chance. The few who had run had been shot in the back. Only these men remained.

Convinced that an attack on the fort will come any minute, Alex Macdonell has the men take up defensive positions. The day, almost the longest of the year, wears on and finally turns to night. No one sleeps.

Five more survivors straggle in. The fifth, a man who had been taken prisoner, brings news that Governor Semple and twenty other men are dead. He also brings an ultimatum from the enemy camp: They have five settler hostages. At dawn, they will kill them, then they'll attack the fort and slaughter every man, woman and child. The settlers' only alternative is to give up the fort and leave Red River forever. If they do that, their lives will be spared.

The messenger's stories terrify those with families. How long can they defend an open fort? Defeat is inevitable. Reluctantly, Alex Macdonell agrees to surrender in return for safe passage north for all, to the protection of the Hudson's Bay Company.

Thus ends the violent day that has come down to us as the Battle of Seven Oaks. As decades pass, it will become synonymous with and inseparable from the story of the Selkirk Settlers. Its consequences are still echoing, two centuries later.

But June 19, 1816, is only one day out of the more than one thousand that are the stuff of this tale, and the gunfight is just the most deadly event in a series of trials, triumphs and failures that make the story of these three years so compelling.

Our story truly begins three years before as our band of hopeful pilgrims are about to set foot on North America's shore. Trial and tragedy are already with them.

CHAPTER 2

ARRIVAL

AUGUST 18 TO SEPTEMBER 16, 1813

HUDSON BAY, NEAR CHURCHILL RIVER.

O n an August afternoon, two ships appear off the western shore of Hudson Bay. Both are under full sail and running hard for the Churchill River. They show no signs of slowing as they enter the inshore shallows. Is this a chase? Britain is at war with the U.S., and the second ship is a fighting vessel — perhaps a Yankee privateer? But no, both are flying British colours. Is some terrifying fleet about to heave into sight? But the horizon remains empty, not even an ice floe to break the monotony on this mild, late-summer day.

Sweeping into the river's wide mouth, the ships glide past a disused stone fort, and quickly reduce sail. Along the western bank of the river, Hudson's Bay men as well as some Dene and Inuit hunters look up, startled, as this dramatic apparition bears down on them. It's not quiet; men shout orders, sails are reefed, rigging and spars clatter and creak. The bystanders can only stare. Imagine a pair of giant airships appearing out of nowhere to drift down your street and past your house. These vessels are vastly larger than anything normally seen in this river. For many Indigenous witnesses, these may well be their first sight of ocean-going vessels. The natural reaction is alarm. In the sub-arctic wilderness, the unexpected is rarely good news.

The ships heave to and drop anchor in Sloops Cove, a snug harbour three kilometres from the river's mouth. Sailors scramble over the rigging and decks to secure the anchorage. Some spectators recognize the Hudson's Bay Company ship *Prince of Wales*, which has been supplying the trade for years. The other, HMS *Brazen*, is Royal Navy, an escort against those Yankee marauders. What are the ships doing here? And why is the activity on the warship so much more vigorous than that on the *Prince*? Watchers can't decide whether to be thrilled, or chilled.

A ship's arrival is a big event in the life of any remote post, probably the biggest of the year. The short northern summer allows for only one or two ships most years, and those invariably head for York Factory — or York Fort, as it is usually called — the Hudson's Bay Company (HBC) northern headquarters, 250 kilometres south. But here it is, the news from home! Letters and newspapers, English food, tea and trade goods. It should be a stellar moment, but Mr. Topping, Churchill's Chief Factor (trader), merely notes in the Churchill Post log:

> Late in the afternoon the Prince of Wales and His Majesty's Ship the Brazen cast anchor in the river. Sent two men to Sloops Cove to fire a [salute], but from the bad weather and the darkness of the night, they would not put off.

In fact the *Prince of Wales*'s longboat had been lowered into the water, and late in the evening Captain Turner was rowed ashore, not to greet Mr. Topping but to scout sites for hospital tents. The ship is riddled with deadly typhus. Turner's crew, normally twenty-five, has been reduced to eight fit for work. Several sailors have died along with five passengers, a mixed group of Scots colonists bound for Lord Selkirk's settlement, far inland.

Informed of the situation by Captain Stirling of the *Brazen*, which has no sickness, Topping orders that the cargo for the post be taken off so the ship can depart as soon as possible for York Fort. Passengers should remain on the ship.

Too late. Passengers and ailing sailors are being disembarked as fast as Captain Turner can manage it. The *Prince* will go nowhere until his ship is free of contagion and his seamen well enough to return aboard.

Topping sends his own boats to collect Churchill's cargo, but the men are ordered "on no account to go on Board the Ship. Our Indians also were called together and desired to keep away from Sloops Cove." This does not go down well with Indigenous hunters, who are understandably curious to see their first European women. Grumpily, they declare their intention to leave for their winter camps, but Topping begs them to stay and hunt fresh meat to supply the sick, "which after much entreaty they consented to do." He also sends all his available fresh meat and vegetables "for the relief of the sick people."

The ninety or so passengers put ashore are mainly Highland farmers. Their ultimate destination — Red River — is deep in the heart of the continent, where they will join an advance party to establish the first permanent agricultural colony west of the Great Lakes. They range in age from one to sixty-five, and half are women and girls. One of them is my great-great-grandfather, Sam Lamont, a 22-year-old millwright contracted to build a mill to grind the colony's grain. They had expected to land at York Factory, where the colony's governor would meet them with boats to convey them 1,200 kilometres inland.

Now, they have rocky ground for a bed and sails for a roof. Over half are fevered with typhus. A crossing that had started with so much hope ends as badly as anyone might imagine, short of sinking. Their leader and doctor, William LaSerre, is among the dead. Quarantined in the open, kept distant from the Churchill Post, neither comfort nor hygiene is possible. But these are Highland farmers, no strangers to adversity, and after eight weeks at sea, just to be on dry, unmoving ground must be some relief.

There is nothing 1813 medicine can do for typhus, so the patients must put up with fever, chills, aches, coughing, vomiting and diarrhea until the war between microbes and immune systems is resolved.

Two weeks later, the passengers and the *Prince of Wales* are taken out of quarantine, but Captain Turner makes the drastic decision *not* to go to York Factory but to head straight back to Britain to avoid being trapped by ice already forming in Hudson Strait. He orders all cargo unloaded and sets about preparing his ship.

He has not reckoned with William Auld.

On September 9, Auld sweeps in like the wrath of God, which, as HBC Superintendent of Northern Factories, is pretty much what he is. Topping had sent a fast boat to York Fort to warn him of Turner's intentions.

"I immediately embarked in an open boat in the middle of the night," Auld later writes. "I got to Churchill in 45 hours, drenched with salt water, the sea breaking over us for 3 or 4 hours without mercy." He shoots off a furious letter to Captain Turner: "For the last 12 days York Fort has been entirely destitute of Oatmeal and only 3 barrels of Flour remain." He rages about the disastrous effect on business if the *Prince*'s trade goods are not delivered to York Fort, not to mention the burden on the HBC of caring for these wretched Scots. He demands an answer "immediately."

William Auld is, to put it plainly, generally despised. Though he has had a long and respectable career with the Hudson's Bay Company as surgeon and trader, he has been promoted beyond his competence.[1] He has alienated most of his subordinates, many of his Indigenous clients and even his own employers.[2] In his letters, he reveals himself as officious, arbitrary, rigid, petty and relentlessly negative. In many ways this book is a tale of dubious leaders who make decisions that thwart success and court disaster. Auld is the first afflictive example.

Auld summons Captain Turner ashore and threatens to replace him as captain. It works. "After some time, Capt. Turner consented, and orders were given to re-ship the cargoes destined to York Factory." The cargo is hauled back aboard, freshwater barrels are filled, and finally, to everyone's great relief, Turner admits forty-eight of the healthiest colonists back on board. The sick and recovering will be kept over the winter in Churchill and sent on in the spring.

---

1   J.E. Foster, "William Auld," *Dictionary of Canadian Biography*, biographi.ca/en/bio/auld_william_6E.html.

2   Auld has been forbidden from writing directly to the governors (board members) of the HBC.

Next morning, both ships hoist anchor and head for the sea. HMS *Brazen* clears the river, but a strong tide drives the *Prince of Wales* aground. Turner manages to work her loose, but can only return to Sloops Cove, where he lightens her load, dumping most of his fresh water, one of his heavy anchors, assorted cargo and — alas — all the would-be colonists. Thus unburdened, the *Prince* escapes to sea, where she and *Brazen* set course for York.

The close to ninety Scottish farm-folk left behind discover that Churchill, though one of the oldest trading posts on the bay and glorified with the name "fort," is no more than a scatter of ragtag buildings barely fit to house a few officers and a dozen or so servants (as all employees are universally known in these days). There is no shelter for long-term guests, certainly not ninety, most of whom are women and minors. The shoreline is rocky and windswept. To winter under tents is unthinkable. Yet there are no trees large enough to provide logs for cabins. The prospects are unpromising.

And those arctic breezes lifting their kilts are not getting any warmer.

CHAPTER 3

SCOTLAND

1813

SUTHERLAND COUNTY, SCOTLAND, EARLIER THAT YEAR.

It is March, and the Clearances have come to Kildonan, a tiny parish on the vast estates of the Countess of Sutherland in the northern Highlands. One of the great social crimes of British history, the Clearances have been advancing across the Highlands since the late eighteenth century, dispossessing small farmers in favour of great flocks of sheep, whose wool and meat pay the great landowners far better than the pitiful rents they can squeeze from tenants. Cast out, their victims face degradation, destitution, even starvation.

And now they are here, in Kildonan, in the person of a sheepman named Reid, who appears one day to assess the valley for its grazing potential. Furious locals run him off posthaste, and, filled with dread and fury, decide to march to Dunrobin Castle to confront the countess herself.

As it happens, the lady is absent, enjoying the social season in London, so it is her agents, Patrick Sellar and William Young, who hear that a Kildonan mob is coming fast, bent on hanging them and burning the castle. They hastily swear in and arm a few dozen townsmen as "constables" and send for soldiers from nearby Fort George. The mob arrives in Golspie, where Young and Sellar face them, backed by some

11

Church of Scotland ministers. The agents threaten arrest or worse, and the ministers throw in eternal damnation. The sheriff reads the Riot Act, but the Gaelic-speaking Scots can't understand the English gibberish, and anyway, no one is rioting. Instead, the thwarted rebels grumpily leave town. A few hours later, a detachment of infantry and artillery arrives. Finding no one to shoot, they follow the tenants back to their strath but again find no one willing to take up arms. The soldiers rough a few people up, arrest others, ultimately release them, and leave. It is the Rebellion That Wasn't.

The Improvers, as the clearance set style themselves, get to work with callous efficiency. Each family is given mere days to gather belongings and livestock and vacate the only homes most have ever known. Resistance brings on brutality. The able are forced out at gunpoint, the sick and aged are carried out to lie in the open air, and vacated houses, generally built of drystone, have their thatched or sod roofs broken down or set afire, to ensure people can't return. In exchange for what they thought was their birthright, the countess promises tiny lots in a coastal village called Helmsdale, where new houses will be built for them. If they choose to become fishers, boats and nets will also be provided.

They are not fishers and they don't believe the lady's promises. The future is bleak, perhaps impossible. So when recruiters from the great lord and colonizer, Thomas Douglas, Earl of Selkirk, arrive with offers of land in a fertile valley far over the sea and beyond the reach of Improvers, it is small wonder that they jump at it and resolve that very year, that very month if possible, to put the countess and her lackeys behind them and build a new Kildonan in a new world.

Thomas Douglas never hoped to become the earl. Four brothers had to die childless for the title to pass to him, perhaps explaining why his interests developed so far beyond the traditional narrow focus on family pride and fortune of a senior Scottish peer.

Born in 1771, Douglas is a product of the Scottish Enlightenment. He believes that society and economics are governed by unseen and unwritten laws that are susceptible to manipulation for change, an insight that will shape the modern world. During a visit to Paris in 1791, he sees it in action as France frees itself from the Bourbon yoke. A few years later, observing the post-revolution Reign of Terror from a safe distance, he sees the disastrous consequences of letting change get out of hand. He embraces reform, but is no revolutionary. He believes strongly that the class structure of Britain should be preserved. Still, society should be reformed to enable the poor to prosper, and aristocrats have a duty to make that happen, financially and politically. At the same time, the poor must be "sensible that they received their aid from the good will of their superiors" and that aid should be "administered by those who contributed it,"[1] so that there can be no doubt to whom they owe their good fortune.

By the time Douglas conceives of the Red River Settlement, he's inherited the earldom and its fortune, married the "vivacious" and well-connected Jean Wedderburn, and already tried his hand at two significant social-engineering projects. Both are colonial experiments, involving relocating Scottish and Irish families to planned and administered settlements in British North America — one in what would become the province of Prince Edward Island and the other in southern Ontario (Upper Canada) near the U.S. border. Both have some success but have also been plagued with problems, chiefly the result of insufficient planning on Lord Selkirk's part and incompetent leadership from the men he appointed to administer them.

He now turns his eye to the middle of the continent and the reportedly rich and ready-to-cultivate flood plain of the Red River, where it is joined by another major waterway, the Assiniboine, at a place called, appropriately, The Forks. His lordship has never seen the chosen place for the very good reason that it takes hard months of travel to get there from Scotland, and when you finally do . . . let's just say there is nothing to attract an earl. Nonetheless, he is convinced it is the best candidate for a new settlement. In British eyes, and British law, this land is under the control ("ownership" is too strong a word

---

1   J.M. Bumsted, ed., *The Collected Writings of Lord Selkirk* (Winnipeg: Manitoba Historical Society, 1984), p. 94.

at this stage) of the Hudson's Bay Company; in 1670, King Charles II, who had also never been there, granted the HBC a trade and colonizing monopoly over 3.9 million square kilometres of land, lakes and forests, or what in Europe might be called, well, Europe (minus Russia). By using his own fortune and that of his wife's family, he acquires a significant ownership share of the HBC with which he is able, not without difficulty, to persuade its managing committee to let him exercise the colonizing clause in its charter. He chooses to ignore the dour and vocal opposition of the North West Company (NWCo), the corporate organization of hundreds of independent traders who have been challenging the HBC's monopoly for forty years and more. The Nor'Westers, as they are called, built Fort Gibraltar to dominate The Forks and anchor their western trade routes. They hate the idea of an "HBC colony" on their doorstep.

Selkirk casually brushes this potential obstacle aside, to be dealt with later.

The First Nations who might be expected to challenge the HBC's claim are not even aware of it, since the European model of land ownership is inconceivable in their traditional use and occupation of land. Land can no more be owned than can the wind or sky.

The moment his land grant is confirmed in 1811, the earl puts his latest experiment into action. He appoints as "governor" Captain Miles McDonell,[2] a colonial soldier and gentleman farmer whom he met on a trip to North America and quite liked. McDonell, too, is a stranger to the country west of the Great Lakes, but no matter. From London, Selkirk dispatches him immediately on an expedition to choose, claim and prepare a site for the proposed settlement. At the port of Stornoway a few weeks later, McDonell meets forty or so Irish, Highland and Orkney workmen waiting to sail on a ship called the *Edward and Ann*. Matters get off to a bad start: weeks of delay combined with confusion and disagreement over their terms of service put these men, mainly labourers and roustabouts, in a seriously bad temper by the time they

---

2   The customary spelling of McDonell's name is now "Macdonell," but I am using the spelling that is invariably used, including by himself, in these documents.

finally sail in July. It is already too late to get all the way to Red River before freeze-up.

They spend the winter of 1811–12 in a camp on the Nelson River, upstream from York Factory, at a clearing in the boreal forest. It's cold, the food is bad and there is nothing to do. McDonell has never before "commanded" civilians and his military style gets the men's backs up. The bored Irishmen get out their shillelaghs and exercise them on the heads of the Orkneymen, who respond in kind. The Highlanders are little better and McDonell has all he can do to maintain life, let alone order. By spring, his labour force has been significantly reduced by the number of men injured, fired, restrained and sentenced to return on the first ship to Britain.

In August 1812, McDonell and his party, now just eighteen strong, finally reach the forks of the Red and the Assiniboine, where Miles puts on his regimentals (dress uniform) and claims the land for Selkirk with all the pomp of throwing out the first ball at a Little League game. His bemused audience of North West Company clerks, half a dozen freelance traders and a few First Nations men listen politely, cheer obligingly, then happily take him up on his offer of a tipple.

McDonell decides to winter his people a hundred kilometres south of The Forks, on the Pembina River, where buffalo herds are close by to supply meat. They build a proper fort and name it Fort Daer, a Selkirk family name. They are joined by a newly arrived group including many more workmen and several settler families who sailed late in the year from Sligo, Ireland. Everyone settles down to another grim winter marked with more strife and bad temper, partly due to McDonell's poor management skills.

SCOTLAND.

Lord Selkirk has his recruiters out finding likely settlers. At first he thinks the Irish are his best prospects. Then in March 1813, he hears about the Kildonan troubles and, over a heart-to-heart with the Countess of Sutherland, gains her blessing in recruiting her former tenants. Not that she could stop him, having so rudely disowned them, but form is important to the earl, as is getting along with his social equals.

The actual men and women who will people his colonial ventures are not particularly important to Selkirk. His interest is in the social experiment itself: can emigration solve the problems of the dispossessed and thereby reduce social unrest at home while simultaneously benefiting the Empire? Still, Highlanders are close to his heart, as is the suffering caused by the Clearances. He has a great deal of respect for the clansmen's industry, hardiness and determination, so they get his nod.

He concocts a scheme whereby he can get the British government to underwrite most of the costs of resettlement by offering his Highlanders as soldiers in the ongoing war with the United States. In return, the government will send their families to Red River and put them on farm lots (bought from his lordship) where they will be joined at war's end by their menfolk, should they survive the war. While he waits for the government's verdict, Selkirk sends his recruiter, a man named Sergeant McDonald, to Kildonan to test the waters and see how many might be amenable to risking death for a farm. Sergeant McDonald, however, oversteps his brief and presents this scheme as an offer, not a hypothetical solution. This turns out to be just what the market was waiting for, and not only do men volunteer eagerly, they set about selling their livestock, furniture and tools in preparation for departing Scotland's sacred shore.

The government considers the earl's proposal and politely declines it. Never one to take the first no, Selkirk submits another draft. The government says no again. Another attempt gets a louder NO! By the time Selkirk has the men at the War Office changing their postal addresses, many Highlanders have put their worldly wealth where their mouths are, with all bridges burnt.

Selkirk may be rash, but he is no charlatan. He recognizes his obligation, takes responsibility for the misunderstanding and thinks fast. Apparently he is at his best (or worst?) when he's thinking on his feet. He comes up with another offer, which is complicated and involves the settlers putting up their own money, if they have any, along with some of his to get to Red River and acquire land. Those with no money will rent to own. It is not what they were expecting, but in for a penny, in for a pound. Many volunteer, in fact far too many to accommodate in one year. Choices must be made. Close to one hundred men, women and children are selected to go to York Factory on the June ship, and thence to Red River that fall. That they need to invest their own savings leaves a sour taste in many a mouth, along with a distinct if unstated feeling of being owed, but the alternative — poverty in Scotland — is far worse, and they tell themselves that all will be resolved once they reach the land of milk and honey.

CHAPTER 4

THE VOYAGE

JUNE 12 TO AUGUST, 1813

STROMNESS, ORKNEY ISLANDS, SCOTLAND.

N inety Highlanders, along with two officers and several special-
ized tradesmen, have gathered in this rugged seaport where
HBC ships take on water and food for the voyage to Hudson Bay.[1]
Lord Selkirk has come to see them off and smooth any last-minute
snags. As he loves to do, he spends time writing a long letter to Miles
McDonell, his agent and governor, which will be carried on the ship.
He describes the colonists' resistance to the Clearances but excuses
it as an excess of Highland spirit which led them "to think the lands
their own." This absurdity quelled, they opted for emigration. He
explains the terms:

> You will lay out land for them in as favourable and convenient
> a situation as possible and give them all the assistance that can
> be afforded to forward their work. Though they are working
> for themselves and on their own bottom, I feel quite as much
> interested in their success as if they were in my own immediate
> employment.

---

1   See Map 1.

Those who can afford it will buy their land for five shillings an acre; those who can't will lease at half a bushel of wheat per acre per year. Yes, he repeats, some of them went too far in opposing eviction, but were faced with "a ruinous and unjust encroachment on their property."

Along with the settlers, he sends out much-needed tradesmen, including a carpenter, a blacksmith and, of course, Samuel Lamont. "Lamont," writes Selkirk, "is the Millwright of whose character and skill I have a very good account." His salary is £30 a year, when a common labourer makes £20, and a doctor £50–£100.

Among the settlers, one stands out for the earl. He writes of George Campbell, a 25-year-old, with his wife and year-old son, as "not connected with the Kildonan people. He is wealthier, and his respectable appearance and manners lead me to hope that you will find him an acquisition to the Settlement." Selkirk's liberality toward the Highland rebels shows how far he could think beyond narrow class prejudices, but his belief that George Campbell's respectable dress and manners would equate to a valuable settler shows how much he is still in thrall to them.

Selkirk's letter describes William LaSerre, the young doctor he has chosen as the group's leader and overseer, but who will sadly die on the voyage. He then describes LaSerre's assistant, Archie McDonald, who will soon have responsibility thrust upon him by LaSerre's death. He "appears to deserve all that has been said in his favour. His abilities are very good and his manners popular . . . tho his inexperience requires some direction."

He cautions McDonell, a Roman Catholic, on the subject of religion: "The Sutherland men are rigid Presbyterians . . . I trust that everything will be avoided that will alarm the prejudices of these people." He advises McDonell to keep mum about his Papism: "We must treat with delicacy the feelings of men who have never lived with any but their own sect," until "after a little personal acquaintance they will be convinced that an R.C. may be a very good man."

On the ordnance or military arms of the colony, he notes they have four small cannon and a number of "wall pieces," guns smaller than cannon but too big to carry. He tells McDonell apologetically that he was hoping to send out "three or four" artillerymen to train the people in their use, but none came forward. But at least the artillery will "add to the respectability of the colony."

This is an example of Selkirk's chief fault: hasty planning leading to omissions and improvisation. The number of times he and McDonell discuss the need for a military force at The Forks is disturbing. Potential enemies in their minds include hostile Indigenous peoples and Americans, but especially the Nor'Westers, who have made clear their opposition. In a letter sent the previous year, Selkirk said he'd come out when he could bring a military escort; he thought 500 men should suffice. Five hundred men! The whole colony has fewer than 200 men, women and children. Why is he sending peaceable farmers with families into a situation he will not visit without a small battalion behind him? McDonell will later try to fashion the reluctant Highlanders into a sort of militia. The cliché that a gun in unskilled hands poses more danger to the bearer than his foes will prove true.

On June 16, when the sojourners finally board the *Prince of Wales*, excitement, apprehension and sheer energy animate the wharf. This is it — the day hope conquers despair. It is also the day Scotland is left behind; conflicting emotions battle it out. As soon as he has seen the last passenger tucked away, Selkirk writes McDonell again, assuring him that the passengers are fully paid up to Red River and owe nothing but "all the personal assistance which they can in working the boats" from York Fort to The Forks. He describes the baggage restrictions for each passenger[2] and other particulars. Then he adds two points that seem to be simple housekeeping details but will have profound and unforeseen consequences.

> [Any baggage] of inconvenient size is to be deposited at [York] Factory until an opportunity is found of bringing it to the Settlement . . . These people have no right to expect any species of supply [in Canada] but if any article appears to be

---

2   [4] "All to be put up in packages not exceeding 30x15x12 inches, two allowed for each adult, one to each child under 15, besides blankets." Essentially two average backpacks for everything you own in the world, winter and summer.

The *Prince of Wales*'s passenger list at Stromness, June 1813. Samuel Lamont is number 88.

(Ship's logs, *Prince of Wales* log/C778/Archives of Manitoba/HBC Archives) of urgent necessity, it may be furnished, taking a promissory note for the value.

He restates the glowing opinion he has of this group, especially the well-bred young man he has mentioned before:

> George Campbell is a man of Station rather superior to the rest of these passengers and should be treated with some distinction — he may be allowed a few extra packs of baggage if this can be managed so as not to give umbrage to the rest of the settlers.

Indeed, Mr. Campbell will distinguish himself, but not as his patron expects.

ABOARD THE PRINCE OF WALES.

At sea, the passengers are crowded into a relatively airless space called the tween decks, but the fair summer weather allows those who wish it to spend hours on deck in fresh air and sunlight. One day out, they join the *Eddystone*, another HBC ship bound for Hudson Bay, and HMS *Brazen*, the naval escort or "convoy" that will protect them from prize-hunting Yankees. This proves a wise precaution, for just a few days later, in the quaint language of the log, "The Convoy spake a strange sail." Sure enough, it's an American privateer and it has a prize in tow already. The *Brazen* immediately sets course to intercept and the privateer flees. Two days later, the *Brazen* returns. She has recovered the prize, a small schooner called the *Daphne*, but the Yankee escaped. The passengers are thrilled.

Three weeks later, they see "isles of ice," another novelty for the landlubbers. Then, on July 30, an ominous entry: "John Thompson quartermaster taken very ill." This news is soon eclipsed by the appearance of "Esquimaux," coming alongside in kayaks and umiaks, offering to trade.

This interlude marks the end of routine on this voyage. Two days later, the sickness spreads, and on August 6 the first death — "Andrew Portella, seaman" — is recorded. Next day, with more sailors falling ill, the bedding is brought up on deck, the passenger cabin thoroughly scrubbed down, and a "carpenter employed cutting [a] hole in the ship's side to give more air in the Tween Decks to the sick." Another hole is cut the next day but it's not enough. On August 15, a frantic officer, probably Captain Turner, scrawls in the log, "The groans and cries of the Sick on one side and the Delirious on the other is dreadful beyond description."

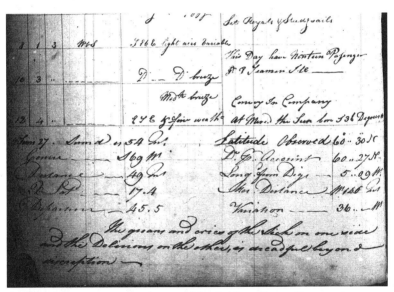

Ship's log, August 15, 1813. Note the entry, "This Day have Nineteen Pasengers & 8 Seamen Ill." (Ship's logs, *Prince of Wales* log/C778/Archives of Manitoba/HBC Archives)

The next day, August 16, the captain orders a course change: "Hauled up for Churchill," says the log, and the passengers' fate is sealed.

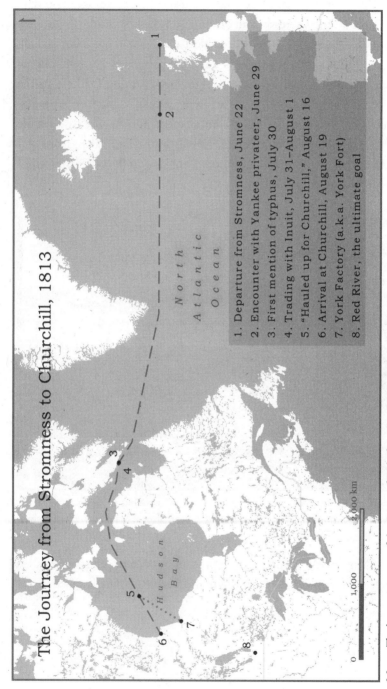

The Journey from Stromness to Churchill, 1813

North Atlantic Ocean

Hudson Bay

1. Departure from Stromness, June 22
2. Encounter with Yankee privateer, June 29
3. First mention of typhus, July 30
4. Trading with Inuit, July 31–August 1
5. "Hauled up for Churchill," August 16
6. Arrival at Churchill, August 19
7. York Factory (a.k.a. York Fort)
8. Red River, the ultimate goal

0   1,000   2,000 km

Map 1. The long sea voyage of the *Prince of Wales* from Scotland to Hudson Bay, 1813.

PART II

MILES McDONELL

(Archives of Manitoba photo collection, Personalities — McDonell, Miles, p. 1275, N16074)

CHAPTER 5

AT THE TUNDRA'S EDGE

SEPTEMBER 20 TO CHRISTMAS, 1813

CHURCHILL FORT, NEAR HUDSON BAY.

As the Highlanders watch their ship disappear over the icy swells of Hudson Bay, leaving them stranded, the Churchill Post log records a "stiff gale." At Churchill, stiff gale means a blast that could peel the skin off an apple, and winter may arrive any time. That same day, Mr. Topping decides that they will move to a creek (also named Churchill) twenty-four kilometres up the river, "this being the best place we know, and the only place where there is wood sufficient for Building, Fuel, etc." Although distant from the supplies they will need, it is out of the worst blows off the bay. That alone could make the difference in survival.

The day before, a battered little boat had limped into Sloops Cove from York Fort, carrying a waterlogged angel of mercy, Dr. Abel Edwards. On his way back to England after a year as colony doctor at Red River, he has consented to remain at Churchill to care for the marooned immigrants. The journey from York Factory has been trying. Undaunted, Edwards goes immediately to the sick tents.

The next day, the Post log records thirty-one colonists being sent off to Churchill Creek along with provisions and lumber that had been in the cargo of the *Prince of Wales*. There they find a suitable bit of sheltered woodland and begin to prepare a winter camp.

Responsibility for the colonists has fallen on Archibald McDonald, twenty-three, engaged last spring by Lord Selkirk to second and assist William LaSerre. He had been near-giddy with delight at the prospect of learning the arts of bleeding, purging and treating injuries. Suddenly he finds himself superintendent of the emigrants, a post he does not feel ready for. Selkirk's colonial experiments are quasi-military in structure, and his "officers" are to take command and to be obeyed. To be hired as an officer, one must come from a Good Family, meaning landed, professional, wealthy or all three. Archie McDonald is the educated son of a "tacksman," or gentleman farmer and land manager. In class-bound Britain, this is qualification enough to put him in charge of ninety independent, headstrong and capable Highlanders.

It does not help matters that William Auld, the highest-ranking HBC officer in the country, harbours an abiding loathing for the whole colonization scheme, which he views as distracting and damaging to the fur trade. He transfers disdain for the project onto those involved in it. To another HBC man, he writes that the Highlanders' "filthy and indolent habits are fostered and cherished by the shameful and familiar mismanagement of McDonald," a "boy" who allows "the sick and the hale to live together." The previous Sunday, for example, he says the Highlanders refused to repair boats to carry settlers to Churchill Creek. McDonald told Auld that neither he nor they would work on Sunday. Before HMS *Brazen* left port, Auld considered asking the navy to take McDonald home in irons but feared the spread of contagion: "A ringleader is thus preserved to lead the whole to the miserable fate which cannot fail to overtake these creatures." Auld goes on that he demanded McDonald bring the healthy across the Churchill River from the typhus camp to prevent their contracting the disease. McDonald refused, stoking the fires of Auld's rage.

Although McDonald is not privy to Auld's letter, he knows he will have to defend himself. In a report to Lord Selkirk next spring, he will write that he scrupulously kept "the sick and the hale" under separate canvases and declined to bring the uninfected across the river because it would double his work and possibly spread the contagion to the locals through "contaminated bedclothes." Far from ignoring Auld's advice, he says he never got it: "Not a single person even came near me while at Sloops Cove. Even

Mr. Auld did not give me those private and friendly directions I certainly was looking out for, to regulate my management." He acknowledges the settlers' aversion to Sunday labour, common to all strict Presbyterians, but says they did their share and more of the work despite this.

He can say none of this to Auld as it is happening because he desperately needs the Company's help, and Auld is the Company.

He receives a letter from Miles McDonell, waiting helplessly and hopelessly at York Fort, instructing him to put himself under the command of Auld and Dr. Edwards. McDonell unintentionally prods the sore spot: "Had Capt. Turner put in here instead of going to Churchill the Sick should have had immediate relief and all of you would have reached your destination."

Instead of spending the winter on their future farms making heady plans for the spring, the Highlanders hunker down in what Auld calls "hovels," trying simply to survive. Although McDonell asks Archie McDonald to send him Lamont, it doesn't happen. Perhaps McDonald wants Lamont with him. They are the same age and, as neither is a Highlander (being from Islay, Lamont is an Islander), both are outsiders to the community. While Lamont is not of McDonald's class, as a skilled and literate millwright he's closer than the simple Gaelic farmers. Moreover, Highlanders can be a testy lot, but as a contract servant, Lamont does not have that luxury. Caught between his flinty charges and even worse superiors, Archie McDonald needs a friend, an ally or at least reliable support. Lamont is the logical choice.

Auld doesn't describe the hovels (the settlers call them huts) on Churchill Creek, but the likelihood is that they follow a design used by northern Indigenous peoples for ages, and even by the colonists' own ancestors in the far north of Scotland. A pit is dug, perhaps waist-deep, and then a low roof frame made from lumber and stunted northern trees is built over it to support boughs or other coverings and a thick blanket of snow.[1] The resulting habitation, low and sturdy in the winter

---

[1]   As late as the 1960s, people said pits could still be made out along the creek's shore. Whether they were from 1813 or not, it at least confirms that this form of construction was in use. (Angus MacIver, Lorraine Brandson, and Bernice MacIver, *Churchill* on *Hudson Bay*, 1982)

winds, would be smoky, probably cramped, muddy when warm, and with little privacy and no convenience. But it would be snug, and for a people starved of comforts, snug is likely just fine, all things considered.

On October 16, Dr. Edwards brings the recovering patients up to join them. Archie McDonald wants to mark this small milestone. He later reports: "I asked Dr. Edwards if it was customary giving Rum on this occasion? He told me it was and wished me to give a dram to all hands at night after putting up," which McDonald does. So the people are all together again, and just in time for the "partridges."

Churchill Creek is a favourite wintering place for that fat little featherball, the ptarmigan. They descend in their thousands and present themselves gormlessly for the slaughter. Europeans call them partridges in these days, and Archie McDonald calls them "the greatest blessing we could have wished for, both for saving English provisions and . . . preventing Scurvy."

Beyond fresh meat, they offer sport. Most of the men have muskets or "fowling-pieces" (shotguns), and they set about the harvest with a will. Over the winter many thousands will go into the Scots' cooking pots. Boiled in oatmeal, they make a nourishing staple while enriching the porridge with their insulating fat. Things are looking better than the castaways could have hoped after their terrible ordeal. What — or who — could possibly spoil things now?

YORK FACTORY, HBC HEADQUARTERS ON HUDSON BAY.

William Auld, returned to York Fort aboard *Brazen*, has escaped "those damned savages from Scotland." But he feels he must return to Churchill, at least until Christmas, to ensure the "safety and survival" of the colonists. It would be in character if he also wants to make sure they don't consume too many HBC supplies.

Just ten days after getting back to York, Auld sets out again, with "four Englishmen and three Indians." This trip isn't a brisk sail like the first. Instead of taking forty-five hours, the journey takes forever, as he and his companions are forced to abandon their boats, construct snowshoes and fur parkas and then slog cross-country over unbroken trails. They finally drag themselves into Churchill Fort on October 30, a full four weeks from setting out.

CHURCHILL CREEK WINTER QUARTERS.

On November 8, Auld journeys up the river to the colony on the creek. He immediately puts a stop to Archie McDonald's rum rations:

> He told me that the most rigid economy was to be used throughout the ensuing winter. Mr. Edwards was to examine the record every night to see what was issued during the day.

Predictably, this will lead to friction in what had been, by McDonald's own account, a relaxed relationship between himself and Abel Edwards. Edwards will join Auld in undermining and contradicting McDonald's judgment at every opportunity, and Auld in turn will reinforce Edwards's bullying. Instead of mentors guiding him through the winter, McDonald will be cursed with a pair of nitpicking petty administrators of the worst sort.

Is there any other pleasure Mr. Auld can strip away from these blamelessly marooned people? You bet: the ptarmigan hunt. But on what possible grounds?

The official story, as recorded in the Post log, is that the settlers might "get themselves lost in the woods from their continually straying about with their Guns. Several had lost their way in the Daytime." Furthermore, they don't dress properly and might well end up frozen. To prevent this, "Mr. Auld this morning went to Churchill Creek and desired those who had Guns to deliver them to Mr. Edwards."

It may be hard to believe that Highlanders are not smart enough to come in from the cold, dress properly or learn bush navigation. And of course it is; Auld has another motive. He's decided that the ptarmigan, like game on the earl's estate, is the private property of the Honourable Company, and so must be purchased. "Surely a dozen Partridges are equal to a piece of Salt Beef," he declares. Since he does not trust the Highlanders to keep scrupulous count, Auld impounds their guns and hires Indigenous hunters to shoot the birds and record their numbers.

From Auld this should not surprise us. The Highlanders' quiet acquiescence is out of character and more unexpected. Later accounts suggest a few guns are secretly withheld and occasional shooting continues to be heard.

Winter settles in. Every week or two several men pull sleds twenty-four kilometres to Churchill Fort to gather supplies — oatmeal, salt meat and other necessities — and then haul the load back the next day. This leads to the most dramatic event of the winter.

On November 24, four men make the trip to the fort and are sent to sleep in the "Indian House," a room or building normally reserved for visiting trappers, "where the colony sleds were ready with the necessaries required." In the middle of the night, according to the Post log,

> men who were sleeping in the Kitchen were awoke by the smell of Smoke and getting up observed a fire in the roof of the Indian House. . . . They immediately ran to wake the four settlers but found them up and Mr. Auld on the Staircase, calling for lights.

The flames rise beyond control. Winter has made liquid water scarce, and snow simply can't conquer a fire of this ferocity, so they turn their efforts to getting food and trade goods out of threatened buildings, especially the "Powder Cases and Barrels from the Magazine." Much is saved, but "in less than three hours, the whole of our dwelling houses, Ice House and Coal Shed were nothing but a heap of burning ruins. . . . Most of our stores and trading goods and nearly all our books was lost."

Auld blames the settlers, who defend themselves. Winter grinds on.

CHAPTER 6

MILES McDONELL

AUGUST 14, 1813, TO NEW YEAR'S, 1814

YORK FACTORY.

Miles McDonell and his small flotilla of boats arrive at York Fort around noon on August 14, ending a month-long lake and river journey from Red River. There is no sign of the expected ship, but it will appear any day now, with its draft of sea-weary settlers eager to start life again in this new country. As he waits, McDonell will be anything but idle.

Forty-six years old and a former soldier, Miles McDonell has been trained to action and is uncomfortable without it. A Scots-born Roman Catholic, he immigrated with his parents to New York colony in 1773. In the American Revolution, they chose the Loyalist side and Miles joined a British regiment at the age of fifteen. After discharge in 1784 he disappears until 1791, when he is farming in Upper Canada with his Scottish wife, Isabella. When she dies three years later, McDonell falls into a prolonged bout of the depression that will haunt his life. The colonial army rescues him, giving him a captain's commission that enables him to support his three children. In 1798 he marries again, but his second wife, Catherine, dies after only a year. By 1802 he is out of the army and back on his farm, where he marries Nancy, his third and final wife. Farming still does not produce the income he needs. He struggles on, living frugally.

Lord Selkirk meets him on a trip to Canada and finds him "a gentleman in manners and sentiments," always the earl's first consideration, and "popular," whatever that might mean. In 1811, when Selkirk offers him the post of Governor of Assiniboia and the Red River Settlement, McDonell, now in England, jumps at it.

Later that year, he sails from England to York Factory with his crew of labourers to prepare the intended settlement site near The Forks. After two difficult years, he has managed to stake out the future settlement and his few farmer-settlers have planted crops which are flourishing, just as all had hoped.

In July 1813, McDonell heads north to escort the expected colonists — our colonists, if you will — to their new home. So here he is, waiting to do just that.

After a day or so to recover from his journey, McDonell's first act is to secure and inspect the boats that will take his people up[1] (that is, upstream) to Red River. At this point he is confident that he has twenty boats at his disposal, more than enough to carry the hundred immigrants with their luggage and boatmen the 1,200 kilometres to their destination.

These boats are double-ended (pointed at both ends), usually about 9–13 metres long and 2.7 metres wide, and weighing 450 kilos or more when empty. This standard model of an open, river-faring craft will one day be known as a York Boat, but at this time, they are simply "batteaux," in the spelling of the time.

The boats seen to, he must arrange for supplies to be pulled from Selkirk's stores, or purchased from the Hudson's Bay Company, which means haggling with its tight-fisted superintendent, William Auld. The two men share a hearty mutual dislike.

Even as he wrangles with Auld, he must finish his annual report to Lord Selkirk. In it he paints a picture of the last year, which, while

---

1   It is counterintuitive to think of going south from Hudson Bay as "up," but that was the universal convention in 1813 and to avoid even further confusion, I will adopt it.

ultimately successful, was plagued by physical hardship and personality conflict, especially between McDonell and his junior officers. This has a familiar ring after his labour problems of 1811 and 1812, and indeed both stem from a character trait mentioned by several others: an unattractive arrogance and general aloofness, even toward social equals like Auld, but especially to those whom society or his lordship has put "beneath" him.

Peremptory arrogance is of course commonplace in this class-bound period, but it does not transfer well to the management of small groups and perhaps especially his junior officers, all of whom are civilians and social equals, unaccustomed to parade-ground discipline. During the winter of 1812–13, insubordination approached outright mutiny, at least in McDonell's telling:

"It is not in my power," he begins, in his report to the earl, "to describe to your Lordship all that I suffered from . . . those by whom I was surrounded, not excepting the Gentlemen serving under me. I shall take the liberty here of touching on this very unpleasant part."

This he does, touching on it for the next four-and-a-half handwritten pages. His two gentleman assistants, Dr. Edwards, whom we know from the Churchill camp, and another "young man of good family," Kenneth McRae, ignored his orders, malingered, wandered about at their whim and were openly insolent. It got so bad that he finally sent McRae off to a hunting outpost, and the bad boys were separated for the rest of the winter. Their bad attitude "spread from the officers among the people. I could not venture to be for an hour absent from the Fort for fear of what might happen." He seems to have made no attempt to counteract dissatisfaction by appealing to the colonists and servants directly. Officers do not consult the ranks on matters of discipline.

Edwards and McRae are here in York with McDonell to catch the *Prince of Wales* for its return to Britain. They too have written to Lord Selkirk, complaining just as bitterly about his abuse of them with overwork and terrible living conditions, his disregard for their safety, his public scoldings and so on. They most certainly give as good as they get, but what stands out about all these communications is how much ink they spend on internal politics and petty grievances and how little on the settlement, the Indigenous residents or the settlers who are the point of this whole exercise.

It must be said that, quite apart from all this personal chafing, there is no doubt that keeping several dozen people adequately fed through the long, long prairie winter was a great source of stress. In McDonell's winter journal, most entries include an accounting of food secured that day and measures taken to find more. It was his constant anxiety.

He tells Selkirk that he has chosen land for the settlers' farms. They are to be hundred-acre strips, each fronting on the river to give each family a portion of the woods that line the riverbank and plenty of clear prairie beyond.

Last year's crops, he says, mainly failed from being planted too late, and yet "the country exceeds any idea I had formed of its goodness. I am only astonished it has lain so long unsettled[2] . . . The land is most fertile and the climate most extraordinarily healthy.[3]" He means that the fevers that make warm and damp climates so dangerous are unknown here.

Finally he turns his attention to First Nations. Neither he nor Selkirk ever doubt or deny Indigenous "ownership" of the land they are invading, but McDonell can't get his head around their concept of possession:

> I am at a loss in what manner to make a purchase from the natives. Those here do not call themselves owners of the soil, though long in possession. It belonged originally to the Cree whom the Assiniboine, a branch of the Sioux, drove off.[4] A small annual present will satisfy the Indians here and should others make a claim a present will satisfy them also.

---

2   Unsettled, but not unused or unoccupied, a contradiction that would be conveniently invisible to most settler-Canadians for another two centuries.

3   Though most self-described "tough Canadians" fear the prairie climate today, and even prairie dwellers tend to whine at winter's length, I never came across a single complaint in the record of these years. The absence of endemic disease more than made up for the icy winter.

4   This is strictly McDonell's reading of matters at the time, whatever the truth of the situation.

He reports that all the "formidable threats against us are blown over" and everyone in the neighbourhood of The Forks seems favourably disposed to the colony. This is another of McDonell's regrettable traits: wilful obliviousness. At least some are anything but favourably disposed.

So much for the past. In the present he must cope with William Auld, who immediately and probably intentionally throws McDonell off balance with a piece of alarming news:

Mr. Cook, chief factor of York Factory, had noticed, after the 1812 colonists had passed through last year, that several of his silver teaspoons were missing. Now the crime has been traced to McDonell's best and perhaps only friends back at Red River, Alexander and Christina McLean.

The McLeans are gentlefolk, socially and financially equal to Miles McDonell and so a cut above the rest of the settlers. They have 300 acres, a hired ploughman and a maid. As McDonell's friends, they are fair game for Edwards and McRae and it is just these bad boys who have laid the crime of the missing teaspoons at their feet.

Auld is almost unseemly in his tattling enthusiasm. He tells McDonell, in writing, that respect for Lord Selkirk alone (underlined three times) has kept him from issuing search-and-arrest warrants for the "Delinquent and Family." "As this is an offence punishable by Death," he enthuses, "we have had much hesitation about the proper line of conduct to pursue." Nonetheless he declares their guilt without "a shadow of a doubt."

His certainty comes from sworn testimony of the young officers. Apparently they had seen Christina with the purloined cutlery and had carefully made a drawing which, when compared with Cook's remaining spoons, matches perfectly. What could be more satisfying than sending their oppressor's only friends to the gibbet? Probably no one expects it to go that far, but the discomfort and shame would be a sufficient and delicious revenge. The possibility that there might be an innocent explanation seems not to have occurred to any of them.

McDonell trusts Alex McLean implicitly and has left him in charge at Red River during his own absence. He is certainly troubled by these revelations but he is not about to jump into the executioner's box with Auld.[5] To Lord Selkirk, he laments,

> I feel extremely hurt at the accusations lodged against Mr. McLean's family . . . Mr. McRae's malice is conspicuous on this and many other occasions. It is very odd that this affair should have been whispered about all winter without ever coming to my knowledge.

Small group politics. There is nothing more he can do until he returns to Red River and gets the so-called delinquents' side of the story. Besides, far more urgent news demands his attention: word arrives of the *Prince's* diversion to Churchill. He waits and frets.

A week later, on September 7, his worst fear is realized — the colonists are stranded for the winter, and will not come to York. "Mr. Auld proceeds immediately to Churchill."

Having sent with Auld the letter telling Archie McDonald to submit himself to Auld and Dr. Edwards, McDonell wastes no time getting ready to leave. He brings Lord Selkirk up to date in his letter and fumes at Captain Turner's decision, hoping that the captain "shall be made to smart severely for his brutal stubbornness." On September 10 he writes,

> Closed my last dispatch to the Earl of Selkirk. At 10 o'clock AM we got underway with 3 boats. Many of our people were in liquor.

The trip to Red River will take five weeks. It is an exhausting marathon of rowing, poling, hauling, portaging and sailing, all upstream, all in open boats. Even for a governor, though spared the brute labour, it is

---

5   Auld's antipathy toward McLean, as toward so many, knows no bounds. Having heard that McDonell left Alex McLean in charge at Red River, he observes, "This summer McLean has the direction [of the colony] and everyone that is under him fears plunder and waste will riot uncontrolled."

certainly no picnic. Braving rain, frost and endless portages, they reach Jack River, the northern entry to Lake Winnipeg, on October 4, making the last stretch in "the shortest time ever known." Impressive, but hard, hard work against strong currents in autumn-shallow streams.

The trip south, through the length of Lake Winnipeg, involves no portages, but still they're plagued with contrary winds and rain. They reach the mouth of the Red in nine more days and The Forks at last on October 15.

McDonell immediately notes that "Mr. McLean has been very careful of everything — used only two bags oatmeal."

The governor is back.

RED RIVER SETTLEMENT NEAR THE FORKS OF THE
RED AND ASSINIBOINE RIVERS.

On October 19, four days after his arrival, McDonell addresses the matter of the Purloined Spoons. The McLeans are ready with their response. Christina McLean gives the first and most fulsome answer:

> Christina McLean [swears] that on the 28th October [1812]
> . . . she, along with her serving maid, Ann McDonald, were
> emptying out the contents of a canteen . . . and on turning it
> upside down, a Silver Teaspoon dropped out which did not
> belong to the deponent and on taking it up asked the maid
> how it could have come there? to which the maid replied that
> she did not know.

At this point Kenneth McRae arrived at the tent door. Christina showed him the spoon, saying it wasn't hers and that she had no idea how it got into her luggage. McRae, she says, looked it over without comment. Later, she regularly loaned the spoon to the officers for their tea or Dr. Edwards's medical preparations.

Her maid and her husband then confirm this, the maid repeating the story of showing it to McRae.

Seems a credible enough response, but still . . . does one point out to someone who happens by that this teaspoon just fell out of your luggage and that it isn't yours and you have no idea how it got there? Maybe in a world where a teaspoon can get you hanged you do. What about the other three spoons? Many questions, few answers.

FORT DAER, ON THE PEMBINA RIVER.

The colonists from the *Prince of Wales* are marooned at Churchill and beyond McDonell's care or control, but he still must look after his few settlers and servants who are already here. Convinced he cannot adequately provision the colony at The Forks, McDonell once again moves them to Pembina, a hundred kilometres to the south, where they reoccupy and restore Fort Daer for another winter of privation and food insecurity. His journal becomes an account of who is hunting where and what provisions are coming back to the people. And the people? They have clearly had enough of this winter-quarters nonsense:

> [Dec. 2, 1813] I stop the provisions of the Settlers' families for this day to urge them to go also to the plains [go hunting]. They are a dead weight on my hands and do not strain to help themselves.

It is hard to believe that, if the direness of the situation were fully explained to them, the settlers would refuse to "strain to help themselves." At any rate his starvation threat does the trick and they submit.

Despite hard times, the winter is not without its distractions. On December 12 McDonell "rides out with all the Gentlemen" apparently for simple enjoyment. The next day,

> Married John Cooper, one of our men, to Mary McKinnon, daughter of a Settler. They make a wedding according to Highland customs. Two Saulteaux Indians dance a reel after

laying aside their blankets and dressing themselves in clothes borrowed from our people.

Then, on Christmas, he distributes pints of unspecified liquor to the people as well as extra rations of food. It's a jolly celebration:

The Highlanders and Irish played several matches at the Hurl[6] on the ice — treated all the people with a dram in the evening . . . They were all very merry and well satisfied, danced, sang Gaelic songs etc. etc.

On New Year's Eve, Scottish Hogmanay, he joins in the hurl-playing, imbibing and dancing. He notes, "The people, although chiefly Presbyterians, made some encroachment on the Sabbath before they broke up."

These entertainments, including the Sabbath encroachments, recur regularly in his journal entries, to the constant drumbeat of "meat brought in," "so-and-so sent to the plains," "Sioux hunting party seen," "sleds of meat," "several deer killed," "three sturgeon caught." Food, and hostile Dakotas (Sioux), are his constant anxiety and preoccupation.

Throughout the winter, the unmistakable cordiality and invaluable help of the First Nations (Dakota excepted) are evident. Saulteaux Anishinaabe, especially the band of a chief called "The Premier," along with unnamed Nakoda Oyadebi (Assiniboine) contributors, regularly bring in meat and fish for trade, though what is given in return is not specified aside from the occasional gift of tobacco or liquor. Powder and shot are probably big items, since there are comments that the "Indians are completely out of ammunition." This relationship of mutual aid and dependence forms the basis for the generally amicable relations that will persist between Indigenous peoples and newcomers throughout the early life of the Red River Settlement. This is especially marked in the warm relations with the Saulteaux band of the immortal and still-celebrated Chief Peguis, of whom more presently.

---

6   Now called hurley, a traditional Celtic game involving teams with sticks and a ball.

The new year is ushered in with goodwill and good spirits, but three hard months of winter still lie ahead. Can Miles get the settlement through them without tripping over his own snowshoes?

CHAPTER 7

STRESS

JANUARY 8 TO APRIL 26, 1814

FORT DAER, ON THE PEMBINA RIVER.

As January establishes its character (cold!), McDonell wastes no time shooting himself in the foot. On January 8, 1814, he issues a proclamation that "prohibits all export [from Selkirk's concession] of provisions of whatsoever nature for one year from this date."

McDonell seems to have no notion of the profound implications of this one edict in the complex social relations on the western prairie, probably because he has no real notion of how these relations came to exist.[1]

It should not require repetition that if the Great Plains "belong" to anyone in the 1810s, it is the Indigenous people of the First Nations, who have been here at least since the last ice age. However, in the previous century and a half, three other communities have come to believe they have an inalienable right to occupy the land included in McDonell's "proclamation."

---

[1] For those who want to go deeper than these few paragraphs, I particularly recommend *The North-West Is Our Mother*, by Jean Teillet, from which many of these facts are taken.

The first is the Hudson's Bay Company, operating under the Royal Charter of 1670, which granted it a trade monopoly over all the lands between Lake Superior and the Rockies, and south from the Hudson Bay to the Missouri River. Since then, it has exercised that monopoly almost exclusively in the northern parts of its concession through its "factories" (trading centres) on Hudson Bay, fed by a system of lesser posts, largely along the Saskatchewan River and its tributaries.

The second, the North West Company, grew out of efforts by Montreal merchants to get a share of the trade despite the HBC's charter monopoly. They tend to exploit the more southern regions where the HBC have few posts, but the two big players have since 1800 come into more direct competition. In the beginning the owners of the rival company, called proprietors or partners, were French, but are now mainly Scottish, still headquartered in Montreal. Their employees are francophone voyageurs from Lower Canada who canoe trade goods every year 1,500 or so kilometres from Montreal via rivers and lakes to their depot at Fort William (now Thunder Bay) near the western tip of Lake Superior, to be dispersed from there to trading posts throughout the northwest all the way to the Rockies. Furs by the bale come back the same way, many coming through The Forks at Red River.

Over the years these canoemen have split into two distinct groups: those who make the return trip every year from Montreal, never going farther west than Fort William, and the winterers, "les hommes du Nord," who stay permanently in the trading territory, delivering their furs to Fort William every spring, restocking with fresh trade goods and returning west to prepare for the next winter. These inland servants are generally known as Canadians, a term in these days restricted to those from Lower Canada (now Quebec). Many have left permanent NWCo employment to become "freemen," those who work under contract from year to year as it suits them.

These men, the freemen and Canadians, are creating the third and most interesting category of new westerners. Les hommes du Nord marry Indigenous women and raise families. Their children are called

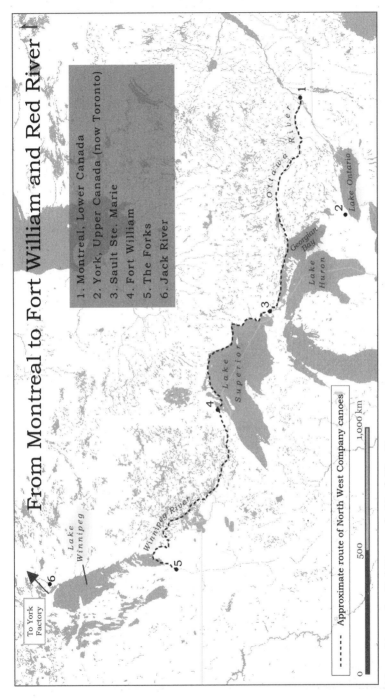

From Montreal to Fort William and Red River

1. Montreal, Lower Canada
2. York, Upper Canada (now Toronto)
3. Sault Ste. Marie
4. Fort William
5. The Forks
6. Jack River

Ottawa River

Lake Ontario

Georgian Bay

Lake Huron

Lake Superior

Winnipeg River

Lake Winnipeg

To York Factory

- - - - Approximate route of North West Company canoes

0   500   1,000 km

Map 2. Montreal to Red River — the North West Company canoe route.

by any number of terms to indicate their mixed heritage, but as they grow up and begin to raise another generation, they adopt the name Bois-Brûlés (burnt wood) — a reference to their skin colour and generally francophone paternity. The Bois-Brûlés are neither "Indian" nor "White," and are beginning to become aware that they are creating a unique social identity of their own. Nonetheless, they have no doubt they belong in the West, the only home they know. They live by the survival skills of their mothers' people and much of the social organization and commercial relations of their fathers'. Their semi-annual buffalo hunts sustain them, and the pemmican they produce — a stew or paste consisting of dried bison meat mixed with bison fat and other ingredients — furnishes a durable, reliable and transportable staple that enables and sustains the NWCo's trade.

Time and expansion have brought the Hudson's Bay Company and the Nor'Westers into more and more direct contact, and their competition has become, at times literally, cutthroat. The result is that both companies' profits have shrunk to almost nothing. Each believes itself in a commercial death struggle.

Nor'Westers have been coming through The Forks unmolested for decades. They take their access to pemmican for granted, and it has yet to be challenged. They are certain, with strong reason, that the laws of Lower Canada validate their trading activities. They will inevitably see McDonell's ban on transporting pemmican not as an expedient of the colony's need, but a ploy by their hated rivals to choke off their trade. For their workforce, the Bois-Brûlés, that could mean loss of livelihood, and the end of a way of life. The stakes are about as high as they can be. McDonell, in his proclamation, brushes all this aside.

Another potential source of confusion is the ambiguous relationship of the settlement to the HBC. The North West Company and its Bois-Brûlé associates will make no distinction between the two and see the colony as an HBC plot, period. That is not an unreasonable position by any means, but it doesn't reflect reality in these first years. Many in the HBC — the Company, as they call themselves — are openly hostile to the Red River Settlement, and the terms of Selkirk's grant by the HBC make it clear that the settlement is his responsibility, not the Company's. Nonetheless, there is an informal cooperation and mutual connection between the two. The governing committee in London hopes the settlement will be a local source of food to replace expensive imports from Britain. But in neither company nor settlement is there any belief that they are united, at least not in 1814.

With the exception of this last item, it is doubtful how much Miles McDonell truly understands of the make-up or history of this world. He has been planning this proclamation for some time, and its language is unambiguous:

> And whereas the welfare of the families forming the Settlements on the Red River . . . renders it my duty to provide for their support . . . Wherefore it is hereby ordered that *no persons* trading for the Hon. HBC[2] or the NWC or *any individual whatever* shall take out any Provisions . . . procured or raised within the said Territory for one twelvemonth from the date hereof.

The proclamation also lays out the geographic bounds of Selkirk's concession, called Assiniboia, "of which I the undersigned have been duly appointed Governor." Described verbally, Assiniboia's boundaries are incomprehensible; translated onto a map, it is enormous.

One glance at the map exposes the Pemmican Proclamation as an unenforceable pipe dream. At 300,000 square kilometres, Assiniboia is almost four times the size of Scotland, far beyond any possibility of effective control by McDonell, even if he truly were the royally appointed governor. But his appointment comes only from the Hudson's Bay Company, and there is no evidence or precedent that the HBC, or for that matter, even the king of England, has a right of governance over this place beyond their own employees and their own

---

2   The inclusion of the HBC in the ban is trivial, since the Company has other sources of supply.

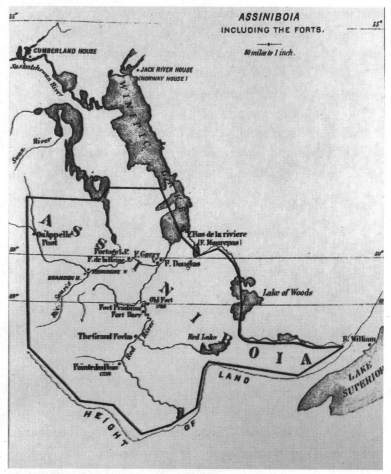

Map 3. Assiniboia, Selkirk's land "grant," as drawn for the Royal Society of Canada. (G. Bryce, *The Five Forts of Winnipeg, Transactions of the Royal Society of Canada,* Vol. 3, 1885)

forts. Their charter is a trade monopoly, not a deed of ownership or claim of sovereignty, no matter what they pretend.

Their competitors are fully aware of this.

By any measure, geographic or legal, the Pemmican Proclamation is an absurd fantasy. Purely logistically, McDonell must know this. So why does he do it?

He probably feels he has no choice. In this second winter in a row of dangerous scarcity, he sees no other route to stave off famine. He's looking at another hundred or more mouths to feed next year and many more again the next and the next, until agricultural production gets well underway. What can he do? Give a military man a problem and he will solve it with decision, determination and orders. The claim on all the region's resources is an act of desperation using the strongest tool he knows: command, backed by implied force. In a situation that calls for tactful diplomacy and delicate negotiation between stakeholders, he has opted for the iron fist and the face of stone.

He makes a risible attempt to forestall an imagined panic among the suddenly de-rationed fur traders with these words:

> Save and except what may be judged necessary for the . . .
> parties within the Territory to carry them to their respective
> destinations and who may on application to me obtain a
> Licence for the same.

In other words, if you beg, I'll give you bus fare home.

The Nor'Westers will not panic, nor will they beg.

That same night, January 8, he throws another of his dance parties in Fort Daer, where "the Gentlemen, men and women enjoyed themselves and encroached on the Sabbath."

The next day, McDonell sends men to post the proclamation about the district. Across the Pembina River from Fort Daer, at the North West Fort, Chief Trader Wills immediately tears it off his gate. The next weekend McDonell throws yet another party, "danced country dances . . . kept it up till near daylight." These entertainments help keep people's minds off such scary realities as "the man sent to Mr. Warren's [hunting] tent returned without meat. No accounts from the plains."

A few days later, his entry mixes good news with bad.

> Lagimonière arrives with his family . . . he has not seen so
> much as a partridge since he left [Stony] Mountain.

Lagimonière is Jean-Baptiste Lagimonière (now spelled Lagimodière). He is a Québécois trapper and hunter who has come back to the Red

River Valley after many years on the western plains. His wife, Marie-Anne Gaboury, was the first white woman on the prairies when she arrived in 1806. They are neither mixed-heritage people nor part of either fur-trade company. The couple will remain valuable, though strictly neutral, friends of the settlement throughout this period. Lagimonière is a superb hunter, making him highly valued by McDonell. Marie-Anne is equally invaluable to the settler women but McDonell does not notice or remark on that. That a hunter like Lagimonière has not seen "so much as a partridge" is ominous.

A week later, three more sleds of meat arrive from the Saulteaux camp of the chief called The Premier. On January 25, McDonell records:

> To save our meat, 1 lb. of oatmeal per ration is issued, to be continued until we hear from the plains [hunters]. Sent a party to the Premier for meat. Sent him some Rum and Tobacco.

On January 28, a party of six hunters arrives with meat, and with them a man named James Barr, who tells McDonell a horrifying story: Barr and a friend were "left on the plains by the hunter Bostonais," hauling sleds piled with frozen meat. They lost their way in the dark and had to spend the night on the open plain, turning up their sleds for some respite from the wind. They could not make a fire to melt snow or thaw any of their cargo. The next day, still lost, they saw a band of "twelve Sioux on horseback, some miles off." One of them was all for throwing themselves on the hunters' mercy, but his partner wisely vetoed that. At last they recognized a patch of woods and there found friends who fed them and welcomed their meat.

This tale is far from unique. Even in the twenty-first century, winter waits like a stalking wolf for the stranded traveller who makes a wrong decision. In 1814, it waits for everyone. Starvation is common, even among First Nations bands whose food eludes them or who become disoriented in a storm. McDonell is not exaggerating the threat. Two days later McDonell records, "Weather extremely cold, 40½ below 0." His fractional precision says it all.

On February 4, he sends off a dogsled to York Factory. In a letter to Superintendent William Auld, he recounts the fever that went through the colony last summer and killed "Hector McLean and a boy about 12 years of age." He also encloses Alex and Christina McLean's depositions regarding the missing spoons. He tells Auld of the Pemmican Proclamation, adding a paragraph which shows just how firmly he intends to enforce it:

> I have sufficient force to crush all the Nor'Westers in this river should they resist openly my authority. On the general rendez-vous of their Northern Canoes in spring, their great numbers might induce them to make a violent effort — but I cannot imagine that the [NWCo] can prevail on their men to act against us in that way. Whatever may happen I am determined that my authority shall not be trampled on . . . We are well armed and I have a parcel of fine active stout fellows that will execute any order they receive.

This is confidence born of several of assumptions that he has yet to test. Success will depend on his being right about the Nor'Westers and "their men," as well as his assessment of his own forces. Prideful insistence on "my authority" is the overriding imperative.

Alex and Christina McLean and family have stayed on their farm at The Forks rather than come to Fort Daer for the winter. McDonell receives word that Mrs. McLean has given birth and is looking for a nursemaid, so he uses this excuse to make a "jaunt to The Forks along with Dr. Holdesworth. We take a nurse down for Mrs. McLean."

While making the four-day trip by dogsled, he describes the Red River technique for overnight survival:

> Slept out 4 nights . . . The usual way in making camp is to clear away the snow with a shovel or snowshoe for a space sufficient for a number of people and their fire. The people sleep with their feet to it. With a single blanket and a Buffalo robe they sleep as warm and comfortable as in a house.

RED RIVER SETTLEMENT NEAR THE FORKS.

McDonell dines with the McLeans and on February 15 christens their son. He notes that one Alexander McDonell is also present, and wants to mend fences over some disagreements of the past.

Alexander McDonell is the leading partner of the North West Company in the region of The Forks and Fort Gibraltar.[3] He is Miles McDonell's chief rival. He is also Miles McDonell's cousin, as well as his brother-in-law, and has become a friend of the McLeans. They are friends and family on opposite sides of a divide which will prove greater than their family bonds can bridge.

His visit over, Miles returns to Fort Daer, another four days on the trail. On March 10, he gets his own little taste of the stalking wolf that is winter:

> Holdesworth and I depart for the plains with Horses. After going 30 miles we lost our road and slept in the open plain without means of making a fire or having anything to eat . . . The wind blew strong from the north.

An endless night of discomfort and probably fear distilled into a simple understatement. Pity the horses! The next day they find their trail again and avoid the lonely fate of too many.

FORT DAER ON THE PEMBINA RIVER.

In late March winter finally begins to falter. "The going is now very bad. The snow is melted in the plains. Nothing but water and ice."

---

3   Fort Gibraltar is on the spot where Fort Garry will be built in a few years. The wonderful replica now standing in St. Boniface is across the river from the original site.

The thaw brings concern over preserving meat so McDonell sends two carts to gather salt at Salt Lake.[4]

On April 3 an "express"[5] arrives from points north, bringing letters from the verbose Mr. Auld. Surprisingly, Auld supports the ban on exporting pemmican but says that instead of dropping a bomb like the proclamation with immediate effect, "that a notice [of intention] in my opinion, and I speak feelingly, would have pleased them and us better." Such a notice would take effect in a year.

Wise words. A year's notice would have been fairer and raised fewer hackles. The time might have been used to work out a livable compromise. Too late now without great loss of face.

Auld has much to say. This is his first opportunity to give McDonell a full account of the calamitous fire at Churchill last November. He doesn't waste the opportunity:

> I was awoke by my consort[6] (nursing a newborn infant) and nearly stifled by the smoke . . . I did not save a particle but the blankets on my bed for . . . my little children, left naked and screaming on the river in a horrid night, Thermometer -32°, while the women were assisting removing goods and powder to a distance. I am unable to describe our distress.

Yet he does, at length, climaxing with,

> . . . but behold us without knife fork spoon dish glass table stool chair bed or bedstead or even wearing apparel except what we had huddled in on the night of our calamity . . . All our poor

---

4   There are several salt lakes in North Dakota. This probably refers to the North Salt Lake in present-day Walsh County. A one- or two-day trek each way, depending on conditions.

5   "Expresses" are mentioned frequently. They simply mean the mail, carried as quickly as possible between posts over land, water or snow.

6   Auld has an Indigenous wife ("consort") and several children for all of whom he expresses great affection from time to time.

men who were hunting and fishing <u>for your fellows</u> have lost
all . . . You thus see the colony is destined to be our ruin . . . for
what — a Phantom! But my <u>loss</u> is no phantom.

You have to admire the deftly inserted "for your fellows." No
opening is missed.

Heart-wrenching as this tale is, he saves his strongest anguish for
McDonell's defence of the McLeans, including a graphic visual aid:

"Oh! I think your exculpatory proofs of McLean's innocence are like those dayly
offered by convicted felons, which never retard their voyage to Botany Bay or —"
(Library and Archives Canada, Selkirk Papers, p. 1265)

April 17 brings a Charlie Chaplin moment to McDonell's journal:

Alexander Smith went out shooting and returned in a great
fright from having seen a bear, which turned out afterwards
to be a Canadian.

Anyone who recalls when police on the prairies wore buffalo coats
will understand Mr. Smith's confusion.

With the thaw, game is becoming plentiful, especially migrating
waterfowl. On April 23 the ice on the Red River breaks up. Winter
is over.

Winters like this one are what the nascent colony is up against if it
is to survive long enough to become self-sufficient. The problems are
real, daunting and hadn't been anticipated by Selkirk and his people in
Scotland. McDonell is on his own in finding solutions. Upbringing,

training and class conventions steer him toward autocratic dictation rather than any kind of collaboration. Combined with ignorance of and indifference to the fur trade, plains peoples, Highlanders or anything but his own stubborn entitlement, this almost guarantees his failure.

Not that anything is inevitable or foreordained.

CHAPTER 8

A WALK IN THE WOODS

JANUARY 14 TO MAY 23, 1814

THE CHURCHILL CREEK CAMP NEAR HUDSON BAY.

April has arrived here, too, in the winter refuge of the Kildonan Highlanders, but not spring, not yet. With temperatures easing, it is decided that before thaw turns the land to swamp, whoever is strong enough should make an overland trek to York Factory, to be ready to start upriver the moment ice clears from the northern streams. Daunting as that sounds — a hike across 240 kilometres of primal wilderness — the winter-weary settlers are eager.

Their young leader, Archie McDonald, has survived the hellish pettiness of William Auld and Abel Edwards and grown more comfortable in his role. He feels he understands his people, and they him. He begins a journal, as all leaders are required to for the guidance of those who succeed them. It starts on April 6 with the trekkers' departure, fifty-one of the heartiest souls, carrying clothing, guns and supplies, or pulling them on sleds: "The guide moved off at half-past six followed by the men and sledges, after whom came the women."

Of the fifty-one, twenty-one are men and thirty women, at least three of whom are pregnant. Three of the men are servants, or contract men, including Sam Lamont. Not counted are the guides and hunters to get them safely to York Fort. Wolves and polar bears are a concern, so the men's guns, confiscated last fall, have been returned to them. A piper takes his place in the centre of the line to lift spirits and encourage vigour. In the late afternoon, they camp opposite Churchill Fort, says McDonald, "several people having developed Cramp,[1] but all as cheerful and hearty as if they were going between houses at Churchill Creek."

Two morning gunshots alert the people every day: the first, usually around 4 a.m., signals them to rise, breakfast and break camp, and the second, an hour later, to fall in behind the guide and march off. The early start allows an early halt while daylight remains for setting up camp and preparing the evening meal. It also minimizes snow blindness from the reflected glare of a low southern sun.

Astonishing to consider the resilience and determination of these young men and women. After six months of a winter such as none had ever experienced — eating a diet poor in so many nutrients, especially vitamins C and D; faced with a trek across rocky, broken terrain with ice ridges, snowdrifts and tangled deadfall; threatened by slavering, winter-starved predators — they are not just willing, but eager. All these obstacles aside, it promises progress, improvement and, above all, change. Surely the greatest privation of sedentary winters before electricity liberated us was the sheer, endless, soul-crushing monotony. So off they go.

On April 7, the first full day on the trail, Archie McDonald writes, "Andrew [McBeath] was disabled by the cursed cramp — I took ten oz blood from his arm."

Cramp and snow blindness will plague them for the whole journey, and Archie McDonald, though his apprenticeship was cut short, is the closest thing they have to a medic. From the evidence of this walk, he seems to have only two treatments in his medical repertoire: bloodletting[2]

---

1   Muscle cramps, especially in the legs, arms and back, and a twisting in the gut are early signs of scurvy, not surprising in people who have had no access to fresh vegetables or fruit. Although preventives are available in the form of cranberry and spruce teas, they taste terrible and are often resisted.

2   Venesection, or bloodletting, an ancient practice, had received a (mistaken) boost in legitimacy around 1800 and at this point was (no pun intended) cutting-edge clinical practice. (J.M. Barry, *The Great Influenza*, Penguin Books, New York, 2004)

and purging. His first recourse is always to open a vein. He bleeds Mary Gunn for snow blindness, then Jannet Sutherland "as a means for checking the damned Cramps." Twenty-four-year-old Jean McKay is four months pregnant, but she gets lanced for cramp just like the others.

When bloodletting doesn't produce improvement he gives the patient "a dose of Jalop." This is jalap, a purgative. He often administers both together.

On April 9 they see two bears, turn in at 6 p.m., rise at 1 a.m., start off at 2. The moon is considerably over half full, lighting up the snow so that dark obstacles stand out and the trail is easy to follow despite the darkness.

On April 11, Charles McBeath is so blind and cramped that they distribute his pack load among others. Against orders he begins eating snow, worsening his cramp so much that he must be carried into camp. Mary Bannerman is bled for snow blindness and purged with jalap. Next day it "blew very smart from the North. The whole of the women and most of the men had their blankets over their shoulders during the forenoon." Blankets. Today's arctic parkas are technical wonders. These people give new meaning to the word "hardy."

On April 13, Jean McKay has an attack of cramp that causes her to stumble: "her foot gave way and she fell on bare ice." Later, in camp, McDonald

> attended her and found her much inclined to vomit, shivering all over, faintish, abdomen tense, pulse throbbing and on closer examination had an haemorrhage of the Vigenae [vagina?] and somewhat feverish.

Archie bleeds her, applies "tepid fomentation" and gives her twenty grains of jalap. "This woman is four months on in her pregnancy and I fear the symptoms threaten abortion." But Mrs. McKay is tough; she survives both the fall and the treatment.

Next day they all take a rest. Jean McKay is feeling better, but he bleeds her again anyway. Also Robert Gunn, the piper, for cramp. And Herman Sutherland. It blows hard all day, but McDonald sends three hunters with two settlers to shoot ptarmigan. They bring back seventy, none shot by the Scots. (Perhaps it was good that Auld assigned ptarmigan shooting to the Indigenous experts.)

Several times on the trip they are resupplied by stashes of food deposited earlier, and by hunters sent out from York to meet them. Hundreds of ptarmigans are devoured, with many, many pots of oatmeal. A blood trail of Archie's leechings marks their progress. Happily, this does not seem to attract any of those slavering, winter-starved predators.

On April 15, they resume the trek, leaving Jean McKay to rest a bit more with her husband Angus, her sister Jannet, Angus's brother George, and Charles McBeath. A hunter and an interpreter stay with them. They are well supplied with food, guns and ammunition.[3]

The rest slog on for three more days, getting lost, finding their way again, finally reaching the Nelson River and tracking its bank south for kilometres before finding a crossing over the piled-up ice. They then backtrack to a campsite six kilometres upstream from York Factory, on the banks of the Hayes River, where they arrive on the morning of April 18. The trip has taken twelve days. Taking out the day of rest, that is over twenty kilometres a day.

After seeing them camped, Archie McDonald hikes the six kilometres to York Factory. He discovers the title far outshines the reality. As described elsewhere by Miles McDonell,

> [York] Factory is built at the distance of a hundred yards from the north bank of the Hayes River, in low miry ground without a ditch. The stagnate water by which it is always surrounded, except when frozen, would be productive of much ill health had they a longer summer.

He goes on to criticize the design as "ill laid out," the construction as poor and the heating as barely adequate. As for the eighteen-foot surrounding palisade, its pickets are so thin and full of gaps, no enemy could be repelled.

---

3   Some histories state that a child was born on this journey. Not true, but this story of Jean MacKay's troubles is the likely source of the error.

Churchill to York Trek, 1814

1. Sloops Cove
2. Churchill Fort
3. Typhus Camp
4. Winter Camp
5. Jean McKay and
   party are left behind
6. York Factory
7. Settlers' Camp

Hudson Bay

Nelson River

Hayes River

To Jack River
&
Lake Winnipeg

0   50   100 km

Map 4. The trek from Churchill to York is 240 kilometres, more or less. The dense and frequent water obstacles (shaded areas) make winter travel a necessity.

Fortunately for Archie McDonald, the hospitality makes up for what the architecture lacks. Best of all, his nemesis Auld is away, off on a tour of inland posts. Archie is given dinner and "very kindly received by Mr. Cook and the other Gentlemen." The chief factor is by all evidence a humane fellow. McDonald speaks up for his charges:

> I expressed my desire to Mr. Cook of giving each of the party a dram but he told me it was his particular instruction from Mr. Auld to give no rum for the settlers and consequently could not deviate from it, tho' he certainly saw the propriety of giving it now. However, they got none.

Even in his absence, Auld has ensured that his petty meanness is carried on. The Hudson's Bay Company can certainly spare a little cheer for fifty honest, trail-beaten, tough but sorely tried women and men who have put up with a whole northern winter of his "economies." Even taken literally, what could a dram[4] each mean? A gallon? Maybe two? Ten litres if they go wild, which few Presbyterians will. Amounts like that are small change in the currency of the fur trade and would not have been in short supply at York Factory. Auld's order is pure spite.

The travellers will spend the next five weeks resting in their tent camp and repairing clothing for the long and (what's new?) arduous trip upstream to Red River. If we go by McDonell's arithmetic of last August, when he had twenty boats and took six with him, there should be fourteen left behind for them. But no — Auld will spare them only two batteaux for fifty-seven settlers and boatmen. These boats will be crowded to the gunwales with no room for cargo beyond survival provisions. They will have to leave almost all their baggage behind.

Sam Lamont is sent to the fort to help the Company's carpenter and blacksmith repair the boats and prepare them for the voyage. As a contract man, not a settler, he is issued cloth for "a pair of trousers, much in want and which he is entitled to." When Archie asks for cloth

---

4   A dram is now generally seen as half an ounce. Then as now it was probably a euphemism for a drink or two of any size, but in the early 1800s a dram was literally measured as four to five ounces of fluid.

to renew the settlers' trousers as well, "Mr. Cook replied that he was sorry he could not in consequence of the strict order he had from Mr. Auld."

The people are divided into five "messes" of ten persons each, to whom rations are issued regularly, and the whole group is treated as a military unit with Archie McDonald the sole commander. He is strict with the rations. On morning of April 25, a Monday, he notes that he told

> Sam Lamont to put up some Shelves in my Tent when to my astonishment he informed me he could not as he had nothing to eat yet, neither had they anything to cook, though the provisions last served out was intended to last until Wednesday.

When the rest voice the same complaint, Archie grudgingly agrees to a small bump in the rations, but after that, "no complaint can be made." They are not allowed to go to York Fort without his permission and are fined when they disobey. One Sunday they are "warned to be clean in the course of the day, as the Gentlemen from the Factory and their wives would call upon us."

Why this degree of control is thought necessary or indeed tolerated by fifty free adults who have generations of experience controlling their own lives and behaviour is baffling to a twenty-first century democrat, but it seems to have been taken for granted by both sides with little grumbling. Of course, McDonald controls their rations, a powerful suasion.

What about poor Jean McKay and her companions, whom we left behind in the snowy wasteland? Archie never mentions them again, but an entry in the York Post log, four days after the arrival of the main group, informs us:

> At 11 AM Jacob Foliman and the Indians arrived with a party of settlers all well but very hungry having spent last evening without food. Treated them hospitably and sent them to the encampment above the Factory.

All survive, and Mrs. McKay is well intact. Her son will arrive on schedule in August.

By May 20 the river is open, the boats are ready and the people are warned to be at the fort on May 22 for sailing the next day. They dutifully show up, and at last that Highland spirit shows up with them.

> They all started forward demanding cloth Trousers[5] for wear going up the Rivers, a greater allowance of Provisions, an allowance of Rum and also a supply of Tobacco to Account.

Mr. Cook remarks that the tobacco is certainly a reasonable request, so McDonald acquires enough for all. But he says they'll have to rely on his generosity for any rum they're issued, and as for new trousers, "I must deny them entirely."

Despite these disappointments, this must be the most exciting and hopeful moment since that beautiful June day on the wharf at Stromness. They are off once again to their Promised Land. All being people of The Book, that phrase cannot but ring in their ears. After all of what has passed, their next destination will be the fertile plains, with all the peace and plenty they could wish for. They clamber gingerly into the boats, arrange themselves, wave goodbye to their winter guardians and push off, undoubtedly to the heart-swelling efforts of the piper.

Next stop, the New Jerusalem. Well, not exactly next stop.

---

5   The alternative to cloth trousers is leather, which is in plentiful supply. In the absence of cloth, leather is used for sails, tents, carry bags and finally clothes. It is universally despised — even by those Indigenous people who have come to know cloth — for its stiffness, its weight and its deplorable nastiness when soaked with water — from river spray, for instance.

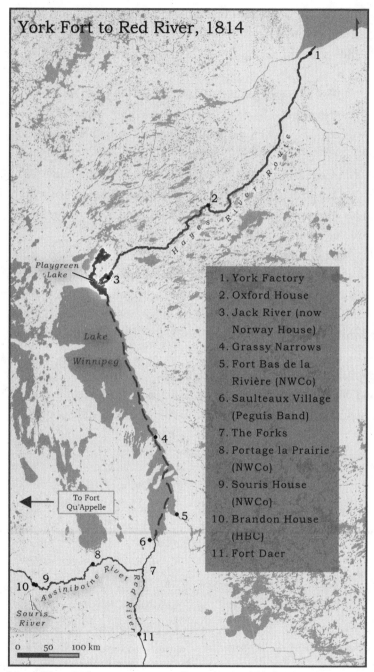

York Fort to Red River, 1814

Playgreen Lake

Hayes River Route

Lake Winnipeg

To Fort Qu'Appelle

Assiniboine River

Souris River

Red River

1. York Factory
2. Oxford House
3. Jack River (now Norway House)
4. Grassy Narrows
5. Fort Bas de la Rivière (NWCo)
6. Saulteaux Village (Peguis Band)
7. The Forks
8. Portage la Prairie (NWCo)
9. Souris House (NWCo)
10. Brandon House (HBC)
11. Fort Daer

0   50   100 km

Map 5. The 1,200 km upstream row, pull, carry and sail from the sea to the centre of a continent.

CHAPTER 9

INLAND

MAY 23 TO JUNE 21, 1814

HAYES RIVER, NEAR YORK FACTORY.

L ake Winnipeg is the great thoroughfare through the heart of
Rupertsland.[1] Broad and shallow, it offers plain sailing from Jack
River (now Norway House) to the mouth of the Red River, 400 kilo-
metres south.

Getting to Jack River is the challenge.

Jack River is around 500 kilometres from Hudson Bay as the ptarmigan flies. But as the batteaux lumber, wallow, wander, drift and are
rowed, sailed, pulled and carried, it is much farther. On a topograph-
ical map, the route looks so convoluted that it seems to promise instant
disorientation and a slow and terrible death by exposure, mosquitoes
and predators. In fact, by 1814 it is a well-established passage that has
been marked, refined and even groomed by nearly a century and a half
of traders and trappers making seasonal pilgrimages in search of pelts
in one direction and European weapons, tools, fabrics and iron pots
in the other. This has created a whole class of skilled river navigators,
called tripmen in HBC jargon.

---

[1] Rupertsland is the name given the trading concession granted by King Charles to
the Hudson's Bay Co. in 1670. It covers "all lands draining into Hudson Bay" —
almost four million square kilometres.

Where the rivers or small lakes are broad and the current slow, the upstream route may be rowed or even sailed. Where it rushes through narrow rockbound defiles, the boats must be "tracked," that is, hauled along from the shore by ropes while men in the boats try to keep them from running aground. Where even that is not possible, there are thirty-three portages or "carrying places" along the route. At each one the half-tonne boat must be emptied and manhandled over generally rough or sodden ground for anything from a few metres to several kilometres, then reloaded and relaunched into the upstream current. For toughened Baymen it is an effortful but familiar routine. For Scots farmers it is a brand new challenge.[2]

Map 6. HBC map showing the intense development of the route from York Factory (upper right corner) to Lake Winnipeg, 1819. (Wikimedia Commons)

---

2   Entering <The Hayes River - A Canadian Heritage River Story Map> into a search engine will lead to a fabulous interactive map with fascinating details about places mentioned on this route.

After launch on May 23, the first day goes well. Both boats are directed by seasoned tripmen, Jonathon Wishart and Charles Flett. In the late afternoon, they pitch camp on the shore and are warned to be ready to launch at 5 a.m. By now, the Hayes River has narrowed, with a corresponding increase in current speed. They have to track all the next day. Archie McDonald divides each boat into three shifts, all of whom he praises for their efforts. He issues everyone "new shoes," presumably moccasins, or "Indian shoes" in their parlance.

The next day, wet snow delays their departure as the boatmen keep the leather sails covered for fear they will get soaked and become too heavy to catch wind. When they do get going, tracking again, McDonald reports the ground "uncommonly bad." He issues the trackers rum as a compensation. Again, he is full of praise for their efforts.

The shoreline gets even more difficult over the next couple of days and more rum is doled out. On Saturday, May 28, after another exceptional day of tracking, he says that everyone hopes that tomorrow being Sunday will be a day of rest. "I was astonished and told them that while on a passage of this nature we must have as few laying up days as possible."

As they go inland, the settlers' dismay at the wild and inhospitable country slowly succumbs to the beauty of the scenery.

After a week, the people are going through their rations faster than expected, which worries Archie, but at the rate they are now progressing,

> the steersmen say they deserve their belly full and we now will get to Jack River in less than 28 days. . . . We got over the flats and carried at the Lower Burntwood carrying place and the South Side handing place and at Morgan's Rocks — always when we carry, the women make themselves very useful and of course walk when the water is shoal [shallow].

And so it goes for days, carrying, tracking, rowing, sailing. Up before dawn, in camp by six. "Weather uncommonly good — no mosquitoes." Occasionally they have to break up ice jams or pole through them. Rum is handed out sparingly. Says Archie, "I find that giving them a dram unexpected makes them enjoy it and more contented than if they had it daily which of course they would then claim as a right." They begin to pull fish from the rivers to supplement the rations, which Archie increases to match the extra effort and quick time they are making. Each person gets oatmeal, rice, biscuits, pemmican and pork, distributed so that "every man and boy gets about 2 lbs per day and every woman 1½ lbs."

On June 4, they arrive at the HBC post of Oxford House to find that the next lake, called Holey, is still fast with ice.

> We put up for the night. Soon after it came to rain and blow most tremendously accompanied with Thunder and lightning. . . . Since we encamped, the ice is giving way a little. . . . There came two Indians to see the white women out of curiosity. I have got them to set some Hooks in the Lake and gave them all a dram.

The fishers come back in the morning with eighty pounds of fish, and receive some more rum. One of the settlers' hooks catches a trout weighing an impressive thirty-two pounds (over fourteen kilograms). Finally, the ice in Holey Lake recedes, and they are able to set sails and cross it, but in the strong rapids at the lake's inlet, the bow stem of one boat is smashed. They stop for the night, and "Sam Lamont and Blacksmith got it repaired." Archie notes the "many Indian camps" they pass, where the people are building the season's canoes.

They arrive at Jack River in mid-morning on June 11. They are twenty days out of York Fort, over a week faster than expected. The settlers' delight in their own achievement is doubled when they run into friends and relatives, people who have been here a year or more. They ask them what Red River is like.

"No country in the world is better by all appearance," says one.

"Fish you can have in great abundance, and as for cattle, they are so plentiful at times that one day I killed a large Bull with my axe," says another. He presumably means bison, which are often called cattle by the newcomers.

One man presents his sister with a maple sugar cake. Pure sweetness, both the confection and the reunions. Jubilant, the Churchill group ask Archie if they can write home to friends and urge them to come out next year. He tells them to wait until they've seen the Red River paradise for themselves — after all, there is only one postal run a year, when the annual ship returns to Britain in the fall. That evening, the settlers drink and dance with HBC servants, a happy respite. Clearly, Mr. Auld neglected to sow his poison when he passed through.

The HBC men urge Archie to move on "with all dispatch," and he takes them at their word. "Party warned to be ready early tomorrow." One afternoon and evening is all their reward for three weeks of unbroken effort and remarkable progress.

Lake Winnipeg (or Winipic, as they call it) is a treacherous body of water, shallow and susceptible to wind, blowing up into whitecaps with almost no warning. HBC tripmen know to treat it with respect. In the nasty weather on Playgreen Lake, the passage into Lake Winnipeg proper, they make slow progress and dare not advance into the main lake. They stay there another day, pelted with sleet and snow.

The wind continues as they finally set off on June 12. They meet some First Nations people who trade them "a few dozen eggs." Later, boats coming north from Red River hail them, and catch them up on the news of the winter, including a version of something called the Pemmican Proclamation and the Nor'Westers' fierce opposition to it. What might they make of this?

A couple of days later, pressing on too long after dark, they realize they're lost. In the morning they engage a passing Indigenous couple to guide them, and by evening reach the narrows that separate the upper and lower basins of this enormous lake, the twelfth largest in the world by most reckoning.

After more bad-weather delays they finally reach the mouth of the Red River on June 20. The settlers are immediately enraptured with the appearance of the country on its shores. Even today it is easy to see why: the relentless sand and spruce of the boreal forest give way to bushy grassland at the south end of the lake as though at the lifting of a curtain. The relief and anticipation of arrival must be almost overpowering, despite the continuing rain.

The next day, McDonald writes:

> Rained very hard last night. During the forenoon several bands of Sottos [Saulteaux][3] met us on the banks of the river and gave us some fish and seemed much pleased with our appearance in the country. . . . We came ashore within a few miles of the Settlement, when the Settlers were so pleased with the situation they were so anxiously and so long looking out for that some of them wished to remain on the spot for the future.

And who can blame them? It may still be a few kilometres to their nominal destination, but the Land of Plenty is under their feet: verdant, fecund soil. The urge to clutch onto the earth and refuse ever to move again is mighty.

The reality is that tomorrow, they will be taken to The Forks and will meet the 1812 colonists and Miles McDonell. This seemingly interminable journey will finally end.

They have no idea of the history they are walking into or the nature of their governor or how close they have just come to blundering into a war zone. All they know is, they are finally here. And here — is *spectacular*.

Tomorrow will be time enough for discovering the terrifying events that have anticipated their arrival.

---

3   Perhaps no single word in this whole account is more variously misspelled than this one — the contemporary term for a branch of the Anishinaabe people who are believed to have fled smallpox a couple of generations earlier from Sault Ste. Marie at the eastern end of Lake Superior. Hence Saulteaux — "from the Sault."

CHAPTER 10

THE PEMMICAN WAR

MAY 1 TO JUNE 20, 1814

RED RIVER SETTLEMENT, NEAR THE FORKS.

B y May 1, while the Kildonan group is still trekking between Churchill and York, Miles McDonell is back at The Forks from Pembina, ready to take on spring and the arrival of the 1813 contingent next month. He visits the McLeans on his first evening, joined by the Nor'Westers Seraphin Lamar and Alexander McDonell, his brother-in-law. Everyone is friends again, at least socially. Three days later, Auld arrives, and things turn sour. When Alexander McDonell comes round to call at Miles McDonell's house, Auld refuses to see him, so Miles must reluctantly turn his cousin away. Afterwards, he writes in his journal, he "walked with Mr. Auld. We met Mr. McLean about certain accusations." The spoons no doubt, but frustratingly, nothing more is said.

On May 17 Mr. Auld goes off. His visit has lasted two weeks; it probably felt longer.

Rumours come from "Indians near the Lake" that the Nor'Westers have "invited them to assemble at The Forks to resist the embargo laid on [pemmican]."

McDonell reports sowing nineteen quarts of wheat seeds and beginning to plant potatoes. Again he mentions the First Nations being asked "to assemble to intimidate us." It's worrying him.

On May 19, "Peguis comes to me with some of his people. Invite them to talk tomorrow." Peguis is chief of the Saulteaux (Anishinaabe or Ojibwe) Nation on Netley Creek, and his band, like the settlers, are relatively recent migrants, having arrived from central Minnesota when Peguis, now about forty, was a child. They settled near the mouth of the Red River, where extensive marsh made fish plentiful and convenient, so they do not compete with long-resident Indigenous peoples who hunt buffalo.

Perhaps this shared newcomer status is part of what attracts Peguis to the settlers. Or perhaps it is the notion of having European food producers nearby as a source and market for trade goods. Perhaps it is a result of his frequently expressed antipathy toward the Nor'Westers for previous insults. Or perhaps it is simply his abundant and apparent curiosity. Whatever it is, Peguis is friendly from first contact and will remain so until his death. He is moderate in his habits and has an expansive, welcoming and inquiring nature.

It is the crucial time of the Nor'Westers' year. With the spring thaw, the winterers who spend the winter trading from remote posts between here and the Rockies return to Fort William on Lake Superior to deliver their annual harvest and restock with trade goods. Soon they will be heading back upcountry and will want pemmican to see them through the following winter. Except they can't have it, if McDonell's proclamation is to have any meaning. That, of course, is the question of the hour.

The day after Peguis's visit, May 19, McDonell writes,

> a boatload of pemmican belonging to the NWCo is coming
> down the Assiniboine River. Swore in Constables and sent off
> a guard to watch the river.

The gauntlet has been dropped. He is prepared to apprehend the Nor'Westers' property by force within view of their fort, Gibraltar, which overlooks the Assiniboine.

The Pemmican Proclamation says nothing against bringing pemmican into The Forks, but McDonell knows that it is coming here only to be distributed to the westbound canoes. Once gone it cannot be retrieved, so it must be confiscated before distribution. The next day, the situation escalates:

> Word is brought early from our guard that the Frenchmen are out in numbers, armed. Go out immediately with all the people well-armed and take two brass field pieces.[1] Messrs. [Alex'r] McDonell and Seraphin with 12 or 14 followers, all armed, had been at our guard early this morning . . . I withdraw part of the men with the artillery in the evening.

The "Frenchmen" are the winterers who need the pemmican. McDonell writes to Wills, the ailing but still titular head of Fort Gibraltar:

> Sir, Having learnt that my Proclamation was intended to be resisted . . . has induced me to prepare for the enforcement of it. Armed parties are therefore stationed on Assiniboine River.
>
> An armed body of [your] men went early this morning to the place where one of my parties is. The consequence of appearing in that menacing aspect might have been serious.
>
> [signed] Miles Mac
>
> PS, I am happy to contribute to your relief by the attendance of the Colonial Surgeon and beg you will freely avail yourself of all the assistance he can render you.

Thus do "gentlemen" threaten mayhem and bloodshed above their signature while offering medical assistance and social consolation below it. He also assures Wills that he will pay for any pemmican he seizes.

---

1   These are light cannon supplied by Lord Selkirk. Just two- and three-pounders, they are small by military standards, but can destroy a canoe or sink a river boat with one shot.

The next day, Peguis makes his promised return visit, bringing a flag and "Pipe of Peace." McDonell reciprocates with a large gift of tobacco.

When no boatload of pemmican shows up, McDonell sends John Spencer, whom he has appointed sheriff, back up the river to find it.

McDonell meets Wills to talk about the proclamation, and records Wills's answer:

> You know that we never acknowledged your authority here. . . .
> To issue such a proclamation, your commission [as governor]
> should come from the Privy Council.

In Wills's view, he is not defying the law, he is defying the Hudson's Bay Company. It's a fair point, but McDonell cannot concede that. Everything depends, in his black-and-white view, on his person being recognized as the embodiment of British law.

Wills says the "wintering Proprietors" are going to gather at The Forks and decide how to proceed. Meanwhile he's giving up nothing.

Sheriff John Spencer comes back with the empty batteau that was carrying the pemmican; the wily boatmen have hidden the contraband en route. He arrests them and puts them in lockup. One day later, the spineless nellies spill their guts: they hid the swag at White Horse Plain, a Bois-Brûlé village some distance up the Assiniboine River. Spencer and two men set out on horseback. The sheriff takes up the story:

> At the White Horse Plain, I called at a Lodge belonging to
> André Poitras, where I lost no time in making enquiry where
> the pemmican was secreted which he readily showed me.

Poitras takes him to the stash, hidden by the riverbank among artfully arranged willows, around which all footprints and other disturbances have been smoothed over. Had it not been pointed out, Spencer says, he'd never have found it. Given that these are hundred-pound (forty-five-kilogram) bags of pemmican and there are ninety-six of them, the boatmen had gone to some trouble. Spencer seizes the bags and takes them by boat to The Forks.

The first confiscation has been effected.

A letter from Brandon House HBC post informs McDonell that NWCo pemmican from their posts at Swan River and Qu'Appelle has been stashed away in Souris House, the neighbouring North West post at the mouth of the Souris River, to prevent "the Colonists" from taking it. McDonell sends off Spencer again, with a posse of five and a warrant for more seizures.

Nor'Wester Dugald Cameron from the Winipic River Post arrives at Fort Gibraltar. He is the first of the "Proprietors" whom Wills is assembling for consultation. Others will arrive over the next week.

Later that day McDonell writes, "Mr. Wills and Mr. Sutherland will wait on me tomorrow to propose an amicable adjustment." You have to hand it to Wills; he is trying his best to contain matters peacefully.

Wills, Cameron and McDonell's cousin Alexander show up to parley. They acknowledge, according to McDonell, his authority as governor and justice of the peace. McDonell tests them: he points out that they, the Nor'Westers, are constructing a blockhouse on the river side of their fort specifically to overlook his guard detachment, a clear threat of violence toward himself, as governor.

Amazingly, the Nor'Westers begin dismantling the blockhouse on their return to Gibraltar. Only one more signal is needed to establish good faith, and next day, June 8:

> The NWCo . . . apply for an order for the Swan River provi-
> sions to be allowed to come down, which I gave accordingly.

That was what he was waiting for — a request that implicitly acknowledges his authority.

Out near Brandon House, 200 kilometres west of The Forks, Sheriff Spencer goes to town with his warrants. At the NWCo post, which he calls River de la Sourie, he is not resisted and confiscates 94 kegs of fat, 479 bags of pemmican, 10 bundles of dried meat, and 10 parchment skins. It is a serious seizure, and it won't go unanswered by the NWCo.

At Red River another Nor'Wester partner arrives: Duncan Cameron, not to be confused with Dugald Cameron, who arrived a couple of days ago. Duncan Cameron is a formidable force in the North West Company, and will rise to arch-villain status at Red River soon enough, but in the beginning he seems as willing to negotiate as his colleagues. He and Miles McDonell meet but they can't come to terms since the NWCo is unwilling to give up any pemmican. Miles writes, "We part to meet tomorrow." (He then adds, matter-of-factly, "Learnt the untimely death of my daughter in December last year at St. Andrew Rivière aux Raisins."[2])

That night, there is a dance at Fort Gibraltar and several colony people attend, including his friends Alex and Christina McLean. This irritates McDonell because it smacks of fraternizing with the enemy.

Next day he gives Duncan Cameron and other newly arrived North West partners a tour of the colony's "improvements." They talk some more, but Duncan Cameron is a man who plays to win, as does McDonell. Once more they find no common ground.

On June 15 a furious McDonell fires off a letter:

> Gentlemen: Information has been brought to me this moment that Mr. Howse [an HBC man] . . . was attacked in the plains this morning by an armed force of your people and brought a prisoner to your Fort.

Free him or face the consequences, snarls McDonell. When they don't he has his servants arrest and imprison twenty Nor'Westers with several canoes. He calls in outlying work parties and prepares for a fight. The Nor'Westers respond by demanding their men's immediate release, "unless you mean to declare War against us, as indeed your motions seem to indicate."

War. The word is now on the table. To *Captain* McDonell, this is a challenge. He fires back,

---

2   This non sequitur, dropping the death of his daughter dryly into an unrelated paragraph, is typical Miles McDonell. He is a complicated man and subject to pronounced emotional swings, but he does not share them with his journal. Like most of his class he would view the expression of them as unseemly.

I am aware of all your hostile preparations, the arming of your people to intimidate us, but all this will not do . . . Our taking arms is in consequence of your having done so.

The Nor'Westers respond by declaring they intend to take Howse to Montreal and try him for "burglary."

McDonell mounts a show of force, leading seventeen armed men and a cannon past their fort to establish a battery threatening anything on the river. Once more he tries on his favourite argument, calling himself the "Government legally established here, against which you have taken up arms." He promises to arrest any of their people "found in arms," and to detain any canoes or boats attempting to remove pemmican from "his" territory.

Escalation meets escalation. More guns, more gunmen. To top it all, the Nor'Westers are running low on their pemmican supplies and 300 canoes are expected in the next week or so, all needing provisions for the coming year. They are every bit as determined as Miles McDonell. It seems that nothing can stop this game of tag from making the final leap to bloodshed. To avoid it will require an eleventh-hour intervention worthy of Charles Dickens. Happily, this is exactly what happens.

McDonell says he and Peter Fidler, the colony surveyor, are just sitting down to dinner when he gets a note from Fort Gibraltar: Mr. McDonald has arrived and sends his compliments. This changes everything.

This McDonald — Le Bras Croche (Crooked Arm) to his voyageurs, John McDonald of Garth by his own styling — is a senior partner in the North West Company.[3] He is described as "pugnacious and daring," a man who carries a pair of duelling pistols in his luggage and likes to use them. He is on his way back to Montreal from the Pacific coast, by canoe and horseback. He is a dangerous adversary, but a canny businessman. No hothead, he is comfortable giving something to get more.

McDonald joins the two colony leaders for their meal.

---

3   C.M. Livermore and N. Anick, *Dictionary of Canadian Biography*, biographi.ca /en/bio/mcdonald_john_1866_9E.html.

McDonell reports, "After a good deal of talk he proposed to send 10 canoes to the Bay [later this summer] to bring up oatmeal for the settlers if I would let them carry out their pemmican [now]." This offer to replace the calories later that the NWCo needs now is a brilliant stroke, a win-win in today's terms. McDonell says, "This was immediately agreed and we rode directly to the camp to prevent any accident."

Together the two men ride out, passing quickly from group to group. The scene they ride through is a battlefield poised: "3 or 4 Indians painted and armed going towards our Camp — turned them back." At the Nor'Wester camp, "Mr. Duncan Cameron, a number of Canadians and about 7 Indians, all armed for war." They jointly give each and all the order to stand down and return to quarters.

Disaster averted.

The Nor'Westers' trade is saved without loss of face and at low cost. Le Bras Croche's timely arrival has probably saved lives.

McDonell's long June 17 entry concludes with,

> Mr. McDonald, Mr. Howse and 3 Gentlemen Partners came
> to my house to settle matters. They stayed late.

In the midst of this cordial parley, Sheriff Spencer arrives and triumphantly announces that all that booty he seized out near Brandon House is on its way down the Assiniboine on boats. To his shock, instead of gratitude and congratulation, he hears it will be immediately returned to the Nor'Westers per this agreement. He instantly resigns as sheriff, says McDonell, "so much hurt at the provisions being parted with."

The Nor'Westers present McDonell with a letter. They remind him that "for the existence of your infant colony . . . mutual good offices should exist between us and you . . .":

> We are happy that things at present promise to terminate
> amicably and that we have come to terms, though very hard
> upon us, yet which we are willing to agree rather than come
> to extremities.

The letter is signed by five Gentlemen Partners (of whom two are named John McDonald). Miles replies in admirably concrete terms:

> When the provisions seized at [Souris River] arrive, 175 bags
> shall be delivered to you, as you have agreed to send Canoes
> to Hudson Bay to bring up oatmeal or other provisions for the
> Settlement. I shall deliver a bag of Pemmican for every bag of
> oatmeal of 90 lbs weight.

And thus ends, if only for the time being, what is already being called the Pemmican War. So far, so good.

On June 19 McDonell again welcomes visits from Peguis and another band chief called The Premier, both of whom promise their friendship. June 20 is a day of two momentous events. The significance of the first is not immediately apparent, but Miles records it in his journal:

> Capt. Grant came to see me — a good quiet Indian.

He has just met Cuthbert Grant, a man neither quiet in the historical sense nor an "Indian," in the First Nations sense, an example of just how loosely that term could be used. Grant,[4] in his early twenties, is the son of a Scots-born North West partner and "a Métis woman, probably of Cree and French descent."[5] He is literate and at least bilingual, educated in Montreal and possibly Scotland. Even at his young age, his potential is being recognized as a trader and leader among the Bois-Brûlés, thus the honorific "Captain." Though educated as a European, he is by choice unequivocally a man of his people and of the

---

4   Much more information can be read at the *Dictionary of Canadian Biography*, biographi.ca/en/bio/grant_cuthbert_1854_8E.html, and in his biography *Cuthbert Grant of Grantown*.

5   George Woodcock, *Dictionary of Canadian Biography*, biographi.ca/en/bio/grant_cuthbert_1854_8E.html.

plains. He is also a career Nor'Wester, born and bred. His impact on the settlement will be profound.

Later the same day, McDonell records the second, even more momentous development: "Mr. Archibald McDonald arrives with 51 Settlers . . ."

It seems reasonable to think this would be the high point of his day, even his year — the settlers have arrived! But no, it isn't even the high point of the sentence: ". . . with 51 Settlers and brings accounts of there being no provisions at YF." This changes everything again. If there are no provisions at York Factory, then there are no bags of oatmeal, and the Nor'Westers can't fulfill their end of the agreement. Miles hurries off to add a postscript to his letter of agreement:

> By the boats just arrived, I have found that there is no oatmeal or other provisions to be spared from YF, which renders it unnecessary to send down canoes to the coast. — MMcD.

This postscript seems on the surface to render the truce agreement null and void. It also reduces the historic arrival of the Highland families to an afterthought in McDonell's power game.

A soldier is a soldier is a soldier. But at least nobody is shooting.

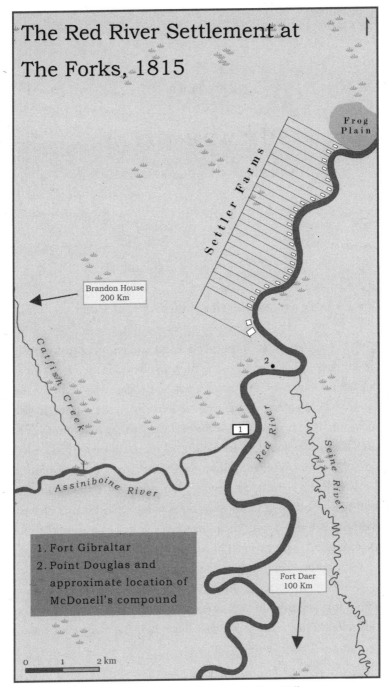

Map 7. The immediate Forks environs, after a map by Peter Fidler.

CHAPTER 11

SUMMER IDYLL

JUNE 21 TO AUGUST 25, 1814

THE BANKS OF THE RED RIVER,
A FEW KILOMETRES NORTH OF THE SETTLEMENT.

Wholly ignorant of the powder keg and festering turf war they have just sailed into, the fifty sojourners from Scotland have been left on their own for most of a day on the grassy banks of the river that is to be their home, their future and their escape from atavistic feudalism. They have arrived in the best week of the best month of the year.[1] The grasses and trees are a mural of greens in every shade, bright and still new-looking, magnificently fragrant with life and promise. The Red River is full and flowing, but relatively tranquil after the flood-rush of a month before. The air is redolent with a mix of spring wildflowers mingled with the pungent compost of an alien clay: Red River gumbo. They can smell its fertility; its richness pulls and sucks at their feet as they clamber from the boats.

The west wind carries the scent of 1,500 kilometres of unbroken prairie: thriving timothy and sweetgrass, wildfire smoke, marshy funk and buffalo musk. The forest that lines the bank contains trees that

---

[1] It still is. This description was originally written in the same week of the same month, two centuries later.

recall home, a welcome relief from the endless wall of conifers that has screened their view of North America's possibilities until now.

Archie McDonald, with his judgments, his expensive accent and his Right to Decide, has left them to prepare the settlement for their arrival. They are all equals here: Gaelic, unselfconscious and spontaneous. For some, the promise of this place has captured them already, while for others the many unknowns and the vast distance from loved ones complicate their relief.

Some give themselves over to exhaustion, collapsing on their backs to stare at the clear blue from a bed of soft vegetation, free at last of rock, hard benches and water, water, water. Others poke at the ground and tear up native flora to assess the soil. A few venture in search of the highest rise to see for themselves what endless grassy plain really looks like. A couple of hardheads even decide they've already found their future homesteads and are staking imaginary boundaries.

And Samuel Lamont? He's no farmer, nor even a settler. He's there to build a horse-driven grist mill, and is probably already about it, closely examining the riparian trees with an eye to those which might build walls or be strong enough to support millstones and horses and heavy iron hardware. Even at twenty-two he has a practised eye.[2]

The days rival Scotland for their length. As the sun at last begins to lose its grip, does the piper unleash his drones and assault the ears of young Indigenous hunters spying through bushes on the opposite bank? Probably. It's unlikely that the people go to bed early, finding themselves too excited, too eager, maybe even too homesick, in the face of a year of dreams suddenly made waking reality.

They certainly rise early next morning. On June 22, McDonald, who spent the night at the settlement, records: "Went back for the people and arrived with them about 9:00. Capt. McDonell visited them in the course of the day." What Miles may have said to them we can only guess, because his journal merely remarks, "Settlers arrive — 31 men, 3 women and 17 girls."

---

2   Today, a walk along the "monkey trails" (informal paths) of the river bank in Whittier Park, exactly opposite the first settlement, feels like it must have that day in 1814, before the western bank was cleared.

Where he got those numbers he does not say, but he will repeat them in a month or so, suggesting a disappointing indifference to the settlers as individuals. It is likely the count done on departure from Churchill by Archie McDonald — thirty-one females and twenty males[3] — is closer to the truth.

On that same day, McDonell sends a young "officer," John Bourke, with Sheriff John Spencer and others to Jack River and York Factory to bring back what supplies they can. About twenty-five now-redundant servants go with them, to return to Britain or back to their jobs with the HBC. He has doubtless used the opportunity to cull his ranks of last winter's "refractory" servants.

The settlers spend the day getting their tents and campsite set up. They are introduced to the local catfish, "which they think a great deal of," says Archie McDonald.

Summer is fast advancing. Over the next few days they will plant forty bushels of potatoes and some of the younger women will be set to weeding barley sown earlier. Necessary work, certainly, but their fun is in speculating about the future. Archie reports that the men are discussing land conditions and where they might want to live once plots are assigned.

McDonell has established the colony's base at a sharp bend in the river which he has named Point Douglas, about three kilometres north of The Forks and the NWCo's fort. He has built a habitation for himself and servants, and is now enlarging it to accommodate his officers, storage for furs, supplies, weapons and equipment, as well as a large barn for farm activity. It is getting to be a compound, but not a fort. There is no wall or protective palisade. He is evidently not especially worried about defence, despite the spring's unrest.

The home farm, to be worked on Lord Selkirk's behalf, covers most of Point Douglas. The settlers' riverside plots march north from its boundary and away from the North West post.

Just a week after their arrival, their Highland contrariness fully

---

3   For a more complete list of trekkers, see the one compiled by George Bryce in the Appendix.

restored, the men show up at McDonell's headquarters and declare that they don't want to settle near The Forks. Furthermore, unless they get their lands in Pembina, a full hundred kilometres upriver, they will appeal to Lord Selkirk and await his response. Why they would demand land they have never seen or been close to is one question. What they intend to do for the year it will take to get word back from his lordship is a greater one. "Such resolutions, of course, could not be heard of," writes Archie McDonald.

Archie summons a settler named John Matheson, from Aultbreakachy, "whom I know to be a young man I can reason with." He reads Matheson an article by Lord Selkirk himself, regarding an earlier group of settlers the earl sponsored. They too kept finding fault with the lands offered to them, over and over, until "time and expense forced them" to choose when they found the only lands still available inferior to their first options, but "must settle there with diminished resources." Matheson is duly impressed and promises to talk sense to his friends. McDonald observes that the newcomers were much taken with the land when they got here, "and I am convinced that they would be still if it was not for two or three old [i.e. 1812] settlers we have got here that are good for nothing." It seems a little soon for him to have formed that negative opinion on his own, but he is probably correct about the source: who else but those earlier settlers would be in a position to suggest this? Yet why would they urge a move that would cost them more precious growing weeks and put a hundred more farmers in year-round jeopardy from hostile Dakota? Perhaps the North West Company played a role.

It is disturbing how quickly local politics seem to have infected the new arrivals.

The next day, the women continue their planting and weeding[4] but the men stay in camp, presumably chewing over their options. Late that night they come to Archie McDonald, caps in hand, "begging forgiveness for their obstinacy, and they would be willing to take allotments wherever proposed."

---

4   The women are paid for their labour at a rate of one shilling and sixpence a day, which is close to what the lowest-paid male labourers make.

Just in time, as Auld will arrive the next day. No one would want him wading in on these growing pains. As it is, Auld immediately disapproves of the arrangements made with the Nor'Westers and declares that, had he been here, "it would have been different."

The next day he and McDonell discuss many unspecified subjects, and the day after that, Auld leaves.

That same day, some of the "girls," no ages mentioned, accept an invitation to visit Fort Gibraltar. McDonell reports that they are "civilly treated, but discouraged by Mr. [Duncan] Cameron who said that it was a pity to see such fine girls come to such a country." Archie McDonald is not happy: "In the evening I spoke to the girls. They are warned not to go near the French House as all they will hear there are disagreeable lectures." Nothing is said about the agreeable company they might also encounter among these dashing, mostly young, adventurers. A girl can get a little peakèd after a long year of the same old Presbyterians.

The newcomers are rapidly getting their eyes opened to the realities of their new home. Far from the empty lands awaiting human settlement they've been picturing, this place is a hive of activity. As later archaeology will prove, The Forks had been a crossroads for millennia, and remains so in 1814. Nor'Wester winterers are still coming through, with their rough manners and frontier dress. So are First Nations canoes with paddlers speaking several languages and eyeing the latest arrivals curiously. The Nor'Wester fort is an impressive structure surrounded by an imposing defensive palisade.[5] The clerks and partners who inhabit it can put on a fair show of European flash and refinement when they are so inclined. Most of all, the fiction that this is Lord Selkirk's land, an extension of his estates in Scotland, must be raising serious questions in the newcomers' minds. In Scotland, as they know from bitter experience, the laird would just have these strangers evicted. No one seems in fear of that. Yet the governor tells them that Selkirk is indeed the lord of this land.

What else might not be as they hope and expect?

---

5   Its beautifully reconstructed replica bears that out today.

Archie McDonald and Peter Fidler, the HBC's surveyor now loaned to the colony, have been laying out the farm lots. On July 3, they are out again with the surveying chain, staking twenty more lots, "each a hundred acres and 3 of which in breast of the river." A squared acre is about 209 feet (64 metres) to a side, so three along the river translates as 627 feet (192 metres) of river frontage. That also means they are 33 squared acres long, which works out to 1.3 miles (over 2 kilometres). So roughly 200 by 2,000 metres of land for each family. That is far more land than any of them could dream of in Scotland, and double the size recommended by Lord Selkirk for future lots, so these settlers have to be pleased, and they are — sort of. They would not be Highlanders if they didn't suspect catches.

McDonell's plan was for the settlers to build their houses in clusters of five or six, for mutual protection and support. Not unreasonable perhaps, but the prospective landholders will have none of it. On July 8, says Archie, "I went down with the Settlers to [show them the lots]. Many told me that they would not consent to build their houses in a cluster, but every man would build on his own respective land."

When Archie reports this to his chief, "Captain McDonell agreed to it rather than have them dissatisfied." One imagines a good deal of eye rolling, sighing and muttering under the breath, but McDonell is learning the lesson of every would-be autocrat put in charge of free civilians: choose your battles.

On July 12, the lands are assigned. Through a clever series of lotteries — first with large self-defined groups drawing for group tracts, then subgroups for smaller ones, then individual holdings — they manage to distribute the settlers so that families and friends are settled close together while no one is given favour over anyone else. There are no complaints! Or as Archie McDonald puts it the next day,

> I went down and put each family in possession of his farm at which they were so highly satisfied, as there was no symptom of partiality or fraud, that in the evening no one would change his lot for another's.

Congratulations all around. In the series of momentous days that have marked out the journey so far — casting off from Scotland, leaving Churchill, leaving York, arrival at the settlement — this one must feel like the *triumph of hope*: their very own land, secured by occupation. Families immediately move to their lots and each proclaims its presence with a tent.

When Miles McDonell visits each lot a couple of days later, he is warmly received. It is a high point in governor-settler relations.

It's a happy time. Auld acquaintance is forgotten (in both meanings of the word), and all eyes are on the future. On July 22, John Matheson, that reasonable 23-year-old from Aultbreakachy, marries Barbara Sutherland, twenty-one. "They got a round or two of the pipes and a dram before they went away." So hardly a break in the urgent work to be done.

The men begin by clearing and preparing homesites. Many choose to live among the riverbank trees, though these apparently are not stout enough for building. Good timber must come from stands along the La Salle River, a tributary of the Red a few kilometres upstream from The Forks. Crews are dispatched to cut and raft the logs.

Even Miles McDonell has a good month. Food, mainly in the form of catfish and sturgeon from the rivers, is plentiful. On July 13, he seems to foresee the end of hostilities with the NWCo: 296 bags of pemmican arrive in boats, and he sends 196 of them to Fort Gibraltar, where they will soon be carried off to the northwest posts beyond Assiniboia's boundaries. Relations between himself and the Nor'Westers are cordial again. More ominously, the boats sent to Jack River for supplies return with nothing but the mail from York Factory. As McDonald had told Miles, supplies up north are meagre. Much depends on this fall's ship from Britain.

Nor'Westers helpfully tell McDonell that, at their Turtle River post far to the south, the Brûlé practice of hunting buffalo from horseback is driving the herds too far from the post for hunters on foot to reach. On July 21 Miles issues another proclamation, this one "prohibiting the running of the buffalo with horses." Again, he is striking at the heart of the Bois-Brûlés, people of the buffalo, for whom bison chases are central to their way of life. Another questionable decree, another self-inflicted wound in relations with the neighbours. Another case of Miles McDonell misreading his audience.

A few days later Miles prepares for his own trip to York Factory, to meet the incoming ship and escort supplies and this year's settlers back to The Forks. He will take with him sworn statements from the men who were at Churchill the night of the fire last November. These affidavits will go with his annual report to Lord Selkirk. He can't let Auld's charges of negligence stand uncontested.

He will also be taking Archie McDonald's report. Archie is feeling good about life, and it shows. His report is all compliments for the people on their journey from York to the Red River Settlement, he is sanguine about the Nor'Wester threat, minimizing the Pemmican War. He assures his lordship that the settlers "never were happier and more content in Kildonan than they are here already." He hopes the earl can visit soon, and ends on a high note:

> The Settlers have been writing home to their friends, and I am afraid from their very favourable accounts that more Emigrants may offer themselves than your Lordship can possibly bring out the first year.

On July 25 McDonell sets out for Jack River and York Factory. He takes fourteen men in two batteaux and a newly built schooner, "a stout boat of 35 feet keel and 11 feet beam, all built of oak, finished in May by Donald Livingstone . . . it is called the Cuchullin."[6] McDonell installs himself in a batteau along with his young clerk, James Warren, and the blacksmith, James McDonald, who is going back to Scotland. Just before they reach Lake Winnipeg/Winipic, they put ashore to pick up a singular travelling companion, Chief Peguis of the Saulteaux Anishinaabe, and his "attendant," to use McDonell's term. Peguis has never been to Hudson Bay and has never seen an ocean vessel. He will be Miles's personal guest.

---

6   Cuchullin (pronounced *kyu-KULL-in*) is one of the spellings for a hero of Irish folklore.

In his absence, McDonell has left Archie McDonald in charge of the people and Peter Fidler as caretaker of the colony. Fidler is a career Hudson's Bay Company officer who arrived at York Factory in 1788. He trained in surveying and map-making and is a master of the craft.[7] A strong supporter of the settlement, he is also a hard custodian of its stores and supplies.

Life on the Red River continues to run smoothly through late July and August. Hay is harvested, houses are built, crops are weeded. This is a competent group of farmers and they require little supervision or instruction. The officers' job is mainly to make sure they have what they need to carry on: timber for building, tools for tending the central farm's crops, and of course food, since that will continue to come mainly from central stores until the individual farms produce enough.

On July 29 Fidler notes the completion of a kitchen building for the Point Douglas compound. He has four men constantly at work on a "Large House," and more on a smaller house, for officers and tradesmen. Fidler is not afraid to be tough; on August 8 he writes,

> The fish at this season is very soft and watery and bad, had a dispute with the people about always making them eat only fish. I kept firm and would allow them nothing else whilst fish could be got and keep the pemmican until winter. They all went quietly back to the work, allowing the justness of this reasoning.

But the next day, he grumbles that "the mowers refuse to eat fish. Those lately come from the Highlands, they are the worst to please."

Archie takes the mowers' side and Fidler grudgingly concedes to allow each cook a gallon of oatmeal or flour a week, "which is too much . . . I am positive they make improper use of some of it." What might constitute the improper use of a few handfuls of oatmeal or

---

7   The spellings we use today for many places, most notably Saskatchewan and Winnipeg, come from him. A sketch of Fidler's career can be found at biographi.ca/en/bio/fidler_peter_6E.

flour? Perhaps an extra biscuit or bun? A secret spirit-still somewhere, producing minute amounts of alcohol?

Over the next three weeks, a daughter is born to William Sutherland and his wife, who like Jean McKay must have been pregnant on the trek from Churchill to York. Jean herself gives birth on August 23, a healthy boy they call John. Peter Fidler grimly reports the collapse of the potato house roof, but generally he is pleased with the progress of construction.

In late August, Archie McDonald's journal ends, not to resume until January. Probably a volume was simply lost. At any rate we shall hear no more from him in 1814.

On August 25 boats arrive carrying the remainder of the Churchill colonists, those who could not make the overland trek to York last spring. There are thirty-three of them, "mostly old people and children," reports Fidler, including "a deaf boy, 9 years old, dumb, got his leg broke and an arm out of joint on the passage up. He is a poor creature, a miserable object." This is Alexander Sutherland, whose father, John, died of typhus last September. His mother, brother and sister came from Churchill in April, leaving Alexander in the care of another brother, 16-year-old Donald.

Reunited with his mother at last, Alexander has had enough — he dies just three days after arriving. It may have been of some comfort to both of them that he died in his mother's arms, but this intimate tragedy can nonetheless stir hearts two centuries later.

It cannot, however, reach the heart of Peter Fidler. His journal entry for the day reads,

> Paid several Canadians off, mostly in Liquor at the rate of a day's work for ½ pint British Brandy. The crippled boy died this morning, a fortunate circumstance both to itself and mother.

Meanwhile, way up north, in a river far, far away —

CHAPTER 12

BREAKDOWN

LATE AUGUST TO SEPTEMBER 11, 1814

YORK FACTORY, ON HUDSON BAY.

McDonell, Peguis and party land at York Factory after a month-long journey from The Forks. They're welcomed by "Auld, Thomas, Cook and all the gentlemen of the factory."

McDonell can only talk Auld out of "one barrel of Beef and one of Pork for our people. There is very little provisions here." This makes him anxious for the arrival of the supply ship, which may have provisions enough to ease the threat of winter starvation. Like the year before, he spends much of his waiting time revising and completing his report to the earl.

He holds back no drama as he describes the brinkmanship of the Pemmican War: "I felt the weight and responsibility of the whole upon myself . . . The NWCo had 120 Voyageurs and 200 or 300 were expected soon . . . My small band of 28 men had only a house for its defence and the Settlers families could not be protected. A defeat must have been in every way disastrous for us."

He then turns to the new settlers. The 1813 colonists, he says, are qualitatively different from their predecessors: "Those of 1812 . . . did very little and were always doubtful of the issue. The Servants we had cared not how little they did, so long as they were paid their wages. None of them cared for settling on the land."

He is pleased with Archie McDonald, "a fine active young fellow and has been most attentive to the welfare of the people he brought with him."

He declares his belief that the Indigenous population "of this District" (without defining whether he means The Forks area or all of Assiniboia) is about 4,800 souls. "Free Canadians" (again, no definition), about 2,000. This is one of the few times we get a glimpse of the scale of society in Assiniboia. Seven thousand souls is hardly an empty land.

McDonell cannot avoid one of his favourite themes: the boil on his fundament that is William Auld; in particular, Auld's campaign against Alex and Christina McLean. He expresses "regret" at the affair of the teaspoons, which he insists resembles malicious gossip rather than serious complaint. As evidence, he cites a notation by McRae on the back of his drawing of the teaspoon: "A CHOICE MORSEL," it reads.

Setting aside his report, he, Auld, Edwards and Cook compare Cook's spoons to the one brought from Red River. McDonell confides to his journal, "We all find it belongs to [Cook's set] and I give it to Mr. Cook as his property."

Now, he and Auld compare depositions on the devastating Churchill fire of last November. They don't match, in a way that McDonell finds terribly upsetting. He does not record the details, nor does anyone else, but enough clues exist to piece it together: the colony men swore that they heard Mr. Topping, chief factor of Churchill, say that the fire was probably the fault of recent Indigenous occupants of the "Indian House," but Topping has denied saying or believing any such thing, throwing responsibility back on the colonists. James McDonald, the blacksmith who arrived with McDonell, is the only man present whose name is on the discredited statement; he is to be charged with perjury.

McDonell does not resume his report to Lord Selkirk. Instead he retreats into himself. He doesn't even talk to his journal, just jots ambiguous phrases: "unwell," "had no sleep," "distracted on account of state of [Red River Settlement] matters." The story as it unfolds comes through the eyes (and words) of his heretofore implacable enemies, William Auld and Abel Edwards. To their immense credit, both men rise above their antipathy.

Dr. Edwards, still waiting for his lift back to England, notes McDonell's downturn and comments that in the next few days it "increased to a considerable degree in the course of which he frequently exclaimed that the Colony would be ruined. . . . [He bewails] the scarcity of provisions here and the impossibility of his men getting inland without them." By August 29, the doctor is alarmed, as are Auld and other officers. Thomas Thomas,[8] the man who is replacing Auld as superintendent, offers to destroy the false depositions, if it will help. Burning the papers, says Edwards, produces "a great and instantaneous change in Capt. M, who now appeared quite calm and joined in a dance which Mr. Auld had [arranged] entirely on his account."

The relief is fleeting. Next morning the demons are back, and McDonell calls for Edwards, who is horrified by his appearance:

> Countenance wild and distorted, his body convulsed with agony. He had been up all night and was wretched. He had ruined Lord Selkirk as well as the Colony. Nothing but death could relieve him, it was entirely his own fault, etc etc.

Edwards tries to console him as anyone would, but Miles insists that "only death can relieve me." Auld joins them, and Miles effectively resigns, begging Auld to take his keys, portable desk and all the colony papers, to which Auld agrees. Miles, says Edwards, "then called himself a villain, that the Colony was ruined by his mismanagement, that he was a wretch — too bad to live and too great a coward to die."

They persuade him to lie down and take away his gun and sword. Edwards stays in the next room. He hears much sighing and restlessness but little sleep. Four hours later, though, McDonell is more in

---

8 Thomas's Welsh parents seem to have outdone even the Scots in name-redundancy. According to the *Dictionary of Canadian Biography*, there was a *second* man named Thomas Thomas stationed at York factory at the same time. They were distinguished as Senior and Junior.

control of himself. His friends Hillier and Sinclair take him out for a short walk. Edwards or Auld stay with him at all times.

No one who has ever cared for a friend or relative in emotional crisis or suffered one themselves can mistake what's happening here. Once again, the drama crosses the centuries undiminished, and does credit to Edwards's compassion and maturity, as well as his powers of description.

Auld, too, rises above pettiness, and writes a letter that he gives to McDonell the next day:

> Dear Sir, — I now fulfill my promise to you by undertaking to provide a Gentleman from the [HBC] who will be capable of a Locum Tenens[9] in consequence of your determined resolution to resign the office of Governor of the Colony.
>
> You will here see a new proof of our anxiety for your personal comfort and happiness which is the hearty wish of us all here.

McDonell replies gratefully and hands over the keys and papers of office.

Later the same day, Edwards reports the arrival of a British man-of-war, HMS *Rosamond*:

> . . . two officers landed at YF . . . They acquainted us that the Prince of Wales is at no great distance and also informed us of the number of Colonists on board, etc.

The gentlemen and naval officers dine together and turn in.

When they rise the next morning, September 1, Miles McDonell is a new man. According to Edwards:

> Capt. McDonell quite recovered and in most excellent spirits. Indeed, the contrast of this day with yesterday is great in the extreme, and if I had not seen him myself, I could hardly credit it.

---

9   Someone who temporarily fills an office in the absence of its usual incumbent.

Whatever the crisis was, it has blown over, never to return. Miles asks for his keys and account books back and reassumes the title of governor.

So what had happened that caused the profound reversal of mood, especially since the burning of the depositions resulted in only a brief respite? If it is not simply brain chemistry, there is only one other change in material circumstances: the arrival of the ships.

Captain Stopford of the frigate *Rosamond* had brought news that the number of Red River–bound passengers aboard the *Prince of Wales* was only fifteen, almost all of them tradesmen, and one a qualified doctor. This may have tipped the scales. McDonell had reason to believe there might be as many as two hundred fresh colonists. Just trying to fill two hundred stomachs on top of those already in the settlement must have seemed an impossible challenge. Oatmeal shortage and insufficient pemmican must have been tormenting him with visions of mass starvation under his command. No wonder he considered the disgraced officer's traditional way out.

But fifteen people? A trifle! And a doctor, too, no less. This is a blessing, not a curse. The *Prince of Wales* arrives. Within days, McDonell is back to himself, damning the newcomers as "a troublesome set of people" who "will do little good. They are people of expensive habits." He busies himself with the accounts ("in a most disorderly state") and winter supplies ("Get 3 barrels of beef from YF. Oatmeal not yet landed").

Hallelujah, Miles is back!

Auld's effort to help him calls for a slight revision of McDonell's assessment of his long-time nemesis. Resuming his report to Selkirk, he writes, "He is a man of strong parts — can be a warm friend and a most bitter enemy, is possessed of a vast deal of policy and intrigue." The ships bring a sheaf of correspondence from Selkirk. In his acknowledgement, Miles confesses, "I am distressed and miserable at the backward state of the Red River Settlement's accounts and feel the justice and weight of your Lordship's reproaches."

He strongly requests a visit by Selkirk himself — "there are many regulations wanted for the Colony which I feel myself entirely unequal to make. . . . As it is, I am completely harassed and yet there is so little done." This is as close as he can come to admitting his recent crisis, and there is no mention at all of his short-lived resignation.

Even on the McLeans, McDonell backtracks, declaring their depositions to have been burned as well:

> That family has occasioned me a great deal of trouble. I thought them injured and endeavoured to support them, but there are so many collateral circumstances told that I am a good deal staggered as to the propriety of their conduct.

It's not a surprise that McDonell doesn't mention the extent of his breakdown, but he must know Lord Selkirk will hear about it. Like most large corporate cultures, the Hudson's Bay Company is a snakepit of "policy and intrigue," to use McDonell's own phrase, and information is currency. In the same dispatch bag with Miles's report goes a letter to Selkirk from Thomas Thomas, the incoming HBC superintendent. Thomas is not about to be part of any cabal to protect McDonell. He writes to Selkirk:

> It seems that your agent Capt. McDonell has met with difficulties which he did not foresee . . . for after his arrival at York he requested Mr. Auld to take on himself the charge of the Colony and gave him the keys of his Desks, which keys Mr. Auld returned at his request the day after. Cannot say what induced him to resign in this manner, but he was so greatly distressed as to excite the Compassion of every officer present.

Thomas closes by advising Selkirk to get the details from Hillier and Edwards. Why he believes this letter is necessary is not clear; probably the corporate climber's instinct for getting ahead of any hint of collusion in a cover-up.

He reads the situation correctly. This news will not go over well with Lord Selkirk.

CHAPTER 13

ALIEN ENCOUNTERS

AUGUST 25 TO MID-SEPTEMBER, 1814

ABOARD THE HMS ROSAMOND, ANCHORED OFF YORK FACTORY.

Peguis, Miles's friend and guest, has disappeared from the narrative. What he did between their arrival at York Factory and the appearance of the ships is lost to history, but we have a very detailed record of his response to the wonder he has come to see. He had presumably seen depictions of sailing ships, and their technology would be no challenge to a man of his intellect. When Captain Stopford invites him aboard the *Rosamond*, he does not hesitate. One of the ship's officers, Lieutenant Edward Chappell, records the event.[1] Stripped of the worst of its racial condescension, the excerpt reveals the genuine regard Peguis inspires in Chappell:

> An Indian chief arrived at the Factory from Lake Winnipeg, and some of our officers brought him on board. He staid with us two days, and as he was the Chief of one of those tribes who still maintains their primeval manners, untainted by European

---

1 Edward Chappell, *Narrative of a Voyage to Hudson Bay in His Majesty's Ship Rosamond* (London: R. Watts, 1817), pp. 163–168 (available on Gutenberg.org in various formats).

civilization, a full description of him may not be thought unentertaining.

. . . As far as I could collect, his tribe are properly called Sotees, or people who go up and down rivers. But they have been styled Bongees by the British, from their being addicted to mendicity.

The chief was about five feet eight inches tall, and to all appearance about 30 years of age . . .[2] [He wore a] coat of coarse blue cloth tawdrily ornamented with tarnished lace and adorned with should-knots [epaulets?]; a round hat with a red ostrich feather in front; a very coarse white shirt with frills and ruffles; a pair of red stockings, yellow garters and black shoes that were presented to him on his arrival. If we add to all this finery his native ornaments, such as a neckband of wampum or bead-work (a badge of dignity among the Indians) a long string of beads suspended by his hair from each temple, and a number of large metal links of the coarsest workmanship dangling from ear to ear, his appearance will naturally be imagined to border on the grotesque. His thighs were entirely naked as he could not be prevailed upon to fetter them with breeches; and the cartilage of his nose had been perforated.

He appeared a very intelligent man and was highly delighted with everything he saw on board the ship. . . . A skyrocket struck him quite with astonishment. . . . He was a great egoist and the general tenor of his conversation ran upon his dignity. He observed that he was a Governor, like ourselves, and when snow became deep upon the ground his tribe were going out to make war upon the Swee [Sioux] tribe. He exulted that he had already killed two of the Swee nation with his own hand . . . We presented him with a cutlass at which he was delighted . . . [he had a reputation for] courage and wisdom. Indeed, his remaining two days with us, perfectly at ease, is a proof of the former quality, particularly as we were

---

2   Peguis is actually about forty.

all utter strangers to him, and he had neither seen the sea nor a ship before in his life . . .

He had two wives, four sons and six daughters, and when I presented him with a few spangles and beads he gave me to understand that those trifles would be received with great pleasure by his children. . . . It surprised us much to observe with what degree of exactness he copied all our methods of eating, drinking etc.

We desired to hear him sing . . . instantly taking the hint, he rose up and prefaced with a long speech which we of course could not comprehend. . . . Then he suddenly struck off into an air. . . . The subject, we could perceive, was an appeal to the Deity (Manito) to protect the ship from all dangers in her voyage across the waters. We had many other songs from him during the evening, and on special application we were favoured with a specimen of the war-whoop, a most discordant howl produced by striking the hand quick against the mouth and shouting at the same time.

After making fun of Peguis's unfamiliarity with the European bed, Chappell describes the leave-taking:

He seemed to feel a great regret at parting . . . and gave us all to understand that if we should hereafter visit his territories, he would insure us a hearty welcome.

It is an encounter that none of the participants is ever likely to forget or cease from retelling. It would be wonderful to have Peguis's version.

IN OPEN BATTEAUX ON THE INLAND JOURNEY.

On September 11, 1814, McDonell comes "away from YF in the afternoon with 2 boats, Mr. James White, Surgeon, Mr. John Bourke, Peguis and attendant and 18 men." It is a cold fall and the journey is the usual punishing grind, taking about three weeks to reach Jack River and the entrance to Lake Winnipeg. McDonell spends the calmer moments reading Selkirk's directives on many topics, and getting to know his new doctor.

James White is twenty-five years old and unmarried. He had served for two years as acting assistant surgeon on HMS *Beagle*[3] before leaving the navy to complete his studies at the University of Edinburgh. Those studies included Latin, Greek, French, logic and mathematics, as well as assisting a surgeon and apothecary for practical experience. He attended lectures on all things medical and surgical given by eminent practitioners.

In other words, he's a freshly minted medical man with gritty naval experience and the robustness of youth; Selkirk feels lucky to get him. White's compensation is to be £50 a year plus 500 acres of land, should he decide to settle, and the services of two men to work it.

In his instructions to McDonell, Selkirk explains,

> White [is] to be your second in command. Give him pointedly precedence over other men on Estab't. When you are absent from the Settlement, he should have charge . . . so far as I see his judgement is good.

Here is the other alien encounter, not James White but Lord Selkirk. This nobleman, who has never set foot in the north or west of America, will now instruct those on the ground how a colony should be run, beginning with choosing McDonell's number two.

As usual, good breeding seems the prime requisite for leadership. A 25-year-old who has never managed or commanded even his own practice is now to be second in charge of the fate and welfare of a couple of hundred men and women, in an environment totally unknown to him. He will step in and take over as leader should McDonell have an accident or catch his death. This is not advice, it is Orders From The

---

3   HMS *Beagle* is the vessel which, in the 1830s, will carry Charles Darwin on a voyage that will change the world.

Earl. Who has not felt the burn of getting instruction in one's partic-ular domain from people who have no understanding of it? Imagine how McDonell may have received this one. If he has misgivings, he's right — White is another in a chain of poor judgments by the well-meaning earl.

The most significant piece of mail in the 1814 pouch is the longest memo Selkirk will ever write to McDonell, more than fifty handwritten pages covering sixty-seven enumerated topics and dated last April. One imagines the earl, housebound by late-winter squalls at the family seat in Kirkcudbright, stewing away over the reports coming back or simply exercising his fancy over something that is maddeningly out of reach.

Selkirk begins by expressing pleasure that the NWCo had not succeeded in stirring up the First Nations. "It is a satisfaction," he says, speaking far too soon, "to think that the most trying period for the settlement is over." But he is disappointed at how little progress has been made, considering "the great value of labour and expense of all kinds that have been devoted to the object." (This is the reproach McDonell acknowledged in his report.) He hopes this will change once the people are on their own lands and "working for themselves."

Selkirk affirms that there will be no great number of settlers this year due to the backward state of the settlement, and the delay at Churchill. He notes that the HBC has recalled Mr. Auld, who "has proved himself utterly unfit for such an important charge," and replaced him with Thomas Thomas, "a real man of business, possessed of sound judge-ment and of a distinct open mode of dealing." Miles might disagree if he knew of Thomas's tattletale letter to the earl, but that's a problem for another day.

Much of the memo deals with administrative minutiae, but a few topics stand out, particularly the business of obtaining rights to the settlement's lands from the First Nations. This is the first time Europeans have had to deal with Plains First Nations over actual territory, and the collision of two utterly incompatible concepts of land rights is a delicate matter. Wisely, Selkirk appreciates this. His analogy is feudal — the First

Nations have "domain" in the medieval sense, that is, right of restriction or assignment over all the land of their nation and, like a vassal lord, Selkirk must obtain their blessing to occupy and govern some of it.[4] To this end, he agrees to McDonell's earlier suggestion of offering annual gifts as a form of rent, just as his forebears had paid fealty tribute to the Crown. He doesn't know what form these rent-gifts should take, but he has firm ideas on how they should be distributed:

> The amount of the present should be proportional to the numbers of the tribe and the closeness of their vicinity. Those who are at greater distance may receive some present less considerable, both because there is less probability of injury from them and because they have less interest in the hunting of the reserved district, the loss of which must be held out as the ostensible reason for the pension.

"Ostensible" seems an interesting choice of word, as does "pension." These are not terms that would be used in a land deal in Scotland. He chides McDonell for not specifying the amount or type of "gifts" that would be appropriate. He needs to budget for them, dammit! In the meantime he advises periodic gifts to "keep the Indians in good humour."

For Selkirk, these musings are purely hypothetical, but for McDonell, they are right here with him: Peguis is Indigenous Sovereignty personified, if that phrase had any meaning back then. Neither man has the vocabulary to express what Selkirk is asking. For Peguis, ownership is restricted to personal belongings, and the idea that the land itself can be among those is a concept that will take a long time to grasp. We know that Miles is relatively generous in gifts of tobacco and liquor and ammunition, but how can he communicate that, in exchange, Peguis is expected to give up *all* access to large tracts of land, forever, whether or not others are occupying it?

---

4   They don't, of course; they simply occupy the land they use and protect it from outsiders until they move on, either by choice or by force, to occupy other territory. Which does not mean they don't *value* the land they occupy as highly as any European landlord.

Selkirk is very concerned to get a mill built as soon as possible, and reminds McDonell about Sam Lamont, "I am informed that Lamont is a good mechanic who understands his business, though he certainly looks a dull fellow."[5] He then discusses the merits and demerits of windmills, waterwheel mills and horse-driven mills as though McDonell and "a good mechanic who understands his business" might have trouble figuring it out themselves from conditions right in front of them. He comes down on the side of a horse-driven mill, which is what Lamont is in fact intending.

Selkirk realizes that Lamont's one-year contract has expired. He encourages McDonell to renew it in a way that will minimize cost to Selkirk and transfer maximum risk to the millwright himself, using reasoning familiar to any sketchy twenty-first century entrepreneur:

> I would [propose that] Lamont be tenant of the mill for a number of years, he giving his own labour in construction and repairs and paying a portion of the [cost of construction] from his profits.

In other words, let him work for food and lodging and then when (and if) the mill is finished and if he wishes to stay on in the settlement, he can begin recouping his costs (and paying his lordship) from the profits — if there are any. And by the way, Selkirk adds, maybe the blacksmith should supply the hardware for the mill on the same basis, free labour now and a further share later of the highly hypothetical profits.[6]

The earl complains about how much luxury food McDonell requests for his own table — chocolate, coffee, biscuits, butter and cheese. While he is thinking along these lines, he wonders why he is being asked to send out and pay for materials that the country can surely supply, such as pitch and tar and sugar and salt and even door hinges, glass and nails. He does not suggest who should be supplying

---

5 Seems an uncalled-for slash at my great-great-grandad. But there it is.

6 As a lifelong freelance worker myself, I heartily hope my ancestor told him where to put his offer. In my experience, whenever you are asked to invest labour freely now for a share of some reward your employer might reap later, in circumstances you cannot control, walk away. Always. Tell your children.

these things, nor does he address (and may not realize) the considerable manpower and time that would have to go into their collection and production. Glass and nails?

On the payroll and its drain on his fortune, he tells McDonell to get men off salary as quickly as he can and onto some form of piecework or by-the-job payment. He goes on at some length about men he doesn't know doing work he is "left to guess at." Selkirk suffers the perennial anxiety of the absentee investor: that his funds are being used carelessly by people he can't supervise. Closed up in his study in blustery Kirkcudbright, the earl goes on and on.

He dismisses the McLeans' alleged crimes as "too base" for belief. On the other hand, he gives a certain credit to the very nasty reports of McDonell's behaviour written by Edwards and McRae, the bad boys of 1812–13. Miles is probably too harsh with his subordinates, he suggests, provoking an overreaction from them in return. Nonetheless, the young popinjays are out of line and to be disregarded.

He ends by telling Miles to stop being so blasted conciliatory and friendly with those Nor'Westers, especially Miles's cousin Alexander. They can't be trusted and any accommodation encourages the colony's opponents inside the HBC. More advice from a man who knows nothing of the situation on the ground.

Not surprisingly, McDonell records nothing of his own reactions to this alternately encouraging and infuriating screed. He has learned to be discreet when it comes to his superiors. But his eyes must ache from rolling, his arteries strain with blood pressure. Happily, he has endless physical challenges to take his mind off office politics. Row, you blighters! Row! Damn this infernal rain!

His two boats reach Jack River after three weeks of misery and struggle. There, they find the *Cuchullin*, the colony schooner, come from Red River to meet them. McDonell stays three days, writes a few letters, and sets out again on October 4 in a northerly wind and driving snow. For this leg, he has the larger schooner and just one batteau. With any luck, this will be a routine sail over open water. Luck, however, has missed the boat and there is no such thing as a routine journey on Lake Winnipeg. The voyage is a nightmare, but all survive.

At long last they reach the settlement: "Dressed 6 of our men in Regimentals [Redcoat uniforms] and reached The Forks at 3 PM," October 19, 1814.

Just in time for the hornets' nest.

CHAPTER 14

SEPTEMBER TO HOGMANAY

SEPTEMBER 1814 TO JANUARY 1815

RED RIVER SETTLEMENT, NEAR THE FORKS.

In September and October 1814, during McDonell's absence, Peter Fidler[1] records energetic progress: potatoes dug and put into storage, crops cut and threshed, fishnets woven, cabins finished, roofs sodded, charcoal stocked for the blacksmith, a flagstaff erected; one crew of five builds a farmhouse, a sheep barn, a stable, a "low house" and a hog sty, demonstrating not only laudable industry but a few of the many English synonyms for shelter. The collection of "joined" buildings at Point Douglas, the governor's compound, measures eighty by seventeen feet (twenty-four by five metres). Fidler looks upon everything and, with few exceptions, sees that it is good. Left alone, the colony has every prospect of a flourishing future.

It will not be left alone.

The first clear indication of what lies in store is recorded by Fidler on August 30, when Miles McDonell is weathering his crise-de-l'âme in York Fort. A flotilla arrives at Gibraltar carrying a number of ranking Nor'Westers, some in counterfeit British army uniforms. As they pass Point Douglas and the settlement compound, the whole

---

[1]   Archie McDonald's journal being missing, Peter Fidler's journal is the only record of the colony for this period.

company fires a volley into the air, and, says Fidler, "by their sound, they seemed loaded with ball or shot." Ominous — salutes are fired with gunpowder only. Ball or shot implies a threat. His misgivings are warranted. Three weeks earlier Alexander McDonell (NWCo) wrote to John McDonald (Le Bras Croche), the North West partner who had brokered the truce last June:

> You see myself and our mutual friend Mr. [Duncan] Cameron on our way to commence open Hostilities against the Enemy in Red River. . . . One thing is certain, that we will do our best to defend what we <u>consider</u> our rights in the interior. Something serious will <u>undoubtedly</u> take place. Nothing but the complete downfall of the Colony will satisfy some, by fair or foul means, a most desirable object if it can be accomplished. So here is at them with all my heart and energy.

"Open hostilities," "Enemy," "Nothing but the complete downfall," "fair or foul means" and finally "here is at them with all my heart and energy" — these are not figures of speech, or empty bombast; they are orders, direct from the North West partners. Alexander McDonell took a serious drubbing at meetings in Montreal over the summer ("A general censure has been thrown out against me at Headquarters") for what the Montreal partners consider his weak response to the Pemmican Proclamation, a blatant assault on North West trading rights. They make no distinction between the HBC and the settlement, so the settlement must go.

Some of the "regimentals" Fidler notes are dress uniforms loaned to Nor'Westers by legitimate army officers; others are fakes whipped up by NWCo tailors. They give the deliberate, but wholly false, impression that the wearers are commissioned officers in His Majesty's Service. Miles McDonell has done the same thing to impress the First Nations and the Bois-Brûlés. With the single exception of McDonell himself, who actually holds a commission in the army (though irrelevant out here), none of them have military appointments. This does not deter them. Fidler writes on September 1:

> Mr. Cameron calls himself a Captain and Alexander [McDonell]
> a Lieutenant, though [their uniform] is only clothes got at the
> Portage [la Prairie].

Duncan Cameron,[2] the senior and most determined of the newly arrived Nor'Westers, begins his campaign immediately, attacking Miles McDonell's ban on hunting buffalo from horseback.[3] He tears down the posted order and replaces it with his own, telling the freemen and Bois-Brûlés to hunt how they wish and offering to hire every hunter to prevent them hunting for McDonell and the colony.

Over the next few days, tensions escalate. It begins on September 3 with an attempt to seduce some of the more tractable colonists. At a party given by Nor'Westers, they make "a considerable present" of clothes, fabric, tea, liquor and sugar to Alex and Christina McLean.

Having shown an open hand, they close it into a fist. Out on the prairie, Cameron and his men ambush Fidler and John Spencer, the once-again sheriff. They take Spencer and lock him up in their fort, charging him with the theft of their pemmican last spring.

This action stirs the settlers to a state of community outrage that takes the officers by surprise. Spencer's straightforward personality and honesty have made him the most popular of the leaders, and the settlers are more than ready to fight for him. Fidler and Archie McDonald have their hands full controlling their people, and even declare the arrest legal. Stunned, the settlers stand down. But later, when the Nor'Westers put Spencer into a canoe and begin taking him away, the guns come out again and the officers are ignored. Someone fires a warning shot and others load a cannon and prepare to fire at the canoe carrying Duncan Cameron. Only Spencer's wailed entreaties deter them, and his captors whisk him downstream and away. When Cameron returns without Spencer, several men try again to shoot him,

---

2   Cameron is about fifty, and, like Miles McDonell, Scottish born to parents who immigrated to New York and later, as Loyalists, to Canada. He has been in the fur trade for thirty years. See Jennifer Brown's short bio in the *Dictionary of Canadian Biography* online.

3   See Chapter 11.

but again Archie McDonald stops it. Spencer "was greatly beloved by every Settler and Servant at the Settlement," remarks Fidler.

This violent and spontaneous reaction by the Highlanders harks back to their response to the Clearances, and should remind Archie McDonald and his fellow officers that Highlander acquiescence is not to be taken for granted. That Archie could restrain them suggests he still enjoys a good deal of respect, but using it to defy their determination will cost him dearly and come back on him this winter. Settlers will later testify that the arrest and abduction of John Spencer was a turning point when the optimism of the idyllic summer began to turn into something else.

Alex McLean, still in close touch with the Nor'Westers, tells Fidler that there are warrants out on all those who helped enforce the Pemmican Proclamation. Mr. Holdesworth, the HBC man who carried the proclamation to Brandon House, decides he cannot leave the main house for fear of lurking "Canadians."

On September 7, Fidler sends a man named Crier over to Fort Gibraltar to fetch a couple of fellows he has engaged for the harvest, but the Nor'Westers instantly recognize Crier from recent confrontations. They surround him, rough him up and threaten him at sword point before he gets away.

Matters have gone from the tranquility of summer to the tensions of last spring seemingly overnight. Fidler backs off into defensive withdrawal, focussing on colony administration, harvesting crops and preparing for winter as he awaits the return of McDonell to decide their next move.

On October 19, McDonell finally returns, his arrival echoing that of the Nor'Westers — "dressed six of our men in Regimentals." Fidler, greatly relieved, "fires seven cannon on the Captain's arrival."

Peguis takes his leave of McDonell with "three big kegs of Indian rum and tobacco to treat his people." Then, military man that he is, Miles immediately rises to the Nor'Westers' arrest of Spencer with his worst decision since the Pemmican Proclamation. He dispatches Fidler to Fort Gibraltar with "an order for them to quit the place they now occupy at the forks before the expiration of six months." He writes similar orders for

NWCo posts at Winnipeg River, Turtle River, Brandon House, Carleton House, Fort Dauphin, Portage des Prairies and Rivière Qu'Appelle. Nowhere, though, is any suggestion of how he might back up his edicts. Without enforcement, he has done nothing but poke the bear, stir the hornets' nest, throw gunpowder on the fire. And winter is coming.

The settlers' food production for their first summer is impressive considering their late start, but comes nowhere near sufficient to feed them until next summer. Even the provisions McDonell has brought back from York Fort are not sufficient, so once again, the hunt is going to have to fill the gap. Just three days after his return McDonell sends the *Cuchullin* south to Pembina/Fort Daer with twenty-two "men, families and women" to pass the winter.

On October 27 he "registers two baptisms." The crop of babies sown in the Churchill darkness continues bearing fruit.

On October 30, McDonell concludes, "By a calculation made after taking an account of the provisions on hand, we can supply to the settlers till the first of May." He will hand out provisions once a month. The next day, "Mr. and Mrs. McLean and the children dine with us by invitation. I wish to detach them from the constant intercourse they have with the N.W. Fort." He seems to have heard Selkirk's admonition that he should be more sociable. In his journal, he uses "we" and "us" frequently this year.

By November 10, the Red River has frozen over. On the 12th he passes the evening with the McLeans, his new best friends again. What stands out about this friendship is its uniqueness. Miles socializes with no other couples outside of weddings, a child's baptism or a general party. The McLeans, of course, are on his side of the invisible line defining "gentlefolk." Bourke, the storekeeper, White, the surgeon, and McDonald, the overseer, qualify through their upbringing and education, but Sam Lamont, though literate and numerate with a practical education as a millwright, does not, let alone the blacksmith, carpenter and other skilled trades; and forget the simple labourers and farm families. Class structure is as secure as Lord Selkirk could wish.

This is not just a matter of social injustice; it is central to the many troubles that will plague the settlement. By so casually wearing the cloak of authority and never taking "the people," as he invariably calls them, into his counsel, McDonell sabotages the loyalty and solidarity so vital to the settlement's success. As an army officer, he is accustomed to having orders obeyed without question. As Highland farmers, the people have learned they are right to mistrust the entitled class and look to their own salvation. Gentry and plain folk who need each other to prevail in this unforgiving experiment will spend the winter growing apart.

On November 16 a great fall of snow, "upwards of a foot," curtails activity. The hired men are a little testy about not having been invited to recent weddings, so McDonell calls a snow day and attempts to make amends:

> Indulge the men with a pint of Rum each to drink in their quarters. Self and Gentlemen went in for a while.

He is far less indulgent with some of the settlers, who he complains are demanding "articles" out of colony stores. They are probably remembering all the articles they were forced to leave in York Factory when Auld squeezed them into two measly boats. The promised later delivery of their baggage has not materialized. McDonell will acknowledge the problem, but the general stores are intended just for top-up and replacement. They are not sufficient to meet heavy requests for fabric, tools, kitchen utensils and sundry supplies. It irritates McDonell that they won't take no for an answer. There is not a word about a community meeting or any sort of consultation to reach an understanding between suppliers and supplicants. Just raised eyebrows, clucks, dark looks and perhaps stern lectures.

What's more, despite their trigger-happy defence of Spencer, some are now refusing to train with the informal militia McDonell has organized under the few men with military experience. A few have declared emphatically that this is not what they signed up for and they will have no part of it. McDonell's response is to punish them ("Refused supplies to Sutherland for not taking a musket"). The fissure between governor and governed widens.

On November 28, "Lamont and two men begin to procure timber for the mill." Sam has evidently signed on for another year.

In early December Miles complains about the men's tardiness getting to work and their habit of "sitting up late at nights and visiting the NWCo Fort, contrary to orders." There are few things more certain to put a military man out of sorts than defying explicit orders.

His crankiness turns on the doctor who is still treating the Nor'Wester clerk Wills. "Mr. White went this afternoon to the NW Fort and stayed late. He took tea with Mr. Cameron." We can almost hear the growl in that last sentence. "Forbad Mr. White to visit anyone but Mr. Wills [without permission]."

On December 10, Robert Gunn, the piper who had lifted spirits on the long tramp from Churchill to York, becomes the first 1813 settler to publicly desert to the other side:

> Robert Gunn, piper, has been for two days and nights at the NW Fort, after promising formerly that he would not go there. We learn that he and two others are on treaty with Mr. Duncan Cameron to leave the country.[4]

This is indeed an ominous development, but it is almost immediately displaced by a small but significant scandal. Like isolated communities everywhere, this one undoubtedly lives for gossip, and this morsel is juicy. McDonell records in his journal that "Betty McKay is delivered of a bastard female child."

Babies born out of wedlock, called "natural children," are neither especially rare nor in themselves scandalous, but this one is special because Betty "makes oath" that the father is Abel Edwards, the doctor. Now gone to Britain, he left nothing for the care of his child.

A righteous twenty-first century response might be that the reprehensible cad used his position as gentleman and doctor to seduce and exploit a poor Scots lass without parents and then abandon her to her fate. There may well be an element of that, and Edwards is certainly

---

4   This will become clear soon enough, but "leave the country" means to take up an NWCo offer to transport him to Upper Canada by boat.

destroyed as the moral paragon Auld claimed him to be.[5] But as usual grey reality does not fall neatly into black-and-white stereotype.

Betty is indeed a Scots lass without parents, but she is twenty-four years old, no callow girl.[6] Not to impugn the poor woman on slim evidence, but we also cannot assume the seduction was all on Edwards's part. As to her abandonment by the bounder, it is unforgivable if done knowingly, but since conception likely took place in March, the surgeon may have known nothing of the pregnancy when Betty left with the April group for York Factory, one more pregnant woman on that trek. Quite possibly, she did not yet know it herself.

Blame, beyond moral turpitude, is disappointingly hard to place. Still, Archie McDonald must be feeling delicious schadenfreude. Edwards made his life miserable at Churchill, and now Edwards is a fallen idol.

Throughout November and December, McDonell records families going to Fort Daer at Pembina, but there is no general exodus as in former years. Many people stay in the settlement to safeguard their property and care for livestock. Their log cabins are sufficiently finished to withstand the cold, while Fort Daer's limited accommodation has been neglected over the past summer. There is another reason as well, which they don't share with the officers.

In mid-December, McDonell orders his "sergeants" to muster and drill the settlers, still determined to create a militia from these hayseeds. A few men turn out but most make various excuses not to take up arms.

Whenever sightings of buffalo are reported, hunters set out on foot in pursuit. Some are successful, and sledfuls of meat come up from Pembina from time to time.

---

5   Auld wrote to McDonell that last winter Edwards had been "preventing not only the diseases of the body from breaking out, but those moral evils far more destructive in their consequences."

6   She lives with her uncle, Alexander Gunn, and his other niece, also named Elizabeth McKay.

At Christmas, Miles just reports "gave a dram to our people," and the next day invites everyone, settlers and servants, to gather to "play at the hurl":

> There appeared to be some animosity between them [i.e., settler vs. servant] which was like to turn serious. Two gallons Rum were drank — one from McLean, one from Mr. McDonald. Our Servants invited the Settlers to take a drink with them. In the course of the night some wrangling took place between them.

A collateral victim of those two gallons of rum is the settlement's boar: "He had been let out last night and was killed by the dogs." We are left to wonder at the source of the wrangling, but divisions are deepening.

On December 29, Miles rides down to George Campbell's house, making a stop at Andrew McBeath's. These are probably just seasonal visits with a dram or two lubricating them, but it is worth remarking that this is the first time he has mentioned George Campbell since Selkirk recommended him so highly for his social station and refinement. Campbell is a younger version of Alex McLean; that is, a gentleman farmer. Given Selkirk's enthusiastic assessment of him, one might expect McDonell to cultivate the 26-year-old and his wife as he has the McLeans, but no. Perhaps personality differences are at work here. Whatever the impediment, he will have strong cause to regret, or at least question, his neglect of Campbell.

Hogmanay, the last day of the year, is the principal mid-winter celebration in Scotland and that tradition has come over with the immigrants. On New Year's Eve, "our people, according to ancient highland custom, beat three times around the House and repeated the like ceremony at Mr. McLean's." On January 1, 1815, McDonald and John Bourke, with some of the men still feeling the cheer, go over and exchange friendly salutes with the Gibraltar people. McDonell hides out at the McLeans "to avoid the solicitations of people coming for Rum to drink."

No one works on January 2, but by the 3rd, McDonell is grousing again: "Plagued a great deal by the Settlers coming for articles out of the store, which is the case every day."

It will set a tone for 1815.

CHAPTER 15

BLEAK AND BITTER

JANUARY 2 TO MARCH 10, 1815

RED RIVER SETTLEMENT, NEAR THE FORKS.

Personality and behaviour differences shape the course of the next six months. On one side, Miles McDonell and Archie McDonald are very much Old World, authoritarian and class conscious. They are also "honourable" by their own lights. That is, they behave as they say they will and they respect the forms of British law. This will emerge as fatally naïve and rather absurd on this lawless fringe of empire. Even more so when compared to the character of their chief antagonist, Duncan Cameron.

As the son of a middle-class Scottish family, well educated and literate, Cameron is not unlike Archie McDonald, though considerably older and richer in experience. Years in the fur trade have accustomed him to the easy informality of the western plains. He is smart, cunning, affable and charming, with the common touch that Selkirk's officers lack entirely since the well-loved Sheriff John Spencer was removed from the scene. He is also utterly ruthless, focussed completely on the goal expressed by Alexander McDonell's letter of last August: "the complete downfall of the Colony . . . by fair or foul means." He bears no trace of the sense of fair play that will hamstring McDonell and McDonald. The North West partners have ordered him to destroy the colony and they don't much care how he does it but, to give peace a chance, they have authorized him to bribe the settlers and offer them free passage to Canada.[1]

McDonell seems largely unaware of what has been taking place under his nose for the ten or so weeks since he returned from York Fort. Archie McDonald, however, is fully aware of the subtext in the settlers' demands. On January 2 he records,

> I must observe here that the settlers are very troublesome to us in the Store way . . . Indeed [when refused] they will immediately threaten to leave the country and go to those who will give them everything they want — the NWCo.

There it is — the settlers are beyond just complaining; they are now openly threatening to leave the colony. Cameron is giving them the means and they intend to use it if they don't get what they want.

The effect is preserved in a letter written to Cameron by James Smyth, a 59-year-old husband and father of three. Many of the settlers are uncomfortable in English and most are illiterate. That Smyth can write English puts him in an elite of sorts, yet his letter embodies the unsophisticated vulnerability of the poorer settlers.

> Fort Dair Dec 24th 1814,
>
> Honored Sir,
>
> I understand that your honour have proposed to relieve a poore distressed people By taking them to Montrall next spring I hoap that you will count myself and family in the number as I assure you that I was still against the taking of the pimiken. There is a [lot?] of men weating the Result of my [request?] which I assure you they will fo[llow] my example. . . . If the

---

1   Technically, Canada, Upper and Lower, extends to the western tip of Lake Superior by this time, but in this context it means the more settled area east of Lake Huron, along the lesser Great Lakes and down the valley of the St. Lawrence.

Capt. McDonal hears of my gowing with you he will not let me gow down in his boates . . . there is soom people says you have power to take them and some says not, Now I cojure you by all that is sacrid to let me know your Athority that we would not be deceived . . . Sir pleas to send me a few linds [lines] by the first opportunity to let me know how I'm to cheuve [achieve] your compliance with will forever be obleidg.[2]

— Your Hum'l St, James Smyth

The final lines of James Smyth's letter as transcribed by McDonell's clerk, likely James Warren. (Library and Archives Canada, Selkirk Papers, p. 1293)

It is clear that Smyth is sincere. His distress is partly due to the increasingly abrasive relationship with his own "superiors," but equally, it has been conjured, sown and assiduously nurtured by Duncan Cameron himself. Cameron has been waging an insidious campaign of disinformation and fear even as he has been cultivating the settlers' friendship and trust. The depth of it will only become clear to Selkirk's men when it is far too late.

---

2   It is interesting to note that this is quoted not from the original letter but from a fair copy made at the time. The copyists, or writers, as they were called, always copy verbatim, reproducing any errors or idiosyncrasies faithfully, often noting them.

Cameron's answer to another settler's letter is dated January 10, 1815, and begins,

> I am very glad that the eyes of some of you are getting open at long last to the situation you are placed in in this barbarous country and that you now see your past follies in obeying the unlawful orders of the Plunderer and highway robber.

He says he is willing to forgive men who are not bad themselves but have been made so by bad leaders and bad advice.

> The greatest enemies ever you had is Lord Selkirk, Doctor Auld and Miles McDonell . . .
> In pity to your deplorable situations . . . I will be very happy to take so many of my fellow Countrymen out of bondage. . . . I do not ask a penny for passage or provision. . . . We will oblige ourselves to get lands for those that come to take them and will throw no one on the Highway as Beggars.

He then warns them to take care not to let Christina McLean know what they're doing, "for she would sell her own brother to [McDonell]."

From Cameron's letter to disaffected settlers. (Library and Archives Canada, Selkirk Papers, p. 1743)

The *Prince of Wales* and the *Eddystone* trade with Inuit people near the Upper Savage Islands, Hudson Strait. Watercolour by Robert Hood, 1819. (Library and Archives Canada/MIKAN 2836426)

Settler flotilla leaving York Factory. Watercolour by Peter Rindisbacher, 1821. Rindisbacher came to the Red River with his family in 1821, aged fifteen, and stayed until 1826. (Library and Archives Canada e008299428)

A wearisome portage on the journey from York Factory to Lake Winnipeg. Watercolour by Peter Rindisbacher, 1821. (Library and Archives Canada e008299434)

Cold night camp on the shore of Lake Winnipeg. Watercolour by Peter Rindisbacher, 1821. (Library and Archives Canada e008299440)

Arrival at the Red River, greeted by Saulteaux people. Watercolour by Peter Rindisbacher, 1821. (Library and Archives Canada e008299442)

Anishinaabe (Saulteaux) hunter, possibly Peguis. Watercolour by Peter Rindisbacher, c. 1821. (Archives of Manitoba, B22 box 2, N3753 N3754 CT66)

Bois-Brûlé family in dress clothes. Watercolour by Peter Rindisbacher, c. 1825. (Courtesy of Ernest Meyer and the Winnipeg Art Gallery-Quamajuq)

A family of Anishinaabe (Saulteaux) on the Red River. Watercolour by Peter Rindisbacher, c. 1821. (Library and Archives Canada e0082994589)

Indigenous family fishing where the Seine River meets the Red with the settlement and Fort Douglas in the background. Watercolour by Peter Rindisbacher, 1821. (Library and Archives Canada e008299458)

A party of Dakota (Assiniboine) hunters. Watercolour by Peter Rindisbacher, before 1825. (Denver Art Museum: Gift of Mr. and Mrs. Sam Gary. Photography by Denver Art Museum)

Fort Daer (RRS) and Fort Pembina (NWCo), on the Pembina River where it meets the Red. The soldiers outside Fort Daer place it well after 1816. Watercolour by Peter Rindisbacher, before 1826. (Library and Archives Canada e008299397)

Hunting bison (buffalo) on snowshoes. Watercolour by Peter Rindisbacher, c. 1822. (Library and Archives Canada e008299397)

Anishinaabe (Saulteaux) hunter in winter. Watercolour by Peter Rindisbacher, c. 1822. (Library and Archives Canada e008299450)

Ice fishing and socializing at The Forks, winter 1821. Fort Garry (HBC) is under construction where Fort Gibraltar used to stand. The church is post-1816. Watercolour by Peter Rindisbacher, 1821. (Library and Archives Canada e011161354)

A view of the Red River Settlement, 1817. Pen and ink from pencil sketches by Thomas Douglas, Lord Selkirk, 1817. (Archives of Manitoba)

Parallel to Cameron's campaign to drive a wedge between settlers and officers is another to convince settlers that despite all surface appearances, the "Indians" are absolutely intent on murdering them all, man, woman and child, at the first opportunity, even though all evidence contradicts this. Cameron convinces many that only his firm hand is holding the First Nations back and that with spring he will lose that authority and the Indigenous men will become the savages that Europeans call them.

The officers' social separation from their own people keeps them from full awareness of these machinations. Nor does anyone from the settlers' side cross the line to inform them. Archie McDonald can only guess at the meaning behind the sullen grunts and insolent glares, which he rarely interprets with generosity or even much curiosity.

On January 3, he notes that "Duncan Cameron gave all the settlers he had up last night a keg of liquor to bring home this morning." And next day, "I saw Robert Gunn among the people who act as recruiting sergeants for Cameron."

Two days later comes the sad news that Mr. Wills, Dr. White's Nor'Wester patient, has died, apparently from the long-term effects of alcohol addiction. Archie McDonald, Miles McDonell, John Bourke, Alex McLean and the doctor are invited to the funeral, where "Mr. Cameron treated us with a few glasses of wine. Weather very cold." Regard for the late Mr. Wills seems genuine. He tried hard to broker peace last June.

On January 9, more sad news: Betty McKay's infant daughter, the "female bastard child," dies. McDonell sends Archie and the doctor to examine the body for signs of violence. They return with a verdict of natural death.

High among the settlers' grievances are the property bundles they were forced to leave at York Fort last spring. They were not brought down as promised, and they don't believe McDonell's new promise for next summer. Some want to go up to York on foot over the ice and bring the bundles south at breakup. But McDonell doesn't trust them any more than they him. Says Archie McDonald, "We suppose this plan is principally from those who are determined to go with the NW to Canada." He refuses, effectively holding their property hostage.

The people respond by demanding replacement goods from the colony stores. This causes John Bourke, the storekeeper, "great disturbance." Too bad, since this could be an opportunity for mutual benefit — perhaps a concession to lend articles that can be replaced, or at least to extend credit against the distant goods. An openness about inventory might get the Highlanders' agreement to a rationing system. Instead the bosses fall back on the old patterns: we decide, you accept. On January 14 Archie posts a spiteful note outside the stores building:

> Notice is hereby given to all the Settlers that from their constant application to this store for some time past and from the liberal supplies they have received, no demands can be attended to by the Storekeeper for the space of two months.

Archie is behind in the accounts and no doubt under great pressure. His journal keeps a running tally of his truly long hours toiling on the books since last June. Pressure on inventory just makes it harder. In his mind, his difficult job is to manage and their equally difficult job is to deal with it. Intransigence is the refuge of the overwhelmed.

On McDonell's orders, some disused huts are restored to functionality and fitted out as a school for the colony's children. John Mathieson (called Senior to distinguish him from the young man from Aultbreakachy) is hired as teacher. The curriculum is not mentioned.

Archie McDonald, on McDonell's orders, notifies several men that they are to go to Pembina/Fort Daer to help with the buffalo hunt. They all refuse, giving various excuses — none of which are the truth, which is that they believe, courtesy of Duncan Cameron, that McDonell wants to use them to attack the Nor'Wester fort at Pembina and steal its pemmican. No hint of that actually being the case is recorded, but since neither side addresses it, the men go on believing what they have been told and McDonald goes on believing they are lazy and unwilling. His response is to alienate them, as he records snarkily:

Many Settlers here today but as we have all got quite tired
of them and their demands they got no audience, so they all
went up to the NW fort.

When others come asking for a bit more pemmican, "those people
who refused to go to the plains, of course, got none."

Next day, even Sam Lamont is feeling the stress. Lamont and his
crew have finished sawing the lumber for the mill, and are set to begin
preparing the building site, but something goes awry. Sam refuses John
Bourke's order to return a tent that had been covering the sawing pit.
When McDonald repeats the order, Lamont is "rude enough to tell me
no and to send a horse for it." Presumably, Archie does so.

At this point McDonell leaves the colony to go to Fort Daer to
oversee the buffalo hunt and see them through the winter. Alex McLean
and Dr. White go with him. Command devolves to McDonald, who,
after all, saw these people through a worse winter at Churchill.

Pouncing on the opportunity, Duncan Cameron sends a letter over
to McDonald, inviting him and Bourke to join him for dinner Sunday
"if it is not high treason" to do so.

Archie responds in the same spirit, declining not through fear of
treason but because he is already pledged to Christina McLean for
Sunday dinner. He spends a pleasant evening with that lady, treating
her to a ride around Point Douglas in his cariole (dogsled).

The next day is Provisions Day, the day the food for the month is
distributed, and Archie reports to his journal that "it is rumoured that
Settlers intend to attack the Storehouse if they do not get what they
want." Rumours and "the intriguing Mrs. McLean"[3] regularly appear in
proximity. She is a woman with her ear to the ground and, being a woman
among women, probably gets to hear more than her husband does.

Monday, McDonald is on his guard, not just because of the
rumoured attack but because he too has something to hide: he has
reduced the monthly food allowance. The Highlanders trail in, collect

---

3   Alexander McDonell of the NWCo uses this phrase to describe her in a testy
      exchange of letters with his cousin Miles in 1813.

their allowance and go. "They were not told," says Archie, "neither did they perceive it." This is a new low. It is hard to square it with the Archie of a year ago, when he and the Highlanders were united against William Auld.

Two settlers eventually smell a rat. Hector McLeod challenges McDonald, who promptly shows him the door, whereupon McLeod and others head to Fort Gibraltar and Cameron's largesse. Others hang sullenly about, alarming McDonald. "I supposed this might be the beginning of what was reported yesterday. I got my two pistols loaded, determining to knock down the leader of the mob." It takes the appearance of a Nor'Wester clerk to defuse the situation: "Mr. Shaw of the N.W. came down . . . and had a long consultation with the Settlers before the door of our house." Then Shaw leaves, and the men demand that Archie come out. He does.

"You had better take your provisions and go home," he tells them haughtily. "You may be idle, but I am not."

George Campbell, emerging as the spokesman of the malcontents, responds, "We know you cut our allowance. What will be next?"

This throws a defensive Archie into full self-righteous scold. "Yes, the provisions is less than last month by a pound a man and half pound per woman.[4] Captain McDonell ordered this because some refuse to go out and hunt to feed yourselves and save pemmican for those who can't. Even so what you are now getting, you never did less for in your lives."

"If Lord Selkirk told us how we were to be used, we'd never have come," Campbell replies.

"I believe you are astonished," says Archie (or so he claims), "that such a Nobleman as Lord Selkirk has done so much for you. And so you should be — you don't deserve it now, the way you're going."

It is still only January, but the breach seems beyond repair.

Next morning, January 24, Archie McDonald takes an extraordinary decision for one who has just reacted so pompously to his own people — he pays a cordial visit to the real enemy.

---

4   If that is per day it is egregious, but insignificant if per month. Per week is most likely, but McDonald does not specify.

In the morning went up [and] called upon Mr. [Duncan] Cameron and passed an hour or two with him and took a glass of Rum and water.

He complains that Cameron repeatedly runs down the colony and all connected to it: "How much better it would have been had they gone to Canada," Cameron says, and "Are you yourself such a fool as to think of settling on Red River?"

After trying in vain to counter these barbs, Archie huffs, "I believe I shall never return to this house, if you have no other conversation but these incessant attacks."

Surprisingly, Cameron apologizes and promises to say no more on the subject. Then he walks Archie halfway back to Point Douglas and promises to return the visit soon.

And so he does, just a week later, on February 1. This time his manners are in place and McDonald says he stays "2 or 3 hours and was the best company. I treated him with our best wine."

Nothing illustrates the gulf between the social norms of 1815 and those of the twenty-first century more starkly than the schizophrenic relations in this tiny microcosm on the prairie. On each side the "gentlemen" are more comfortable with their equals opposite than with allies of lower status. Cameron's cordiality may be genuine, though his character suggests that it is more likely cynical manipulation. This doesn't seem to occur to Archie McDonald. Or maybe it does; this cozy exchange of visits will not be repeated.

As January turns to February temperatures drop below −40°C. This brings out McDonald's soft side — "I gave Betty McKay a few things out of the store. She is in great need" — and the hard: he growls that many settlers, "from carelessness," allowed the potatoes in their cellars to freeze in a recent cold snap. "Now they run to us and immediately demand more potatoes." Once again, Archie seems to forget that these people are veteran potato growers. If they have inadequately protected the potatoes against these killer frosts, it is less likely incompetence than misunderstanding just how penetrating the cold can be. They are only beginning to understand the ways of prairie winter. Punishment is probably not helpful.

He takes a horseback ride with Mrs. McLean and John Bourke through the farmsteads down the river. They hear from someone they trust that "all" the settlers are determined to leave and have made deals with Cameron. This finally moves him to rise above his self-righteousness for at least a brief moment. When George Campbell comes by the next day, February 6, Archie invites him to stay, a possible class ally among the disaffected.

Campbell plays it coyly at first, talking as though leaving were the last thing on his mind. Presently he complains that Miles McDonell called him a liar. When he told McDonell that Selkirk had promised him some free livestock on arrival, McDonell (who would have had to have been instructed to do so) bluntly told him Lord Selkirk said no such thing. This rankled then and still does. McDonald offers to make amends by selling him a cow at a knockdown price, but Campbell demurs. Archie drops the price further, "but still Campbell would not have the cow, which makes me think he's bound for another country."

Duncan Cameron goes on offering the settlers everything gratis — food, travel, land in Upper Canada — while the settlement officers punctiliously charge everything they supply to the accounts of settlers who manifestly cannot afford it and who have been deprived of their own belongings without compensation. The officers do this in part because they have no permission to do otherwise and he who could give permission is across the sea. They may even realize that whatever Selkirk has to spend to hold on to his people has to be preferable to starting all over again, but Selkirk does not trust others to make such costly decisions without consultation, so time is on Cameron's side.

February drags by in parsimony and acrimony. Petition and complaint are met uniformly with scolding and rebuff, like this response to Angus McKay, husband of Jean and father of their new baby, when he comes "back for more provisions":

Of course he got none. Neither did I spare him a very severe lecture respecting his conduct. . . . He was told his Pemmican will be reduced next month.

Meanwhile, Duncan Cameron continues his far more crafty and effective campaign, repeating his warning about the hostility of First Nations people at every opportunity. For many settlers, this lie is the deciding factor in winning them over to the dissenters. They make that clear later, in affidavits. A few examples:

Robert Sutherland: "I never saw any appearance of hostility from Indians but was frightened by what Cameron told us. . . . We were told that anyone who remained at RR would be murdered or starved because there would be no provisions for us."

Angus McDonald: Cameron offered him passage, saying he could not leave him to be killed by the Indians. "Had no intention of leaving until George Campbell told me it was my only chance."

James McKay: "I heard Duncan Cameron say he had difficulty restraining the Indians when drunk from killing Capt. McDonell because they had not been paid for their land. I had never found the Indians anything but friendly — many had camped near my farm. But hearing these stories I became afraid."

Haman Sutherland: He was satisfied until fear of Indians arose. "Had no fear myself but heard from Cameron that the Indians intended to murder [us]. When I saw Indians gathering in spring, I feared it was for that purpose. I did not agree to leave the country till I found that all the others were going and was afraid to remain on my own."

Alex Bannerman: "Captain Cameron told me that the Indians would come and murder us all if we remained in the Settlement . . . I was afraid of the Indians, even though they did not trouble me at any time. I never heard any of the Settlers say that the Indians had troubled them."

. . . and so on.

Cameron has groomed George Campbell as his chief go-between. Whether this is Cameron's class prejudice is not clear, but he is clever enough to step into the void left by McDonell's neglect of the young man.

FORT DAER ON THE PEMBINA RIVER.

Far to the south, Miles McDonell is facing his own challenges. Shortly after arriving he hears that some Saulteaux Anishinaabe had clashed with a party of Dakota near "the forks" (now Grand Forks, North Dakota). Six Anishinaabe were killed and at least one Dakota. This of course does nothing to calm fears of "Indians" in general.

The so-called freemen, who may include Bois-Brûlés and (French) Canadians, are firmly allied with the NWCo and harass the colony men wherever they meet. Colony servant John McLeod is detained by some freemen and held for several days. When released he says that he "suffered many indignities and much ill treatment from his barbarous keepers."

On February 16, Miles writes that his notice to quit the territory has now been served on every NWCo post except Fort Dauphin.

RED RIVER SETTLEMENT.

Back at The Forks in the north, February turns to March on a bad note. Visiting Fort Gibraltar, Alex McLean hears Cameron declare that because of Archie's ill use, the people may take the provisions they need by force. McLean reports this to Archie, whose now-typical response is to cut every settler's rations because he has heard that "the obedient ones" are sharing with "those outlaw fellows."

So now he has antagonized "the obedient ones," as well.

On March 2 comes a foreshadowing: a colony servant named Donald McDonell (no known relation to Miles) is seen "spying about the place" carrying pistols and threatening to shoot Alex McLean when confronted. He then takes off for the NW fort, pursued by McLean and John Bourke, now armed. Cameron stops them and addresses McLean "in a very disrespectful manner," to which McLean responds "<u>very manly</u> indeed," according to McDonald.

Three days later, McDonald reports some rare good news: "Sam Lamont the Millwright requested the favour of ½ gallon Rum to his own account to give the rest of the men here as the foundation of the mill is laid. I gave them a quart on the public expense." The completion of the mill's foundation marks the success of their winter's work. Only reasonable they raise a glass to themselves.

However, the next day Archie is complaining about these same sawmen as "excessively refractory of late." They are griping about their provisions: three-quarters of a pound of pemmican, one pint of oatmeal a day with all the potatoes they can eat, "and still they complain. One of them, D. McMillan, came out to the street calling '2 pounds Pemmican or for Canada!' and this in the form of a song."

On this same March 6, Alex McLean challenges Duncan Cameron to a duel for the insults of March 2. McLean has a wife and five children dependent on him. He must be powerfully angry to risk this. Happily, it comes to nothing.

On March 10, Archie whines, "The Servants are giving us much trouble in these days."

It's March. No one on the prairies is happy in March. It is time for winter to end. Surely spring will bring high spirits and relief?

Don't count on it.

CHAPTER 16

LOOSE CANNONS

MARCH 14 TO APRIL 30, 1815

RED RIVER SETTLEMENT.

On March 14, Archie McDonald writes in his journal, "The only pig we have has littered. Unfortunately she has only four young and all are boars. Mr. Duncan Cameron must have two of them provided that so many of the litter survive." Another example of that oddly conscientious honesty or honour the Selkirk gentlemen follow. No matter that Cameron would destroy his enterprise, steal his settlers and probably spit on his toothbrush; if Archie has promised a fellow gentleman piglets, piglets he shall have. It is moot, since the sow herself murders the lot of them, "though a man attended on them all night and during this morning." Even the sow is in a mean March mood. Archie vents his frustration with a long rant about the settlers' laziness and preference for "living off the public supplies."

The public supplies include tools, nails and other construction materials, fabric for clothing and the settlement's common food supply: oatmeal, salt pork and beef, pemmican, some sugar, salt, flour, potatoes and the officers' "luxuries." Stores would also include alcohol and tobacco, trade goods, muskets and ammunition, the heavy weapons supplied by Selkirk, rope, chain, traps, snare wire and whatever else imagination and need can conjure. The food is given out in strict monthly rations; the alcohol on the whim of the officers or at individual expense. Everything is charged to some account, either the individual's or the colony's (i.e. Lord Selkirk) or as a matter of negotiation.

On St. Patrick's Day, Archie gives the Irishmen a half-pint of rum with the promise of another later, but when he comes back is irritated to find that five Scots have joined them, presumably with their refractory tongues hanging out. Then he gets the news from Pembina that McDonell has arrested a Nor'Wester named Bostonais Pangman at Pembina in retaliation for the latter's detention of John McLeod last month. This cheers him up so much that "I less hesitated to give the men the last ½ pint of Rum, so as to make them a little more contented."

From Fort Gibraltar, Cameron demands McDonald or Bourke write to McDonell and tell him to release Bostonais. They do not.

The hired men continue to be refractory. "Our men got [Bargon?] and fat for breakfast, but there was no salt.[1] Consequently they would have none of it and the whole went to work without breakfast." The next general ration to the people is further reduced. Adults now get less than a pound (454 grams) of pemmican a day, and oatmeal is increased to compensate. There is no mention of how people react to this, but relations are now so brittle it probably makes little difference.

Cold weather returns as it often does at the end of March, taxing everyone further. "The day is so cold and exposed that Samuel cannot work at the Mill," writes Archie. "He now is making a small box for me to put the books and papers in."

Archie is in foul temper. He has a set-to with carpenter Miles Livingstone, "who is never otherways but a great plague," over supplies from the stores. Livingstone tells him he has shown himself to be a tyrant, and that has driven the men to Cameron. McDonald has brought this accusation on himself, of course, but it is not entirely deserved. At the same time he is banging heads with settlers and servants, he is negotiating another highly delicate situation with exemplary grace.

---

[1] There are several salt sources within a few days' travel of The Forks, and it is not a commodity they ever lack for long. But the late winter thaw is the worst time for travel, so they will have a few weeks without it.

It begins with the birth of a "natural" daughter to Kitty Sutherland. The baby's father, John McIntyre, is wintering far away at Brandon House, but no one doubts his good intentions and Archie advances many items to baby and mother on his account. Tragically, the baby dies just a few days later and more stores are readily supplied, now for the funeral that Archie solemnly attends.

At just this moment, another baby is born, this time to Anais or Anna McKay and her husband, Will Bannerman. Immediately, Archie McDonald inserts himself into this family's life to a startling degree, going to see the couple and immediately removing their baby and taking it to be nursed by the recently bereaved Kitty Sutherland. The reason for this presently becomes clear: Will Bannerman married Anna just four months ago, when she must have been well along in her pregnancy — with *Archie's* child. Anna/Anais had been a servant in the governor's house last summer, and Archie had taken advantage of her availability with no intention of doing the honourable thing. In marrying the pregnant young woman, Will accepted Anna, but not the child. Archie accepts his responsibility, taking charge of and providing for the baby. It would be some comfort to Kitty Sutherland to have an infant on her breast, however briefly, and in fact she bonds with the little fellow. She and John McIntyre will adopt him, and Archie will be generous in providing for all of them.

All of which is to say that Archie McDonald is not a bad man, just one who has been promoted well beyond his maturity and competence.

If further evidence is needed, it comes in a case of adolescent aggression that any young man would recognize: George Bannerman, twenty-three, comes to the door of the store where McDonald is presiding. Whether George is related to Will is unclear, but he arrives with a good deal of attitude, says Archie, and begins "to give me very insolent and disrespectful language." Archie tells him to move along. Bannerman sneers that he will stand here as long as he wants. Archie retorts that "if I thought it worth my while I would soon turn him away." Bannerman advances, daring him. Another young man arrives and this schoolyard showdown comes to an end.

After pugnaciously recording this, McDonald immediately strikes a softer note: "I gave Alex Sutherland a little provisions for his sister and the infant she is now nursing." Archie's infant, of course.

Word comes from Pembina that Nor'Westers under Cuthbert Grant have waylaid Miles McDonell's clerk James Warren and two others, all of whom they swapped for Bostonais. So that pot has not boiled over.

On Easter Sunday, the breakdown spreads to the servants. They are given a generous ration to mark the day, according to McDonald, but they declare the meat unacceptable and send it back to the kitchen. Archie offers pemmican, but they are sick to death of pemmican. They are given more "meat," but they send that back, too, and grumpily dine only on potatoes and "Indian rice."[2]

Later, Archie asks Sam Lamont, their leader, why they rejected the beef.

"It were as well for us to want it as take what was given," answers Sam. "Meatless bones."

McDonald goes on, "I conversed with Samuel for some time, pointing out the impropriety of [the men's] conduct throughout the winter." He does not record Sam's side of this conversation.

March ends no better than it began. Neil McKinnon takes his daughter out of the McLeans' service, saying, "He shall rather see his daughter drowned than employed by any man that would help Capt. McDonell be against the North West."

April begins on a positive note: "Samuel has the shell of the Mill finished and ready for putting up." On Sunday, McDonald takes a long ride and finds the people cool toward him, but that is nothing new, and he passes a pleasant evening with the McLeans in the company of sympathetic friends. They are all of them about to get the surprise of their lives.

The morning of Monday, April 3, begins as usual. About 10 a.m. settlers begin arriving for the month's provisions and Mr. Bourke begins serving them out.

---

2   This is wild rice, actually a species of aquatic grass, which grows in marshy waters and is gathered by Indigenous people every fall.

What follows is one of the few opportunities to see matters from a different perspective than the journals of the officers, to understand events that take place out of Archie McDonald's sight and knowledge. The following account is drawn from affidavits and courtroom testimony of the men involved. There is remarkable consistency in everyone's recollections, with some remembering more details than others.

Days earlier, there'd been rumours that McDonell and his officers planned to mount a cannon on a boat to prevent settlers deserting the colony by canoe or batteau. Certainly last June they had set a battery on the banks of the Assiniboine to prevent the passage of pemmican. The rumours are probably not true, and what makes the whole business entirely suspect is that the original source of the rumours is Duncan Cameron. Surely, if McDonell and company were planning such things, Cameron would be the last person to hear of it.

Cameron gave George Campbell, as his chief collaborator, two letters of instruction to be read to the men of the settlement. On Saturday, April 1, according to Angus McKay, he, Campbell and John Mathieson of Aultbreakachy met and hatched a plan to carry out Cameron's orders. The next day, after prayer services at Angus Gunn's house, they gathered as many men as they could on the road outside, where Mathieson read the two letters aloud:

My Lads,

I call upon Messrs. G. Campbell, Angus McKay and John Methune [sic] to know those that will be my friends and those that will be my foes. . . . Those who will not obey what they have to say in my name I shall no look longer on as my friends. But those who will obey I shall provide for them and protect them.

The rest of the letter is lost, but numerous men will later attest that Cameron ordered them to seize the colony artillery and bring it to Fort Gibraltar to prevent its use to block the settlers escaping to safety. "To prevent harm but not to make use of" is how Angus McKay will remember it, and to be returned undamaged to Mr. McDonell as soon as the threat was over.

Some will swear that they had grave misgivings about this, but none present alerted Archie McDonald or directly opposed the plan. They either intended to leave the settlement already or wanted to keep their options open.

Which brings the account back to Monday morning, when, according to Robert Sutherland, the people gather from house to house and arrive at the governor's compound. They linger for an hour or two as all make sure they have their month's food before putting the plan into action. John Bourke, the young storekeeper, later recounts,

> I thought the men collected in unusual numbers. . . . At about noon, I was looking out to call someone in when I noticed they had got the cannon on a sledge. I went out to stop them but was took hold of by settlers. I then tried to get into the house where Mr. Archibald McDonald was, but was prevented by people with clubs.

A servant named Kilbride is in the room where the weapons are stored. Campbell, Hugh Bannerman and John Cooper charge in and make for the cannon barrels, leaning on the wall. Kilbride tells them to get out.

"We've come for the field pieces," Campbell tells him.

"You can't have them!" retorts Kilbride, who lunges to intercept.

Campbell sweeps back his coat to reveal two small pistols. "Do not stir," he commands.

Archie McDonald is unaware of anything unusual until George Campbell, Angus McKay and Andrew McBeath burst in and hand him a letter signed by Duncan Cameron. Archie has only to read, "I have authorized the Settlers to take possession of your [cannons] to bring them over here . . ." before he is on his feet and heading for the door. "I was taken hold of by Campbell and party," he says, as were Dr. White and John Bourke.

"Make no resistance," Campbell tells him. "We're taking them so Captain McDonell can't use them to stop us leaving the country."

Archie blusters about consequences to no effect. Then, "A gun was fired [outside] by Robert Gunn."

Cameron and an armed party have been standing by at their fort. When Gunn fires the signal shot they advance to within about 200 metres of the Point Douglas compound and meet the men with the artillery. Their booty amounts to:

2 brass 3-pounders

2 brass swivels

4 iron swivels

1 howitzer

Three-pounders are cannons. Swivels are large and heavy but not quite cannons, designed to be mounted on a wall or a ship's gunwale. The howitzer is a short cannon meant for lobbing bombs over walls or obstacles.

This arsenal is lugged back to Fort Gibraltar, where handshakes, drams and hearty congratulations flow from Cameron and the Nor'Westers. Campbell, Angus McKay, Mathieson and their accomplices[3] take refuge in the fort. Their days as Selkirk colonists are over.

Meanwhile, Alex McLean has stormed into the governor's compound fuming and fulminating as only he can. He was waylaid coming down a trail past the Nor'Wester party. Cuthbert Grant had braced him, but the quick-tempered Scotsman yanked a pistol out of Grant's sash, whereupon the bounders pounced on him, one man choking him from behind until he was forced to yield. He was only released when the whole business was over.

---

3   In a deposition he will give the following February, John Murray will name a full twenty-four men involved in the cannon seizure: G. Campbell, Angus McKay, Neil McKinnon, John Cooper, Andrew McBeath, Angus McDonell, Alexander Murray, John Mathieson Jr., Angus Gunn, William Sutherland, Robert Sutherland, George Bannerman, Hugh Bannerman, Haman Sutherland, Robert Gunn, William Gunn, Angus Sutherland, Hector McLeod, Alexander Bannerman, Donald McKinnon, George Gunn, Allan Sutherland, John McPherson and Alexander Gunn, commonly called the Pedlar.

Archie concludes, "Mr. and Mrs. McLean passed the evening here and we were very much dejected."

Over the next couple of days matters remain unsettled. Parties of rebellious settlers move up and down the trail past Point Douglas, armed and belligerent. At one point "a strong guard of eight or ten men with screw bayonets" escorts "3 dog sleds and 2 Horse sleds passing up to the NW fort with Settlers' baggage." Mr. Bourke reports that he has learned the settlers "intend to plunder the store" for food and clothing before leaving. Archie sets a guard rota to keep watch around the clock. Of the ten men available for guard duty, Samuel Lamont and the cook are exempted as necessary for their own work, and two others are dispatched to Jack River to report the situation and bring help, so the guard consists of six men on 24-hour rotation.

On Wednesday, two days after the cannon seizure, Archie sets men to cutting musket loopholes in the governor's house walls, preparing to defend against armed attack.

He arrests Donald McKinnon, a servant who has deserted, for breach of contract. McKinnon is confined to the mess room. Around 8 p.m., "upwards of 70 men, all armed, surround our houses and disarm our sentries and demand . . . McKinnon." George Campbell and Cuthbert Grant lead the mob. Campbell and Grant rush in, waving pistols at Archie, Bourke and McLean, followed by their supporters, yelling and threatening. This is reminiscent of the effort to rescue John Spence last September, but this time, no one intervenes.

The mob takes McKinnon and withdraws, turning about at the riverbank to fire "a few volleys" into the air. Archie sends a party to bring in the McLeans from their farm for safety. They report that "not a [rebel] passes them without fixed bayonet."

FORT DAER ON THE PEMBINA.

One hundred kilometres to the south and oblivious to all of this, Miles McDonell prepares to return to The Forks. On April 4, he sets out, walking up the still-frozen Red River with his clerk James Warren and six men. They meet two colony men and hear a dramatic version of the cannon seizure, along with the alarming information that a party is on its way to make McDonell a prisoner. They proceed watchfully, and when an Indigenous man overtakes them going toward The Forks they "detain" him so he "might not acquaint [the Nor'Westers] with our approach." That night, they waylay two other suspicious characters and are "well pleased to see Mr. White and a man who were going to Ft. Daer with intelligence of what took place."

The group, now twelve plus their Indigenous detainee, set out at midnight. There is no hostile party, and they creep past Fort Gibraltar as dawn brightens. "We arrived at the house at sunrise and were joyfully welcomed," writes McDonell. "Found only 6 men here."

McDonell quickly organizes a defence. "I made Mr. McLean Captain over our people who formed into a company. Mr. McDonald Lieutenant, and Mr. Bourke Ensign."

Next day, April 8, seeing the Nor'Westers strutting about in armed groups, the loyal men "form a line on the bank of the river." The two groups frown darkly at each, but go no further. McDonell's descriptions sound alarmingly like last June: "Mr. Shaw passed with 13 men armed; Mr. Grant with a party of 6 men passed afterwards; Mr. Duncan Cameron at the head of 8 men arrives with muskets and bayonets fixed."

The humiliation of losing their cannons and then giving up McKinnon cannot go unanswered: "As Mr. Shaw [a Nor'Wester] was passing up in the evening about 6 o'clock, he was made prisoner" by the impetuous Alex McLean and friends. This sparks a melee with Shaw's companions, both sides scuffling and clubbing with pistols and muskets, kicking up so much snow that when hotheads finally try to shoot, they find their primers are soaked and the guns snap harmlessly. A good thing too, McDonell writes later, since any shooting might have been disastrous. As it was, "two muskets and a carbine were broken upon their heads and Mr. Warren was wounded with a bayonet" — serious enough.

Shaw is now McDonell's prisoner, a circumstance guaranteed to torque up the tension without discernible benefit. Next morning, an indignant letter arrives from Cameron, excoriating the colony men for waylaying Shaw and company "like a parcel of assassins when they were peaceably travelling in the road."

Shenanigans continue all week. Spies are seen lurking on the river-bank and McDonell suspects "traitors among our own people giving them information." Shots are heard in the night. At one point, they count thirty-four "rebels" passing, ostentatiously carrying muskets: "Our small garrison turned out under arms."

"We receive information that the blacksmith at the NW Fort is making iron balls for the artillery,"[4] writes McDonell. This is especially ominous.

Worries over loyalty and traitors among them leads McDonell to cross a line: "Proposed to the men to take an oath of allegiance and swear to defend the premises but they [refuse]." Offended, they also ignore an order not to go to bed until given their post assignments "in case of attack." Defiantly, they turn in. Furious "gentlemen" roust them out and organize them according to the defence plan. Even when all but their most loyal followers have deserted them, the leaders cannot bend. The consequences are predictable. Writes Archie: "I who is Officer of the Guard is in the Men's House with 16 of them, on whom I have no great dependence."

About the only bright spot comes when former Nor'Wester John Pritchard arrives, walking into Point Douglas one morning. Strongly supportive and wishing to join the colony, Pritchard quit the NWCo last year and went to Montreal, whence he struck out for Red River in October, walking all the way. Avoiding his former colleagues meant a route of an astounding 5,000 kilometres, but here he is. His commitment buoys everyone's spirits.

On Tuesday, the men who had refused an oath last Saturday are feeling contrite about it. They agree to sign a declaration of loyalty, which McDonell can send to Fort Gibraltar as proof of their determination to defend the settlement.

---

4   This claim will be substantiated later by any number of witnesses. Not only are they making ammunition for the cannon, but carriages to mount them. Cameron evidently sees no reason even to pretend to honour his promise not to use them against the colony.

CHAPTER 17

THINGS FALL APART

MAY 4 TO JUNE 10, 1815

O n May 4, Miles McDonell makes a sorrowful entry that indicates how far the damage has progressed. The momentum is fully with the "deserters." He begins with a long denunciation of Hector McDonald,[1] a piper who came over with the 1812 contingent and who now declares his intention of taking the Nor'Westers' offer. Good riddance, it seems, except that he has persuaded "our blind woman," a widow named Jennet McDonald, to go with him, with her two grown nieces. Apparently Hector told them that McDonell was going to order her off. He sends Archie McDonald to set her straight and even offer her "asylum for life," since she is blind. This seems an act of compassionate generosity and the widow declares that she would accept it, but her daughter has already removed all her worldly effects to the NWCo fort, and she cannot get them back. Now the poor woman will have to endure a trying journey of many weeks to an unknown future.

On May 8 Archie McDonald notes, "Samuel is working at the logs of the mill and 2 men are cutting out the foundation today." On May 13

---

1 This is probably Hector McEachern as no piper named McDonald is mentioned elsewhere.

he adds, "The frame of the mill is up." They expect it to be completed this year, possibly in time for harvest.

John Pritchard, who made that remarkable journey from Montreal, wants a woman. Shortly after arriving at The Forks, he goes up to Fort Gibraltar to reunite with his Indigenous wife, the mother of his son, whom he had left there last year. After two days, he returns, rejected. Miles reports him "quite unhappy."

Unhappy perhaps, but not inconsolable. A mere three weeks later he has set his eye on a woman, the widow of the late Hector McLean, "whom he had seen last evening and was much pleased with." She accepts his offer of marriage after a courtship lasting hours, and McDonell obligingly weds them. As an afterthought he mentions that Pritchard has "settled" on his bride £500, a small fortune, as well as an unspecified extra amount on her infant daughter. A party ensues and goes through the night, with much wine consumed. This leads to frayed nerves snapping.

Archie McDonald writes that a servant named Archie Curry disobeyed John Bourke with such insolence that Bourke felt himself "under the necessity of striking him." This brings in Curry's boss, Duncan McNaughton, the current sheriff among other things, who demands to know why Bourke "struck his man." By way of explanation, Bourke whacks McNaughton's nose "with a large stick." Others leap into the fray, and soon it's Irish against Scots. No word on which nation prevails.

A few days later, McDonell formalizes his defence into the Ossiniboia[2] Royal Militia, naming Alexander McLean, Archie McDonald and John Bourke its officers. Shortly after, Archie gets word that "ten Cree Indians have been brought down to attack the colony." This will become a stock tale of these years. Miles McDonell tells it best: after a couple of days enjoying the hospitality of Duncan Cameron and Fort Gibraltar, "one of the Crees came down [to Point Douglas] much against the will of the gentlemen of the NWCo. But he was so well pleased with the reception we gave him that he remained." The Nor'Westers, explains their guest,

---

2 Miles McDonell always spells Assiniboia with a leading O. I have generally modernized it except in official titles like this one.

had told him the colonists would surely kill him, but look how wrong they were. He comes from the Qu'Appelle district, and when the NWCo men invited him and his friends to The Forks, they promised him a horse, a gun, a big keg and a medal for coming here. Eventually "a young Cree" man arrives and drags their guest away, much against his will.

The Nor'Westers answer this affront by gathering a party of forty armed men and sallying from their fort behind the turncoat piper, Robert Gunn. The militia men rally and meet them on the field. It all ends in anticlimax, to the entertainment of Indigenous guests.

Two days later, three settlement horses are found dead, shot by arrows. This had happened once before, just after the Indigenous group arrived. McDonell doesn't buy it: "Indians are not apt to do such things." He blames employees of the NWCo trying to promote conflict.

Not about to give up, the Nor'Westers go directly to the settlers working their fields to report that the "Indians" are here and about to strike. The settlers stop working, walk up to Point Douglas and, seeing no sign of trouble, go back to work.

The First Nations visitors leave on good terms with the colony. Some are well known to John McKay, an HBC trader at Fort Qu'Appelle, but none were allowed to pay him a visit.

This tactic by Cameron — trying to enlist First Nations people in his opposition to the Red River Settlement — is repeated several times, but never takes hold. Europeans are too important to the Indigenous economy to risk war with the Hudson's Bay Company, and no one has yet tried to take their land; in this corner of the New World, that travesty is still generations away.

The next victory does go to the Nor'Westers, and carries a a slice of salacious gossip involving an appealing young woman named Bethsy McKay, sister of the HBC's John McKay (and the third separate Elizabeth McKay to be mentioned in these pages).

The year before, in the cold and snowy winter of 1813–14, John McKay was factor of the HBC post at Qu'Appelle. Less than a kilo-metre away was the fort of the NWCo. As was common in remote posts, the gentlemen of both companies entertained each other. In this case it was mostly at the HBC post, where everyone appreciated the comfortable house kept for McKay by Bethsy, his unmarried sister, who is herself no small part of the attraction. One of the regulars is the dashing 22-year-old prodigy Cuthbert Grant. Rumour had it that Bethsy's bonnet was set for Cuthbert.

These rumours are confirmed one year later when, in the middle of the night, she bolts for the opposition's fort, to her brother's surprise and dismay. He goes after her but is rebuffed.[3]

Tension continues to bubble and froth. The colony officers propose a ball "amongst themselves and all the women about the place." It is to be an exclusive affair with no pain-in-the-neck servants, thank you. Aggrieved, the men convince the musician not to play. Worse, "they gave very abusive language to Mr. White." White, the doctor, blames this on overfamiliarity between the men and certain officers, especially Bourke and Warren, "at which the latter gentlemen were much offended, so far so that they threatened to have satisfaction," writes Archie. "Under the present dilemma this can be taken no notice of."

Next day it is Christina McLean's turn. She turns the full force of her fury on McDonell and tells him "candidly," writes Archie, "that she will leave the country. And the cause of the expression was merely this: that the Capt. told her that he would be glad if she would make Mr. Pritchard a cup of tea." It would be nice to think it is the sexism that bothers her, but it is almost certainly the offence against her rank as a "lady."

The phony war of taunts and dangerous capers carries on over the end of May and into June. Miles orders swivel guns to be mounted in the second-storey windows of his quarters. Shots occasionally strike the compound buildings, but as harassment, not attack. The weather is June-perfect again, and the fields are doing well.

McDonell has a small HBC house across the Red River taken down, brought across and rebuilt below the compound to overlook the riverbank ravine and anyone hiding there.

A serious disagreement, never explained, between a North West clerk named Mr. Kennedy and Alex (The Raging Scot) McLean brings

---

3   Bethsy's romance with Grant is real and will produce a child, but in 1818 while he is far away in Montreal defending himself against a murder charge, she will leave him. What happens to her after that is unknown.

on the only serious violence of this period. One day McLean, alone in his field, finds himself surrounded by Kennedy and a posse of twelve mounted Nor'Westers. Obviously at their mercy, does he plead a truce? He does not. Archie McDonald records that his response is to launch himself at Kennedy and "give him a hearty drubbing" until Kennedy's friends reply in kind. And in spades. Says Archie, McLean is "much abused and disfigured."

"He is lucky to have got away with his life," adds Miles McDonell. McLean's persona seems always to hover between the outrageous and the absurd.

Next day, Miles reports that the "deserter" women tell those still loyal that as soon as they go away with the NWCo, the "Indians would take to themselves all the white women that remain." It does not seem to have much effect.

On June 5, eleven more men, "chiefly Irish," desert to the NWCo. The governor must be wondering by now if he will end up standing by himself, shaking his fist at Duncan Cameron. Not that he would shrink from that — he is nothing if not brave, this faithful soldier.

June 7 brings a sad climax of sorts. About 2 p.m., four batteaux filled with colonists put out from Fort Gibraltar and sail downriver past Point Douglas and the loyal remnants. This is the largest single exodus of settlers, well over half the colony. The loyalists gather on the bank to watch, armed but not menacing. Most of these people have known each other since their Kildonan days, and intimately for two of the most eventful and trying years of their lives. Miles just says, "The leading boat carried a flag. We counted 42 men besides the women [and children]."

Miles will make a list of those in the boats,[4] a total of 134 souls. Others have left in ones and twos, and a few more will desert after this.

It must be hell for McDonell, for McDonald, for Peter Fidler (now back from Brandon House), and the others to watch this flotilla, an embodiment of the failure of this brave dream, as the boats pull past the mouth of the Seine River to disappear around the northern bend.

---

4   See McDonell's list in the Appendix.

It is easy to imagine even today, standing on the shoreline lookout in Fort Douglas Park; the river has not changed much, nor has that bend.

There is little time to brood. Almost immediately a heavily armed troop of thirty-five to fifty horsemen, mainly Bois-Brûlés, rides out from Fort Gibraltar and north past Point Douglas, rounding up the McLeans' cattle as they go. Duncan McNaughton, colony constable, saddles up and follows, Alex McLean close behind.

The group, under the command of Miles McDonell's cousin/brother-in-law Alexander, halts and begins to set up camp at a place called Frog Plain, about five kilometres north of the Point Douglas compound, just beyond the northernmost settlement farms.[5] McNaughton and McLean demand the return of the cattle but are ignored. As they retreat back toward Point Douglas, McNaughton turns and fires his pistol toward the rustlers. This is no more than a gesture of frustration, but it is replied in kind. "Eight or ten muskets were immediately fired," according to a witness. Remarks Miles, "They owe their safety to the swiftness of their horses."

Later the colony cowherd goes down and finds that they have killed the lone bull and are "frying steaks of him for their suppers."

Cattle rustling is just an amusement for the Frog Plain campers.[6] Their immediate goal is to prevent McDonell from escaping down the river. Duncan Cameron is intent on arresting Miles and taking him to Montreal to answer for his seizure of the pemmican from the Souris River post a year ago. Cameron is at pains to tell every loyalist that the arrest of McDonell will bring safety and peace to the remaining colonists. Everyone knows by now that Duncan Cameron is a liar without boundaries, but what if he isn't lying this time? The loyalist men vacillate over whether preventing Miles's arrest is worth their lives.

The next few days are marked by alarms and fist shaking as Brûlés and Nor'Westers parade past on horseback, whooping and looking fierce in warpaint. The tension breaks for an hour or two when an

---

5   Roughly on the north edge of where Kildonan Park is today.

6   In a comparatively happy ending to this minor atrocity, the cattle are all found two days later, near the Point Douglas compound. Only the bull is missing.

NWCo express canoe carrying mail from Canada arrives, bringing handbills announcing a peace treaty signed last December between Britain and the U.S. The War of 1812 is over. Guns at both strongholds are fired to mark it. On the back of the copy he sends to McDonell, Cameron has written, "Peace all over the world except at R.R."

The guns are reloaded.

CHAPTER 18

SURRENDER

JUNE 10 TO 17, 1815

GOVERNOR'S COMPOUND, RED RIVER SETTLEMENT.

Saturday, June 10, 1815. After sunset, as evening mists form on the river, the guard is alerted to a party of men who have "entered the west ravine, giving the war-whoop." The ravine hides them from the governor's house, so Archie McDonald and Alex McLean venture out with a few men to its lip. Their challenge is met with another war-whoop. McLean, ever proactive, orders James Flynn to shoot. He will say later that he could tell the enemy was about to fire, and Miles will say later that this action was "imprudent," but whatever, it sets off a firefight. Shots are fired from both sides as the exposed men dive for cover.

The men at the house can't join the firing for fear of hitting McLean's party. McDonell orders Warren to go up to the garret and fire the swivel gun over McLean's head, into the trees the firing comes from. This soon drives the infiltrators off, without injury to either side. With adrenalin levels now at "flood," everyone stays up all night, waiting for more. Come Sunday morning, Dr. White ventures out but ducks back when a musket ball whizzes past. The same thing happens to John Bourke and a servant named James Flynn. Suddenly a general firing breaks out from the woods. The swivels upstairs fire back, but the enemy is invisible in the bushes.

Balls come flying through the doors and even the walls of the governor's house, to the great alarm of the inhabitants, who blindly return fire from every opening. Women and children take shelter behind fur bales.

Alexander Murray, a deserting colonist now in Fort Gibraltar, comes out to investigate. From his vantage point he can see the attackers. He later testifies that George Campbell[1] and Cuthbert Grant are among them.

Eventually, the besieging force withdraws. This time there are real casualties: Alex McLean and McDonell's clerk, James Warren. Peter Fidler reports,

> In loading one of the Wall Pieces, the Ball was not driven within 9 inches of the powder. Mr. McLean fired it and had his left hand very much shattered by the bursting of the gun. . . . Mr. Warren standing near had some part of the barrel penetrate a little behind and above his left ear. It made a hole in his skull of near 1¼ inch diameter. Part of his brain came out at the hole. Mr. White immediately attended both and rendered them every assistance in his power.

A musket ball tears through servant Duncan McDonell's arm. Down at the HBC house, erected to cover that very ravine, a complement of HBC employees does not fire a shot, "though their house was marked through with 10 or 12 balls." One of these balls wounds François Munjuinier[2] through the leg.

Warren seems near death and McLean's wound is grave; he will lose the use of his left arm and hand. Nonetheless, says McDonell, "Capt. McLean, while having his hand dressed, insisted on calling for his sword and pistols."

---

1   Campbell's disaffection for the settlement may be understandable, but what would move him to take part in attempted murder of the colonists? What would his sponsor, the earl, think?

2   No two spellings of this man's name noticeably resemble each other, much less match.

His pluck is equalled by his wife's. McDonell calls her a lady of great fortitude who stoically receives the news of her husband's wounds "with the most exemplary resignation."

Though he acknowledges that all the men performed "with spirit and firmness," McDonell learns that they are despondent "and think the cause desperate." Archie writes, "In consequence of the havoc, all our men are willing to surrender."

Rising to the crisis, McDonell calls them together and gives them the pep talk of his life. Their cause is just, he tells them, and far from hopeless. He reiterates a promise he made earlier: a pension to anyone who should be disabled defending the colony. It may also be at this time that he informs them of the approach of a large contingent of Hudson's Bay Company men — over a hundred in all — in a canoe brigade from Montreal, under the command of a senior clerk named Colin Robertson. If they arrive in time, the colony is saved. Whatever the deciding factor, McDonell's pitch lands. They unanimously agree to take up arms once more and "set cheerfully to put the house in a better state of defence."

Perhaps their former despondency was just a post-action adrenalin crash, because their reinvigoration is enthusiastic. They line the walls with fur packs and pemmican bags to absorb the bullets that penetrate. Miles goes to see Alex McLean and finds that Mrs. McLean's maid has fled to the Nor'Wester fort. "She left her mistress, who had brought her up from a child, to attend to her [Christina's] wounded husband alone, and her four young helpless children."[3]

In an unexplained turnabout as dramatic as their earlier re-dedication, McDonell learns that "the greater part of the men" are planning to decamp for Fort Gibraltar tonight. What happened to all that recent resolve? Frightening messages are coming from the NWCo fort that further attacks are planned for tomorrow using the stolen artillery, while all the Nor'Westers want is McDonell himself, they insist. Even as he tries

---

3 Mention of the children brings up a subject that has been conspicuous by its absence — what about the children? None of the journals ever mentions the youngsters, of whom there are at least twenty-two under the age of fourteen. This must all be terrifying for them, but if it is, no journalling man thinks it worth mentioning.

to regroup with the officers, three more "reliable" men disappear into the night. Drastic action is required.

McDonell decides he will slip away and hide himself for some days to make it appear he has escaped and so take the heat off the compound. "[I] named four Gentlemen to manage affairs in my absence and a little before day went off accompanied by Patt Corcoran."

This remarkably long day and night ends with the two men creeping out into the predawn light, bristling with pistols and blades, until they "reach a place of concealment and remain there all day [June 12]." Later he writes that they "heard horsemen hallooing and searching round us. They fired several shots. In the evening we shifted to another place."

For McDonell, it's a simple matter of remaining alive and undiscovered. For Archie McDonald and the officers back in the compound, it is more complicated. First of all, they have to pretend McDonell's gone, even though this means that some loyal settlers, especially those with wives and families, feel abandoned and exposed. Worse, Archie fears that some defectors may already know the truth. "Hyland and Underwood deserted last night," he writes, "and I believe that they knew the Captain's going away [was a ruse]."

Still, at moments like this, McDonell is little short of magnificent in his own way. Not only does he expose himself to extreme danger far from the aid of his people, he actually manages to keep up his journal, no small thing with the clumsy materials of the time. On the second day out he writes,

> Heard some of the half-breeds near us all day. One fellow came within 10 yards. My feelings are on the rack to be hiding myself like a felon, liable to be every moment discovered by the half-breeds. I ought to be there to assist in the defence.

He complains of heavy rain, and "the Miskettoes are intolerable."

Patt Corcoran goes back to the house for information. He returns with the news that the defenders are still resolute, but the strain is telling. All that day, horsemen from Fort Gibraltar had ridden up and down the settlement, vowing to massacre every individual who does not surrender, "which has a very bad effect upon our men."

The NWCo Brûlés address their HBC counterparts directly, telling them either to abandon the colony and the HBC or be considered enemies. This is not their fight. It works. Archie reports that overnight, "all the [HBC] Half Breeds left their stations and also 2 or 3 of the Irish lads."

June 14 is another day of hiding and dodging for McDonell and Corcoran. The Nor'Westers clearly suspect the trick. Notes sent from Archie McDonald and Dr. White say Cameron has arrested the few settlers still on their farms.

In the midst of all this drama, Archie's journal suddenly takes a most personal turn:

> Catherine [Kitty] Sutherland came up from the [Frog Plain] encampment with my little child. Cameron told her yesterday that she must go to Canada, so I have got John McIntyre to come to a final settlement and take her for himself.

Archie will present the couple with £16. That is more than half a skilled tradesman's annual salary, so not a pittance.

By now, Miles has now been gone two nights and two days. Archie takes stock of his forces, which he reckons at thirty-eight men still loyal and willing to fight.

That afternoon, still hounded ceaselessly, McDonell decides there is no point in trying to maintain the charade, so "at 3 PM we left our lurking places . . . reached our house and found our people in good spirits."

Not exactly.

Earlier that day, the Bois-Brûlés at Fort Gibraltar had accepted McDonell's disappearance as real and sent word that now he was gone, they were willing to talk peace. If the colony officers can reach a deal with the Brûlés, Cameron will be deprived of his soldiers. An emissary named Jack Ram duly arrives at about 3:00 p.m. Archie McDonald is momentarily elated but at that very moment, Miles McDonell appears too. The game is up. Ram leaves. Shortly, a letter arrives from the fort, demanding McDonell's surrender.

Miles is crestfallen. "I will give myself up," he offers, "if it will save the colony." Many think that is exactly what he should do. Archie concludes gloomily, "The state of affairs this evening is miserable." He doubts the men he was so sure of just this morning will now even defend the compound.

McDonell's desperate ruse has accomplished nothing, and now he has a difficult decision to make.

FROG PLAIN, NORTH OF THE RED RIVER SETTLEMENT.

The Bois-Brûlés' camp now has hostages — the people rounded up from their farms at the north end of the colony. These include several Sutherlands — Adam, George and Alex — as well as John Smith, his wife and six children, and a woman of twenty-eight named Catherine McPherson. Smith has a sad story. He is in his fifties, illiterate, and uncomfortable in English.[4] He is also quite content with his farm on the Red River and has no wish to leave, but he has his family to think about. He and the Sutherlands have suffered violent threats from George Campbell, Robert Gunn and William Bannerman. This and fear of being abandoned by his neighbours have almost persuaded him to go. Now they have all been dragged to the Frog Plain camp on the threat that "the Half Breeds would murder them all."

The Smith family is held in a tent and guarded by a man with a bayonet. The Nor'Wester Alex McDonell tells them they will be well rewarded if they go to Canada, but he will burn them out if they don't. Smith gamely replies that he would prefer to stay — the soil is better here and the land fit for cultivation without clearing.[5]

---

4   Testifying at a trial in Canada later, he will have a Gaelic interpreter.

5   In the end, despite eight days of detention and threats, the Smiths will stay. So will the Sutherlands, who are hoping their relatives will be among this year's arrivals from Scotland. The ultimate fate of Catherine McPherson is not recorded.

SURRENDER

GOVERNOR'S COMPOUND, RED RIVER SETTLEMENT.

Miles McDonell has a sudden surge of hope. The men are busy strengthening the defences when word comes that a canoe has arrived at Gibraltar with two senior NWCo partners, Simon Fraser[6] and Alexander McKenzie, namesake and nephew of the great explorer.[7] These two are heavyweights, and like John McDonald (Le Bras Croche) last year, they could impose peace.

Except the NWCo is no longer interested in peaceful coexistence. They see the Red River Settlement as a transparent tool of the enemy. McDonell's goose is cooked, though he does not immediately recognize it: "We expect a favourable change since these gentlemen have arrived." Brave and determined, Miles is also thick as a brick when it comes to fur-trade politics.

Dr. White and another officer go out to parley with Dugald and Duncan Cameron, but return late in the evening with no agreement.

White visits James Warren and is pessimistic about his chance of survival.

Archie McDonald has his own Great Adventure in the evening of this day, June 15. His son's adoptive parents, John McIntyre and Kitty Sutherland, are to be married tonight, and are expected at the compound. When Kitty doesn't show, he sends someone to fetch her. Then another is sent, and another, until finally he goes himself. It's about a kilometre to her house, and as he comes close he suddenly finds himself surrounded by armed men. The Bois-Brûlés at Frog Plain have secretly moved south to set up a cannon within range of Government House, hoping to take the defenders by surprise at dawn. They've detained Kitty, John and the others to keep them quiet. They tell Archie to go inside with them. Instead, McDonald draws sword

---

6   Yes, *that* Simon Fraser, the explorer for whom B.C.'s Simon Fraser University and Fraser River are named.

7   His uncle is the Alexander Mackenzie for whom the great river is named, and who, in 1793, reached the Pacific Ocean via the Bella Coola River in present-day British Columbia, becoming the first European — probably the first of any heritage — to cross the entire continent above Mexico, thirteen years before Lewis and Clark.

and pistol. The people in the house call to him to come in and save himself. Instead, plucky Archie lunges at one of his ambushers, gets past him and runs for his life. They start to chase but he's too fast. Archie writes later, "When they saw there was nothing they could do, they fired at me but fortunately I was able to make the House."

Their surprise blown, the Nor'Westers quickly load their cannon, but before they can fire, word comes of the senior Nor'Westers' arrival. They hold off until those gentlemen approve the attack.

The defenders stay up and alert all night, unaware of the cannon trained on their house. Only with dawn, as Peter Fidler describes, "we was surprised to see their great work [meaning earthwork], one 3-pounder and 2 swivels, and the Canadian flag hoisted on the Rampart."

As it happens, the partners have vetoed the cannon assault, but the besiegers are not finished yet. "A five gallon keg of rum was opened for any of our men to drink," writes Fidler. "What with fear and the love of rum, at 8 this morning, 13 of our men were at the battery."

Now the officers' nerve breaks. McDonell says that the gentlemen write him a letter urging that "I should surrender myself to the NWCo for the preservation of the Colony. Our men are again desponding to see themselves so few."

McDonell holds out. At 3 p.m. a letter from Cameron arrives demanding his surrender, which he "of course" rejects. Expecting an attack imminently, he takes stock of his forces and reckons them to be sixteen, including three HBC men. Later he revises this to twenty.

McDonell sends Dr. White and the HBC man, Sutherland, to Fort Gibraltar again to try to get guarantees that the colony will be spared if he surrenders. The emissaries come back with an offer to meet with Alexander McKenzie. Miles meets him, and returns to write, "I must surrender myself to obtain a peace and insure the preservation of the Colony for the summer."

Poor desperate man. He seems the worst choice Selkirk could have made to establish this settlement: aloof, authoritarian, rigid, too proud by half and a disastrous negotiator. Yet he is steadfast and courageous and unquestionably honourable and true by his own lights, something his chief antagonist, Duncan Cameron, can never claim. This is ignominious defeat and he knows it: "This day a twelvemonth, I was in the field with my people. Today I am going to surrender myself to the enemy." And he does.

The Nor'Westers make a show of keeping their end of the bargain, ordering the Brûlés' camps disbanded and communicating the terms of the surrender, specifically that the NWCo "pledge themselves that there shall be peace in the river towards the Colony and HBC for the summer, that they shall cause the half breeds to restore to us the horses they have taken" and more empty words, even as they continue to break a previous pledge by mounting the colony's cannons outside McDonell's place of confinement, to discourage rescue attempts.

Peter Fidler falls for it, writing, "We now consider the war at an end. . . . Peace seems now certain." For a man with over thirty years in this country, he is remarkably gullible.

CHAPTER 19

FIASCO ·

JUNE 17 TO JULY 20, 1815

RED RIVER SETTLEMENT.

O ver June 18 and 19, Archie and the other officers strive to get some sort of normalcy restored to the settlement and recover much of the looted and seized property. Just two days after McDonell's surrender, the colony officers are at Fort Gibraltar expecting to arrange these matters. Instead, as Archie McDonald records, "We were astonished to hear ourselves and the HBC warned to leave this River in the course of 5 days by the Half Breeds, supported by Cameron."

Archie's shock at this pronouncement is either disingenuous or remarkably obtuse. Their own leader had spent over a year claiming sole sovereignty and eviction rights over a company — and in the Bois-Brûlés, a people — who clearly had earned more right than he to be there. Did they really think McDonell's absurd eviction notices would not be met in kind? And the Nor'Westers, backed by their Brûlé work-force, are in a position to enforce the order as Miles and Archie could never hope to.

Archie goes on, "Captain McDonell was quite astonished on hearing it, but told us . . . to satisfy the Half Breeds if possible."

If there was any doubt that Miles McDonell has been living in a fantasy world, this must put it to rest.[1] *Now* he wants to "satisfy the Half Breeds"?

The officers worry that their few remaining loyal settlers are already asking for NWCo protection and that most of the servants, whose annual contracts expire at the end of June, will go over to the "enemy." That same evening, the impotent McDonell sends another letter from captivity imploring them to do what he has not: hold out.

On June 20, several different people write letters to Lord Selkirk. First, there is a letter signed by twenty-eight colonists and servants (among them Sam Lamont), imploring the distant earl to solve this impasse and restore the colony they describe as "a fertile soil, a wholesome climate, [with] Fish, Flesh, Salt, Sugar and Fruit and in truth all things necessary and conducive to our welfare." They leave to him the question of how they might yet create "an asylum where honest and industrious poor may establish their families in honourable independence."

Miles writes his own letter, explaining he had genuinely hoped an agreement had been reached to share resources and coexist but "the whole was overturned by the Agents at Fort William and no part of the conditions were afterwards fulfilled." He describes the campaign to convince the settlers that their lives were in peril from "the Indians" and that their only hope was to flee to the Canadas.

He reports the seizure of the cannon.

He chronicles the people's gradual desertion to the NWCo, complaining that they kept "all the farming utensils, clothing and every other article furnished them by us," and sold them to the Nor'Westers.[2]

---

1   McDonell's name, as Miles Macdonell, is now memorialized on a splendid Winnipeg high school with an illustrious history. Is his inappropriate and incompetent leadership truly something to enshrine?

2   This is true; a number of men will later swear to it. Alexander Murray will say that settlers sold axes, hoes, spades, camp kettles, trading guns and horses to the NWCo. An axe fetched two shillings, a gun three pounds. Alex Bannerman says he sold a copper pan, a shovel, an iron chain, a frying pan and an axe, all from colony stores, for which he received twenty-eight shillings sixpence. On the other hand, most of these people will have property stranded at York Factory which they will never recover.

He takes care to give credit where it's due, praising White, Archie, Bourke and Warren for their readiness on all occasions. His only strong reservation concerns James White's character. While "in the line of his profession he is skillful and attentive . . . he is unfortunately addicted to liquor. I could not therefore have him at any time in command of the settlement."

Although he gave himself up to save the colony, he fears it won't work until force is employed against the Nor'Westers, "but that force must be disciplined troops, not servants or settlers." A hard lesson has finally been learned.

Next day, the Brûlés make starkly clear that McDonell is right. They have bought Cameron's story that Selkirk plans to destroy them as a people and then enslave them. They are prepared to murder and pillage to make sure his drastic scheme comes to nothing. After an early morning meeting with no Nor'Westers present, Archie McDonald reports that the Brûlés refuse to return anything they took from the colony or its people, and indeed if everyone doesn't clear out post haste, the war will resume.

As the officers are digesting this final blow, McDonell's last instruction is delivered from the fort. He appoints Archie, White and Fidler as a leadership troika, with Fidler's duty the colony and people, Archie's the care of the stores, and White's the health of all.

With this, it is over. They can only watch as their governor is ignominiously bundled into a canoe and paddled away. "Captain McDonell embarked with Flynn, his servant," writes Archie. "In the other [canoe] was Duncan Cameron."

There is no mention of a salute or any collective farewell.

Adieu, Mr. McDonell. We shall not see you again.[3]

Still, there is one untarnished piece of good news for this wretched day. Archie records, "I have this evening joined John McIntyre and Kitty

---

3 He will be back for a few months in 1817, but his central role in the Red River Settlement is effectively over. His grief is not. On June 30, 1815, still travelling east, he writes, "read of the death of my eldest son, Alexander, Lieutenant in the 104th Regiment. He was drowned at Quebec 15th September last."

Sutherland together before witnesses." At last! Theirs is a wedding story to enthrall the grandchildren. They are now and forever young Ranald's parents, strong compensation for Kitty's tragic loss, with no taint of the cuckold for Mr. McIntyre.

Such celebrations as can be mustered are abruptly curtailed by an alarm at 2 a.m. A sentinel sees suspicious activity in the willows near the river. Minutes later a fusillade of bullets hits the houses. The men jump to arms and take cover, but "returned not a single shot," says McDonald. Restraint is the better part of valour. After twenty-five minutes the assault ends.

Next morning, the bleary-eyed defenders are wrestling to get boats in the water when a group of riders passes them, bound for the settlers' farms. Soon, Archie reports, "they set fire to all the Houses in the settlement below Mr. McLean's. [Later] they called at McLean's and warned him and Mrs. McLean that if they did not leave [immediately] that they would do the same [to theirs]."

The next day, never giving up hope, Archie hears that "two or three of the [Saulteaux] Indian Chiefs and their tribes will be up to take up our cause."

Sure enough, both threat and promise materialize. The Bois-Brûlés set fire to the now-abandoned McLean house. Within an hour, says McDonald, "it was all in ashes and just then Peguis and Arrow-leg with 35 of their young men passed by the ruins of all the houses that have been burnt. Our flag was raised and the two chiefs led to the Mess Room with their young men."

There, the settlers deliver a very long and florid speech declaring their friendship for the Saulteaux people and their gratitude for friendship in return.

Peguis responds in kind and says

> that he would not allow us to leave the river and that him and
> his men would do all they could to get peace made with the
> half breeds. Accordingly, himself and Arrow-leg and 15 of their
> most eminent men went up to the NW Fort.

They are back in an hour with some hope for further talks tomorrow. "We got the whole of them to tent about us for the night and the two Chiefs slept in the main house." This prevents any repetition of the night attacks, says Archie.

Peter Fidler says that Peguis also makes a special visit to the McLeans, where he congratulates Christina for remaining loyal: "My sister I am glad to find you have sense. You did right not to listen to the people of the [NWCo]. I know them well. They have a sugared mouth and a deceitful tongue. As they have got your friends out of this river, they will drop them like stones as they go along."

Next day, June 25, after meeting with Brûlé and NWCo leaders, the Saulteaux report no success. Every trace of the colony is to be obliterated, but Cuthbert Grant consents that the HBC trader McLeod can stay and take care of the crops from one of the colony houses. According to Fidler, Peguis advises that the remaining colonists retreat to Jack River until they get strong enough to come back. "From this," he writes, "we conclude that we cannot depend much upon him or his Tribe in keeping us in by force."

This is a disappointment, but the Saulteaux are acting in the same spirit that makes them so welcoming to the colonists — peaceful coexistence. For several generations, Peguis's people have been infiltrating lands bordering other First Nations. They flourish by showing themselves to be good neighbours, not by starting wars.

Is there any hope? What about that brigade of HBC canoes that is supposed to be on its way? Some want to hang on, somehow, anyhow, to see if it will magically appear. The leadership (especially Dr. White, according to Alex and Christina McLean) do not believe in the brigade. They believe in survival.

At last, on June 27, they accept the inevitable and board their batteaux. Archie McDonald does not underplay the drama, writing, "Our departure from the Settlement is certainly the most deplorable event that ever happened to British subjects . . . driven from a Country whose fertile soil, wholesome climate, natural productions and beautiful scenery promised ages of happiness. . . . The inhuman and cruel conduct of the NWCo can scarcely find parallel in the darkest page of history . . ." and so on, in the same vein, from a young man who clearly has not actually studied history. He reports that the Bois-Brûlé horsemen rode down to watch balefully as they pushed off, but that the Saulteaux joined the settlers in their boats to ensure they would not be attacked on their way down the river.

McDonald also records the roll of those who "have this day been removed against their will":

1. Mr. McLean	6 persons
2. Mr. Pritchard	3 persons
3. Donald Livingstone	3 persons
4. John McVicar	3 persons
5. Pat McNulty	4 persons
6. Mrs. Stewart	4 persons
7. Alex Sutherland	2 persons
8. George Sutherland	2 persons
9. John Bruce	1 person
10. Duncan McNaughton	1 person
11. Alex McLean	4 persons
12. Martin Jordan	2 persons
13. Angus McDonell and family, described as, "a Canadian forced out and burned out before his face, merely for adhering to the colony."	

This is a partial list and does not include others whose names have been gathered from other lists and references by historians.[4]

The sad flotilla rows on through the night and arrives at Netley Creek next morning. There they are met by Peguis's village and fed,

---

4   Lucille H. Campey, *The Silver Chief* (Toronto: Dundurn Press, 2003). Written on the spot, this list can be presumed accurate, but it does not include the other officers or twenty-one servants or John Smith and family, John McVicar and family, a few more Sutherlands, etc. There are about sixty people in total who appear on various lists collated by Campey, but are absent from the list of deserters. A few people show up on no lists; for example, John McIntyre and Kitty Sutherland and Catherine McPherson.

welcomed and assured of protection. Speeches are exchanged, friendship pledged.

Peter Fidler records Peguis saying in the course of a long and heartfelt address,

> Look at these presents! I wish the Little Englishman (D. Cameron) could see it. When did he or his people ever show such charity? What do they ever bring to our lands but that liquid fire with which they deprive us of our senses in order the better to cheat us of the produce of our winter's toil.

After having shaken hands with every individual[5] he proceeded, "Take courage, my children, gather strength, and return as soon as possible."

Duncan Cameron and twenty-five men paddle by, heading for Fort Gibraltar, returning from escorting Miles McDonell beyond reach of help.

Back at the settlement, the sun rises on chaos. Every building remaining is put to the torch, even the one promised to the HBC trader, John McLeod, who works desperately to get company and colony stores out of the burning house, but most of it goes up in flames. Brûlé horsemen, egged on by Nor'Westers, ride up and down the settlement, trampling crops and burning anything still standing. John Murray, a witness, will later testify,

> [I] was in a little boat with George Campbell's wife on the opposite side of the river. I saw the fire and came over. There was a Mill half-finished by Samuel Lamont burned with the rest.

---

5   Peguis is still remembered and revered in Manitoba. That my great-great-grandfather actually shook hands with Chief Peguis I find quite moving. Alas, his grandson (my grandfather) would return in the 1880s to be part of the process of dispossession.

NETLEY CREEK, NEAR THE ENTRANCE TO LAKE WINNIPEG.

At Netley Creek, the refugees are menaced by a Brûlé patrol from The Forks and ordered to leave immediately or suffer annihilation. Despite contrary winds, they load up and cast off.

The trip down Lake Winnipeg (i.e. north) is a carbon copy of every other — a gruelling, tedious endurance test by headwinds, downpours and swampings, with the added irritant of resentful and insolent servants to salt the wounds. Morale is as low as it can get. Young Warren, still clinging to life, is nursed all the way and is able to walk a bit in the encampments, but he is "very low" and eating little.

They reach Playgreen Lake, a few hours' paddle from Jack River, on July 10. Here they erect a camp and consider their future. The hired men, especially the Irish, have lost all fear and respect for poor Archie McDonald, which drives him mad. On July 12 he punches a labourer named O'Rourke "in the teeth."

On July 20, James Warren dies.

Rock bottom.

PART III

COLIN ROBERTSON

(Library and Archives Canada, MIKAN no. 2939060)

CHAPTER 20

"A WELLINGTON IN WORDS"

JULY 14 TO AUGUST 4, 1815

ON THE WINNIPEG RIVER, APPROACHING LAKE WINNIPEG.

Any casual student of storytelling knows that you cannot have a
string of bad news episodes like the one we have just been through,
with their calamity, pathos and hopelessness, without balancing with
servings of encouragement, resurrection and renaissance. But where, in
this morass of incompetence, colony collapse, and self-serving venality
are we to find it?

If he did not exist, our next protagonist might need to be invented.
Not to oversell this approaching hero, but this story might not have
been written without him. After the ignominious retreat to Jack River,
an observer could be forgiven for wanting out, wishing that somebody
would just put this bloodied and ill-advised experiment out of its
misery. Surrendering to a sociopath? Fleeing in terror and humiliation? Losing everything that your sweat, blood and perseverance have
achieved? Punching your subordinates in the teeth?

Then in marches this Beowulf, this Ivanhoe, this latter-day Radisson,
a dreamer and a romantic but also a man of action, a schemer and a
manipulator whose skill even Duncan Cameron will acknowledge with
the sneering epithet, "a Wellington in Words."

Suddenly there is hope, again.

Colin Robertson, thirty-two, is a senior clerk of the Hudson's Bay Company, leading a new initiative to extend the HBC's posts to "the Athabasca," the country along and around Great Slave Lake and the valley of the Mackenzie River. Now, in July 1815, he is on the Winnipeg River, approaching Lake Winnipeg, a few days ahead of the canoe brigade he himself has raised in Montreal, 140 French-Canadian traders and canoemen recruited to take on the North West Company in territory it has worked until now unopposed, near the northeast slopes of the Rockies. It is a bold, expensive and risky adventure, but he is in a uniquely good position to do this; he worked for the NWCo for six years and knows both their methods and their people well.

Robertson[1] was born in Scotland to a family and class situation much like that of the millwright Sam Lamont. Where Lamont's father was a miller, Robertson's was an artisan weaver, from the time before the big textile mills began crushing their livelihood. Robertson's father put young Colin into apprenticeship to carry on the family trade but he ran away to sea, crossing to New York and thence to Montreal, where he signed on with the NWCo. A go-getter with influential patrons, he did well there and in the process crossed that invisible barrier into "gentleman" status. Like many ambitious men, he does not suffer fools and seems to find them everywhere he goes. This has consequences — remember John McDonald (Le Bras Croche) and his fondness for settling differences with duels? One of them was with Colin Robertson. Both obviously survived, but this may have precipitated the latter's departure from the NWCo, to the regret, we're told, of many colleagues.

Six years later he is leading a high-profile and aggressive challenge to his old firm on behalf of their most hated rivals. During the past year in Montreal he heard much about the Red River experiment from his old colleague, John Pritchard (of the long, long walk), and the picture he painted set fire to Robertson's hyperactive imagination. A letter from Robertson to the Earl of Selkirk is endearing for its enthusiasm ("The prosperity of the Red River Colony is a subject which has much

---

1   Biographical information on Robertson is taken mainly from his entry, written by George Woodcock, in the online *Dictionary of Canadian Biography*: biographi.ca /en/bio/robertson_colin_7E.html.

occupied my thoughts") and for its flood of unsolicited and probably unappreciated advice.

It is not his brilliance that singles Robertson out in this cast of characters, though he is certainly intelligent. It is rather his presence of mind. He is always right here, right now, or even a few steps ahead. In his transition from base to gentle status, he has fully adopted middle-class manners, prejudices and self-entitlement. He is no democrat, but he wears authority with a certain sardonic ease. Unlike McDonell, who bristles at any hint of "presumption," Robertson always has his eye on the goal and plans every move to take him there. His utter self-confidence can be off-putting to colleagues — he seems never to have been well liked by equals and superiors — but he is focussed and effective, making him a popular leader, something Selkirk's experiment sorely requires. And when it comes to dealing with the North West Company, he knows whereof he speaks.[2]

As he enters Lake Winnipeg, days ahead of the main body of his brigade, he takes a couple of days for a side trip to see the wilderness miracle on the Red River for himself. He has heard from passing canoes of the arrest of Miles McDonell and the rout of the settlement. If he had been just a little earlier, he might have made the difference, and it distresses him. On July 14, he enters the river and makes the acquaintance of Peguis and his people. Peguis immediately expresses his disgust for the Nor'Westers and his anxiety to see the settlement re-established. Pressing on, Robertson comes to Frog Plain, "where a number of Mâtives[3] and Freemen were encamped. I went on shore and walked up to the Fort, over the ruins of houses that had been burnt by the white savages."

He knows some of these men and they talk freely to him. They tell him "frankly" that they were paid by the Nor'Westers to drive away the colonists. He listens to them cordially, hiding the anger he feels.

---

2   Finally, he is also the best writer in the bunch, making his journals a pleasure to read and to quote.

3   This is presumably one of the many early variants of "Métis," and would come from Robertson's NWCo experience.

Later he is visited from Gibraltar by Seraphin Lamar, an old colleague. Knowing Lamar's weakness for rum, he "does not fail to administer a good dose of Jamaica," fishing for information. What he gets does not satisfy him.

After Lamar, he turns to his current colleague, McLeod of the HBC, who tells him the recent story from the losers' perspective. Robertson is appalled that the officers surrendered McDonell. It was the colony that was the target, not the governor, and "no good ever resulted from giving up the Leader to the Enemy," he declares.

Almost as astonishing is that McDonell had built no fort, no defensive wall — "Is this possible after three years in Red River?" A few days of effective defence would have been enough, he's sure, because Cameron's Bois-Brûlé "warriors" are actually traders and would have had to leave for their winter posts. "This any man with experience of the North West Company ought to have known." Of course, in that group of Selkirk appointees, there was no such man, until John Pritchard arrived, too late.

In just one afternoon and evening, Robertson gathers all he needs to convince himself who is at fault and what should have been. Heading back down the Red the next morning, at its mouth he encounters a stiff headwind and must stay the night with Peguis and his people. He settles down to his favourite pastime: writing.

He confesses that he thought there was a good deal of exaggeration in Pritchard's glowing account of this place, but "now that I have seen it, it is the finest country I ever beheld." Both riverbanks are clothed with mature trees and ideal for a colony with land beyond the banks "already cleared."

> The woods deepen as you approach the Lake but at points the plains run to the river. Some of these Points are extremely beautiful. . . . A stranger arriving at [one of them] will be apt to look round for a stately mansion to correspond with the scenery.

Most astonishing to him is the land's richness, "the amazing returns which this soil gives to the slightest tillage." He declares one field of "early Wheat" superior to any he's seen in England.

In the morning he strikes north again, to find the camp of the loyal remnants.

WINIPIC SETTLEMENT, ON THE SHORE OF PLAYGREEN LAKE.

Archie McDonald's journal is full of tales of open hostility from the servants. Nonetheless, he soldiers on until, on the day of James Warren's funeral, a man named Decoigne arrives with news of Robertson's imminent arrival. The colonists have been waiting for this and are relieved that he has not been waylaid by the NWCo. They begin to talk of using his brigade, 140 men, to attack "the enemy at Red River."

Before anything like that can happen, they'll have to solve their internal problems. The politics are as volatile as ever, and at their centre is Alex McLean. As people gather for Warren's funeral, McLean loudly tells Decoigne that Dr. White was the cause of their defeat, from his "cowardly conduct" and stubborn denial that Robertson could arrive in time to save them. White defends himself and matters heat up until everyone "disapproved of Mr. McLean's conduct," especially when Christina joined in to support him.

When Colin Robertson finally does arrive, also well ahead of the main body of his brigade, he is immediately disappointed by the camp's slovenly appearance, just a few crude huts with "not even a shed to cover the property brought from Red River, which is in very bad order." This is the misery and despondent apathy of abject defeat, but he makes no allowance for that. The moment the settlers see Robertson they swarm him, urging him to take them back to Red River. They don't trust Mr. McDonald or Dr. White, but they want to go back.

These people have just fled threats, violence and the torching of their homes, yet their only thought is of returning? Remarkable. It can only mean that the prospect of what awaits them back in Scotland is even worse. It touches Robertson deeply, but he tells them that his obligations in England require him to return there on the August ship. He suggests that Mr. Sutherland of the HBC would make a good interim leader, but they know Sutherland and don't trust him either — he agreed to the surrender of McDonell and the abandonment of Red River. Still, Robertson repeats his regrets.

Now his own colleagues put the pressure on. Thomas Thomas and others join the chorus — "They press me so hard," writes Robertson, "that I think I will be obliged to comply." For another day or two these talks go on with various solutions being discussed, none of which include McDonald or White, whom Robertson ignores completely. Archie is offended; he and White are, after all, still officially in charge. When they finally confront Robertson, "he all at once told us that he intended to send every one of the Settlers back. . . . A long plan had been laid down by him and the gentlemen of the HBC without even consulting Fidler, White or myself." To put their noses further out of joint, Robertson makes clear what he thinks of allowing the NWCo to take McDonell. Archie grumbles that it's easy to criticize, but if any of "them" had been in McDonell's place, "they would probably not have managed affairs as well as he did."

Robertson takes no notice, just carries on as though only he is making decisions. He meets with the settlers, who confirm they want no part of McDonald and company. "They want a Gentleman of experience. At all events something must be done to prevent the Colonists going home or the Colony is ruined."

He laments the excessive politics within the group and on this he and Archie McDonald are of a mind. For Archie it is the McLeans. They long ago took it upon themselves to be his judge and jury, and "they assume this dignity in an increased degree since the arrival of Mr. Robertson."

The mutual glowering is interrupted by the appearance of the long-awaited brigade itself, to Robertson's great relief.[4] He now reconsiders

---

4   They had all but run out of provisions weeks ago, and were followed through the worst of their hunger by Nor'Westers in canoes full of food and drink, waving at them and inviting the Canadians to come join them and feast to their hearts' content. Everyone held out and finally Pritchard met them with emergency supplies, not a moment too soon.

---

his own future — he knows that the man leading the canoes, Mr. Clarke, can take the brigade from here.

Still being ignored, Archie festers. He pronounces himself well aware that "McLean" (no more Mr.) has taken upon himself to "censure the [officers] in the name of all the Settlers and Servants of Red River." He and James White huddle and mutter as they watch their authority vanish.

Still, Robertson vacillates, conscious that Selkirk appointed these officers, so their removal is not really in his power. Thomas Thomas has no such qualms. As governor of the HBC he tells McDonald that, given the objection "by the <u>entire Settlers and Servants</u> towards us, that he, Mr. Thomas, should conduct the affairs of the Colony until ship time." Archie's fired.

That does it — Colin Robertson is taking the people back.

Was there ever any doubt? It appears inevitable, but it represents a huge sacrifice for Robertson and his career to forgo both his business in England and his expedition to Athabasca. This seems an almost sacred commitment he is making for the sake of Lord Selkirk and these humble settlers. It is not clear what is at the bottom of this life-changing decision — could it possibly be idealism?

He asks for eleven HBC Bois-Brûlés as well as "an Interpreter and two officers" to help him in "disuniting the deluded young [Bois-Brûlé] men from the Canadian Traders." The officers will be Pierre St. Germaine and Pierre Pambrun of the HBC, and the interpreter's name is Nolin.

Preparations are interrupted by a moment of low comedy that might have been tragedy. On August 2 McDonald reports that John Bourke and the Norwegian Ener Holte (or Holt) were relaxing in a tent when a pistol Holte was examining suddenly went off. According to Archie,

> The ball went through Holte's palm and pipe and lodged in Mr. Bourke's left chest a little above the Hernum and is still under the middle of the Cloircle. . . . The wounds are dressed and I hope the Gentlemen will soon get better.

The injured Hernum and Cloircle[5] will prevent Bourke from leaving with the rest, but he'll be fine. As for the hapless Holte, it is not his last adventure with touchy triggers.

Archie McDonald will not go back to Red River, either. Instead he will depart for York Fort and return to Britain to write an account of his adventures on the Red.[6]

James White, who will return to the colony later in August with the recovered Bourke, immediately sits down to write his wife a letter to be taken back by McDonald and published in newspapers as "From a Gentleman of Red River." In it, he extols the virtues of that Garden of Eden while demonizing the Bois-Brûlés and the NWCo. He describes the desertion by most of the settlers and the eviction of the remainder on threat of death. He praises the Saulteaux for their protection.

In another letter, to a man named Brinkman, he writes more candidly: "Respecting the servants, it will be necessary to observe that almost the whole of them bore a great personal hatred toward Captain McDonell. . . . I was at times much afraid they themselves would carry him off to the NW Fort." He puts this down to McDonell's closeness to the McLeans, especially Christina, who he says is "too fond of listening to and carrying stories. . . . She had somehow or other insinuated herself in an astonishing degree into the Captain's favour."

"In short," he concludes, "if she had been my wife, I certainly should have been jealous."

---

5   Sternum and clavicle, perhaps?

6   *Narrative Respecting the Destruction of the Earl of Selkirk's Settlement upon Red River, in the Year 1815* — London, 1816. Although this is the last we will see of Archibald McDonald, it is not the end of his North American adventures. He will return to Canada in 1816 and Red River in 1818 and later join the Hudson's Bay Co. for a fairly distinguished career. (Jean Murray Cole, the *Dictionary of Canadian Biography*: biographi.ca/en/bio/mcdonald_archibald_8E.html)

CHAPTER 21

RESURRECTION

AUGUST 5 TO 25, 1815

WINIPIC SETTLEMENT, ON PLAYGREEN LAKE.

C olin Robertson assembles all the settlers and servants of the Red
River Settlement and announces that he will be returning to The
Forks three days from now, and invites all "who are inclined" to join
him. He makes it an absolute condition that no one, neither colonist
nor servant, may visit Fort Gibraltar. "To this, they all agreed."

Robertson records the names of the members of his re-establishment
expedition:

> Mr. and Mrs. McLean and four children; Mr. and Mrs. Pritchard
> and one child. The following families remain here until the Fall:
> Widow Stuart and six children; Widow McLean; Mrs. Jordan
> and Miss Kennedy. The Servants that go with me are A. McLean,
> Duncan McNaughton, Samuel Lamont, Michael Kilbride, Pat
> Clabby, Pat Corrigan [probably Corcoran], Jonathon Fowler;
> Norwegians Neils Muller, Petr Dhal and Peter Isaacson; and
> twelve [unnamed] Canadians; officers Messrs. St. Germain,
> Pambrun and Holt, with two Indian interpreters. With
> this corps I take my departure tomorrow, in the hopes of re-
> establishing the Colony at Red River.

He does not mention the cattle, sheep and pigs that will also crowd the boats. Pat McNaulty and John McVicar are also returning with their families. The total is forty-five or fifty people, but on departure day, he makes it three boats and thirty-five men, women and children.

Two days later, he writes, "My boat is full of guides that pretend [to know] the way, but they have passed Pigeon River three times — and now one of the men positively affirms that we are encamped within a few miles of it." He takes it all with good humour.

It is a typical open-boat Lake Winnipeg journey, which is to say, capricious. On August 12 a gale blows up during the night, tearing tent pegs out of the sandy ground and scattering tents and clothing along the beach and into the water. The men dash to retrieve them, but in the lightning-lashed darkness, it quickly becomes a Keystone Kops free-for-all. This too appeals to Robertson's distinctly sardonic sense of humour. "I could not but smile at the ludicrous sight — a dozen men running about in their shirts. . . . While every flash showed a hat or blanket rolling down the beach, the sudden darkness had us running afoul of each other in pursuit."

Pinned down for two days by this wind, Robertson turns to his journal. He observes, perceptively, that McDonell had discriminated against "the families of this country," meaning those men with Indigenous wives. McDonell considered them second-class persons in the colony, "when for the security of the Settlement they ought to have been the first."[1] He thinks the perceived opposition to the settlement by the HBC was really just the bad temper of William Auld, who, he says, was not loved by his officers. If McDonell had just exploited this by courting those officers, he might have "drawn fifty families to Red River his first year, which would have formed a complete barrier against the intrigues of the NWCo." Further, "these families, from their experience in the country, would have been of essential service to the Emigrants on their arrival." Instead, McDonell wrote letters home complaining about the "foibles, failings and manner of living" of the HBC men. These letters were opened at York and read by those men, creating more enemies.

---

1   Robertson himself will marry a Métis woman, and suffer the same discrimination.

Therein lies the difference between McDonell and Robertson — the former trapped inside his prejudices and personal dignity, and the latter constantly looking outward and ahead toward the goal and all means of achieving it.

He hears of McDonell's breakdown at York last September and attacks him on this as well: "This mad scene . . . is the most shameful business I ever heard of and I certainly would not have given it credit, had not Governor Thomas been an eye-witness to the whole affair."

It is August 19 when Robertson finally reaches Frog Plain, where he runs into more Bois-Brûlé men he knows. From the moment of arrival, it is politics first: "Old Deschamps looked very much embarrassed . . . I told them to come up to Mr. McLeod's house,[2] that I had good news to communicate." They do, arriving about ten minutes after him. He engages them, but his real agenda is for them to witness the arrival of the returnees. "My five Canadians with my canoe came up while I was talking to these gentry, and some of the Freemen recognized cousins among them." He distributes rum and tobacco to keep them interested until the first boat of settlers arrives. "They appeared rather astonished when I informed them it was Mr. McLean come to pass the winter with me. One Mâtive observed, 'I hope you will forget what passed?'"

> "Forget that," says I with a forced smile, "Capt. McDonell behaved like a fool! Do you think I'm going to do the same?"
>
> The boat by this time had arrived at the beach. I turned to the Freemen and Mâtives and observed, "A long mis amies, donne Mme McLean a feu de joie au arrivant." [*sic*]
>
> They fired off their pieces. Indians joined them and in every countenance joy and pleasure seemed to be delineated. Are these the men that drove away the colonists last spring? Yes! But they are Frenchmen, and transport a Frenchman to any climate you choose, he is still a volatile Frenchman.

---

2 The HBC trader whom the Bois-Brûlés permitted to stay at Red River.

Later he entertains Seraphin Lamar again, and rum makes the Nor'Wester sentimental. "He went to ask forgiveness of Mrs. McLean and was so overcome at the sight of this lady that tears trickled from his eyes."

Two days later, Robertson selects a spot on Point Douglas to build the fort that McDonell should have constructed, a strategic spot on a curve that commands the river approaches from upstream and down.

Speaking to several freemen and Brûlés, he forms a picture of what went on last spring, of Duncan Cameron's campaign to convince the Brûlés that McDonell's intent was to "reduce them to a state of slavery." Upon firing them up Cameron then equipped them to fight back.

He learns of the arrival last June of Alexander McKenzie, NWCo partner. His unnamed source tells him that McKenzie thought Cameron was being too open about the NWCo's involvement and urged him to make it look more like the Brûlés were acting on their own, specifically by giving them their own room in the fort, "and by that shallow piece of deception deceive the public."

He sends out woodcutters to bring back the pickets for the new fort's palisade.

For three days he has shown the resident Brûlés, men he hopes to win over to his side, the velvet glove. Now it's time to flex the fist inside it, to show them that though he wants to be friends, he will not be disrespected. An instance of "insolence to one of my officers," common enough under the last regime, presents the opportunity. He "checks" the miscreant, leaving us to imagine the details, and to his great satisfaction receives an apology. In return, "I engaged him to hunt for the Fort Daer establishment during the winter. He is an excellent hunter."

He presses his campaign to separate the Brûlés from Cameron, asking if risking death or maiming was really worth the reward that Cameron had promised. They give him the story of McDonell's plan to enslave them. When he scoffs at that, they come back with, "What vexed us most was that when we brought meat to the Governor's house, no one would ask us in to take a glass of rum or even warm ourselves." And there it is — in this rough country, universal courtesy is the ultimate "refinement." You ignore it at your peril.

"And then there was the business of the buffalo," adds Deschamps. "He told us they were his and we must not run them."

"What if I told you that it was your 'friends' the Nor'Westers, who told him to forbid the running of the buffalo?" asks Robertson. At their evident skepticism, he has an idea. "Will you come here tomorrow and go into Mr. Pambrun's tent — you will hear Seraphin himself confess it."

"If that be the case," replies Deschamps, "I'll join the English."

They leave, promising to call tomorrow at 4 p.m. Now he invites Seraphin over tomorrow for "a glass of grog," knowing the old sot will be unable to resist. He cackles to his journal, "I expect much good to come from the line I intend to draw between the NWCo and the Mâtives." If he didn't need his hands for writing, he would be rubbing them with glee.

Seraphin duly shows up and Robertson offers him a chair close to his tent, inside which is Deschamps, close enough to listen.

> I then joined Seraphin and after a little general conversation and paying him a few compliments . . . I asked him how he managed to prevail on the Capt. to issue the Proclamation that gave so much umbrage to the Half breeds regarding the running of the Buffalo. Oh! M. Robertson! That was un grand coup Politique. It was Dugal Cameron that managed that business. I translated the Proclamation into French and read it to the Freemen. But it was sly Dugal that was the cause of it.

Dugal Cameron, of course, was the one who told McDonell that the hunters were driving the herds away from the Nor'Westers' southern posts and induced Miles to forbid the practice in Assiniboia. In Robertson's words, "This was one of the most impolitic acts of Capt. McDonell's administration . . . Dugal Cameron's sole purpose was to stir up the Mâtives, and he only wanted an Edict of this kind to accomplish it."

Though Robertson clearly relishes this sort of intrigue, he seems constantly to be fighting down his urge to rage at the Brûlés for their gullibility and willing complicity. Yet he also genuinely likes and above all *needs* these people. Subterfuge is his only hope: "The authors of all the calamities that have happened are the NWCo. I must endeavour, however painful to my feelings, to make use of such stratagems to separate the Mâtives from that association. If that were accomplished, the Settlement is safe."

CHAPTER 22

DÉJÀ VU

AUGUST 26 TO OCTOBER 11, 1815

YORK FACTORY HBC FORT, ON HUDSON BAY.

On August 26 of 1815, that most-anticipated event of the York Factory year heaves into sight on the eastern horizon: two ships from Britain, the *Prince of Wales* and the *Hadlow*.

It is a replay of 1813 as it should have been. The ships carry settlers, about eighty-four of them, and they have arrived alive and healthy, every man, woman and child of them, exactly where they are expected. Boats and men wait at York to take them up the rivers and lakes at the earliest practical moment.

Aboard the *Hadlow*, spirits are high. A combination of frequent cleaning and airing of quarters and various engaging activities have kept the passengers' health and morale strong, and now they believe they are one giant step closer to reuniting with friends and family whom they have not seen for over two years.

The young man responsible for the settlers (their Archie McDonald, as it were) is a fellow of similar background and education to Archie, but older, with a profoundly different personality. He is sympathetic where Archie is judgmental. He is conciliatory where Archie is confrontational. He is comfortable with himself and quietly humble where Archie is insecure and defensive. Lord Selkirk suggests he would make an excellent sheriff of Assiniboia. Experience tells us to take Selkirk's assessments with a grain of salt, but in this case he may be right.

Alas — his name is Alexander Macdonell. Of all the clans and all the first names in Scotland, why must he share both with one of the Selkirk Settlers' most dire enemies, Alexander McDonell, the North West partner? Madness. There is a slight distinction — he styles his name Macdonell, in contrast to Miles and his cousin Alexander, who both use the spelling McDonell.[1]

These folks have been at sea since mid-June and have no idea what has transpired over the past year. *Hadlow* drops anchor some distance from the fort and, writes Macdonell in his journal,

> A number of people came on board from the Factory, who informed us the Colony of Red River was destroyed and all the relations of the passengers were gone to Montreal. A great confusion now ensued and not one of the Settlers intended for Red River would land, but should return by the Ship to Scotland and at that moment, there was no use to expostulate with them on the subject.

Alex Macdonell and Captain Davidson go ashore, where they confer at length with Governor Thomas. They request disembarking boats for the passengers.

Next day the boats get to the *Hadlow* ahead of Alex, but the people will not budge until he returns. When he does, he tells them the story, he says, "putting the best possible gloss upon it," and they agree to go ashore, where they are given tents and fresh provisions after being "regaled with a glass of rum."

What story does he tell them? What possible gloss could make it convincing? Probably he holds out the possibility that their friends and relations will return when they hear that the settlement has been re-established. To go back to Scotland after all this effort and time, being

---

1 My grandfather was a Livingstone, never to be confused with those déclassé Livingstons. Spelling counts.

further behind than when they left — it's just too awful. And as with all landlubbers, the comforting feel of something under their feet that does not pitch and roll is a strong inducement by itself.

So here they are, taking the next great leap of faith. As for Macdonell, he could not be more pleased with the situation, and himself. He savours every element of this adventure. Next morning he reports that he has slept "in the tent along with the Settlers, covered for the first time in a Buffalo Robe."

The weather is miserable, with sleet and snow or heavy rain delaying departure. The settlers poke about the sheds of York where, to their horror, they discover baggage bundles with the names of their relatives on them. Worse, the baggage is in disarray and stored carelessly, in wet conditions. They immediately take their outrage to the highest level: Robert Semple, newly appointed czar of the Hudson's Bay territories.

Czar is not a great exaggeration. Robert Semple has been appointed "Governor in Chief of all the Territories of the HBC with paramount authority over all Governors of particular Districts."

This includes the Red River Settlement, and marks a most significant change in the status of the colony. No longer can they claim to be a separate entity from the HBC, which nobody believed anyway; now the two are publicly under the same management. Assiniboia and the settlement are now a "district" of the Northern Department.

Robert Semple is thirty-eight years old as he steps ashore at York Factory. Born in Boston, Massachusetts, during the American Revolution, he was raised in England, grew up to be a merchant (of what is not specified) and travelled widely, including Africa and South America. He wrote books about his travels and somewhere he met the Earl of Selkirk, who thought he would make a ripping governor, despite Semple's never having been in the Northwest, met an Indigenous plains-dweller, traded furs or even sat in a canoe in his whole life. Selkirk offered him £1,500[2]

---

2   This is fifty years' salary for a skilled tradesman, seventy-five for a common labourer. For all the social levelling reforms of the last two centuries, the folks at the top have managed to dodge this one.

a year to come and play viceroy. His journals have not survived, a pity because his books reveal a skilled writer who can paint a vivid picture. All we have in his voice are some reports and letters written in an affected style. His flawless spelling, grammar and punctuation bespeak an expensive education. His excessively Latinate vocabulary bespeaks high self-regard. Confronted by wrathful Highlanders, Semple reacts sympathetically, immediately penning a letter to Colin Robertson:

> Sir — Considerable discontent and suspicion having been excited among the Colonists recently arrived by the sight of property belonging to their friends still lying in the stores here.

He urges Robertson to act as soon as possible to correct this and "remove unfortunate impressions of an intent to deceive." He signs the letter and reads it to the settlers, apparently to their approval. Then he adds a postscript below his signature, which he presumably does not read to his audience:

> The above was written to gratify the Colonists who hesitated about departing until it was read to them. — R.S.

So much for not intending to deceive. But the migrants are nobody's fools. Where the 1813 group reluctantly accepted assurances and took only the lightest of baggage with them, this crowd will fill every available cubic centimetre with their belongings, despite the discomfort and extra portaging weight this will create.

They have another letter they need to write, this one for Archie McDonald, who is about to board ship to return to England. They ask him to report favourably on their relatives, and "use all means possible to return them to Red River." Many sign it, with names now familiar: Sutherland, Bannerman, McKay, Mathieson and so on.

This is probably part of the promise Alex Macdonell held out to get the people to come ashore. From the evidence, none of the 1815 deserters will return.

The first group of settlers sets off on September 6. Around forty men, women and children squeeze onto two boats stuffed with their baggage and food for the journey.[3] Peter Fidler assures them that provisions for forty days will be more than enough to see them to Red River. A second set of boats will bring the rest of the people in a few days.

Alex's journal says they depart in a "fine breeze," but soon discover that their boats are leaky. They camp early to repair them. Next day the current is too great for sail or oar, and they must get out and pull ("track").

On putting ashore September 8 in heavy rain they discover that Fidler forgot to load the molasses. Their rations will have less sweetness and fewer calories.

Presently the rain abates. They put in early at Hill River to take advantage of sunshine to dry soggy cargo and further repair their leaky batteaux. Alex remarks on the abundance of berries of all sorts, "also an ermine."

Each day, Alex records the number of carrying places they traverse, often three. He finishes most days' entries with a remark about the people's well-being, something Archie McDonald never did.

YORK FORT.

Governor Semple is getting up to speed, issuing orders and reading reports. He is also writing letters to go back with the ships. He has much to say to the earl about his early impressions, beginning with a severe critique of Miles McDonell:

> Capt. McDonell was careless and profuse in great matters whilst on little points he frequently displayed a niggardly parsimony. . . . At length even his own men and Colonists lost all confidence in him.

Semple has heard, and evidently believes, "that he was under the influence, whether honourable or not, of a married woman, Mrs. McLean. . . .

---

3   Still better than the fifty-seven in two boats forced on last year's settlers.

Her opinion was constantly taken or given in presence of men such as Mr. Thomas Thomas, to his great surprise and disgust."

Semple says that, from what he heard in London, he expected to find Captain McDonell a worthy leader surrounded and brought down by envious scoundrels, "but I do not hesitate to say that I was completely mistaken." Semple is still listening to and believing second-hand accounts.[4] There is much to condemn in Miles McDonell, but he deserves a good deal more consideration than this.

He reads the letters that went back and forth between McDonell and Cameron and disapproves, declaring it sounds like "the war of a low-bred woman or of a NW Clerk, but not of a man, a Soldier and a Chief." And to think McDonell surrendered to these contempt-ible men. "And who was to succeed him — Mr. White? I am afraid his unfitness for command is even greater than Mr. McDonell's. . . . Mr. White has proved himself a slave to liquor."

He apologizes for his very unfavourable picture of "two men whom I have never seen, to whom I wish every happiness," and blames "the weight of circumstances and the desire of laying before you the Truth." Even, it seems, if the Truth is pure hearsay.

In another document he makes clear his own contempt for and even greater ignorance of the Bois-Brûlés, people whom he has never in his life encountered:

> I need not point out . . . the blind malice of our adver-saries who have not hesitated to put arms into the hands of Canadian Half breeds and thus to disclose to that lawless race the dangerous secret of their own strength.

All this before he even leaves the mouldering confines of York Factory.

"For this reason," he concludes, "I consider the Establishment of a white population in the [HBC] Territories as absolutely necessary to future security."

---

4   When, for instance, could Thomas Thomas, that conniving tattletale, have ever heard Miles and Christina discussing anything?

Another newcomer of note is John Rogers. Rogers is that wonderful nineteenth-century character, the Remittance Man, or so it appears. He is in his twenties and has education and optimism to burn, but probably he also has an older brother who is heir to the family title, sweatshop, coal mine or slave plantation, so young John is out to find adventure in the expanding Empire, travelling on an allowance ("remittance") from his family. Such men will become (in)famous in the annals of western settlement. Selkirk recommends him highly but makes it clear that Rogers is not an employee. He is free to go wherever he wants whenever he wants.

Rogers is an enthusiast. From the moment he disembarks the *Hadlow*, he is writing back to Selkirk with useful information about the successful voyage and tips on keeping passengers healthy and happy. If only he had stopped there — but he is brimming with ideas for the colony and the whole continent, all without going beyond, as he himself puts it, "a hundred paces from [York] Factory."

Nevertheless, Rogers is a likeable and willing sort of fellow, up to a point, and will try his best to be useful to the colony. He departs York at the head of two more boats of settlers a few days after Alex Macdonell's group.

Semple himself finally gets away on September 24, but not before throwing a wrench into Alex's plans.

BELOW KNEE LAKE, EN ROUTE TO JACK RIVER.

On September 26, twenty days out of York Factory, Alex's boats are caught up by a "Flying Canoe," paddled by an HBC clerk named Sinclair who has travelled in eight days what has taken the settlers twenty.

"Mr. Semple is heavily loaded and requires one of your boats, that he may travel faster," Sinclair tells Alex. This is an absurd imposition, but Alex feels he can't refuse the governor so all the settlers, their baggage and food supplies are hauled out onto the rocks and the boat turned back downstream to meet Semple. "My anxiety for proceeding is very great," Alex writes, "but I cannot help myself until I can get a boat."

With his one remaining boat, he shuttles people and baggage to the next suitable camping spot and there they stay, fishing by day ("a great rarity for the people") and waiting for Semple to bring their boat back. On the 28th, John Rogers shows up with his two boats. "They breakfasted with us and afterwards they proceeded on through Knee Lake, leaving us."

Next day the beautiful weather seems to taunt him, "this being the fourth day I have been detained." He is feeling quite desperate to get going when finally, at 4 p.m., two boats show up with room in them for the stranded settlers. They pile into the batteaux and, despite the late hour, they shove off, "all well and happy to be under way." The delay has reduced their food to nothing but barley malt, without even molasses, "for which the hands and settlers were displeased . . . Pitched our tents very late in the evening. All well."

They are, Macdonell says, "68 people together in three boats." They struggle on without complaint through a squall that takes off their mast and rain that forces them to land and cover the cargo. They start early and camp late, "children noisy and fatigued."

There are moments of levity. On October 5, as they are hauling their loads across a Duck Lake portage,

> John McDonald, a Saddler from Inverness, got hold of a cask of rum containing the allowance of one of the men and sat himself down in a Bush to regale himself of its contents; when the cask was a-missing, a general Search Warrant was granted and both robber and property were found. He embraced the cask affectionately, swigging its contents as fast as he could, convinced they should <u>never</u> see each other again.

The men throw him into a boat and haul him off. Later:

> William McKay's wife from Caithness, Barbara Sutherland, 35, was delivered of a son, a <u>fine Boy</u>. I thought it advisable to leave one of the boats behind for two days as the woman could not properly be removed.

He notes that the boy is to be named "Selkirk," and that the parson's wife was midwife.

On Wednesday, October 11, they reach Jack River, where Alex meets "Doctor White, and also Mr. Pambrun, who brought us some potatoes and fish."

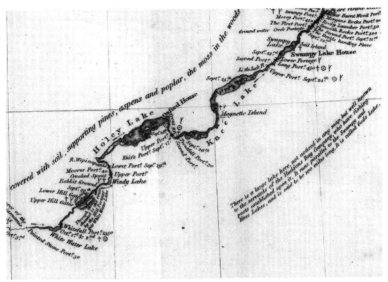

Map 8. Portion of the 1819 HBC York Factory to Lake Winnipeg map showing the landmarks of Macdonell's trip. Baby Selkirk was born at Painted Stone Portage, bottom left. (Wikimedia Commons)

Next day the trailing boats catch up and all together set off for Winipic Settlement, the former refuge on Playgreen Lake, where they lay up for a couple more days to let all the boats and people sail together for Red River. Rogers and Pambrun are going ahead by fast canoe, so Alex gives them a letter for Robertson. And it's a very good thing he does.

CHAPTER 23

"WHEN WE GET WITH WOLVES, WE MUST HOWL"

AUGUST 31 TO NOVEMBER 6, 1815

FORT DOUGLAS, RED RIVER SETTLEMENT.

Robertson has no idea the new settlers are coming. As the newcomers were packing their batteaux at York Factory back in early September, Robertson was telling his journal that Archie McDonald had told him to expect fifty or sixty new families, but he has dismissed this idea, sure that Selkirk would hold back emigration "until the country has assumed a more tranquil appearance." He is betting on having only the people already here to feed and shelter through the winter, and has dispatched John Pritchard to Pembina to begin laying away buffalo meat. This tactic also allows him to hire some Brûlé hunters to bind them closer to the colony.

On August 31, he dispatches Pierre St. Germaine in an express canoe for York, "with dispatches for England." St. Germaine is to bring back news of how many will be coming up to join them from this year's ships.

On September 4, some Bois-Brûlés drop by to report the arrival of Cuthbert Grant at The Forks, and complain that Grant was cool to them when they called in. Robertson suspects this is "for allowing us to return to the Colony." He judges this a good time to break the news to them that in Fort William, when he passed through in July, the NWCo was putting the blame for the whole business in June squarely on the Brûlés, saying they "could not prevent the Halfbreeds from taking up arms against the Colony."

"Oh! What liars!" responds Deschamps, "for M. Cameron sent three or four messages last winter, for me to drive away any of the Colonists that came to my Lodge." Later, when Deschamps had arrived at Fort Gibraltar in the spring, Cameron invited him to join "a number of mâtives and Freemen parading under arms," which he did for fear of being called a coward otherwise. Cameron gave him powder and ball in exchange for his service.[1]

Robertson contracts with Deschamps and his sons to hunt for the colony, but cautions them not to tell Cameron, in case he decides to withhold their share of the reward expected any day from the NWCo at Fort William for their assistance in destroying the settlement. This is not the generous consideration on his part that it sounds; in fact Robertson expects the NWCo to renege on their reward and wants the Deschamps to feel the burn — "the greater a man's expectations, the greater his disappointment will be when not realized."

He ends the day's journal entry with a coda: "When we get with wolves, we must howl," including the quotation marks. This is the first appearance of the maxim that has become Robertson's guiding principle. It is a simple and powerful image, and in stark contrast to Miles McDonell's insistence that propriety and rank are sufficient to settle all disputes. Another example of the crucial difference Robertson's experience makes.

John McLeod of the HBC, during his tenure over the colony lands since the expulsion, had begun building a house of forty feet by twenty by sixteen high (about 12x6x5 metres), but Robertson leaves that to the storage of crops and shelter for the returnees. He moves into a crude "hut à la campagne" and gets on with the work.

Sam Lamont now makes one of his rare appearances. On September 7, Robertson writes,

---

1   For more detail on Cameron's method, see Joseph Boudre's deposition in Note on Sources.

> Sent two men to saw boards and two to square Logs — I have
> only one good Axeman among the Colonial servants and that
> is Samuel Lamont. I am sorry to employ him at this rough
> work as he is a very superior and well behaved man. He came
> out here as a Millwright — however in the present situation
> of affairs, we cannot pay that attention which deservingment
> often demands.

It's not exactly a knighthood and "deservingment" is not exactly
a word, but it stands in solid repudiation of Lord Selkirk's dismissive
"looks a dull fellow" in his memo.

By September 9, Robertson and the Bois-Brûlé Deschamps are talking
again. Deschamps tells him that he has spoken to Cuthbert Grant and
told him "that Cameron had thrown the blame of the whole business of last spring on the mâtives. Grant's reply was that he would not
believe Cameron guilty of such a thing."

Can Grant have been callow enough not to realize that this is exactly
what Cameron would do? Or is he just lying to further the Nor'Wester
cause? The latter is the only reasonable, if disappointing, conclusion.

Cuthbert Grant will presently emerge as the founding leader of the
increasingly self-aware Métis Nation. He embraces his Brûlé identity
with pride, vigour and a good deal of grace. At this stage, however, he
is a Nor'Wester first, and Bois-Brûlé a distant second.

Next day, September 10, Robertson records,

> Messrs. [Duncan]Cameron and A. McDonell are returning to
> the River with a strong Brigade. . . . Ordered a number of
> portholes to be cut out in the big house and cleared away the
> brush wood to a considerable distance round the buildings.

Again, the man of decisive action. There has not yet been time to
build a palisade around the new government compound, which he has
dubbed Fort Douglas. Nonetheless, he fortifies what he has. He also

puts even more men to bringing in the grain, "as I am afraid of it taking fire after the arrival of Messrs. Cameron and McDonell."

Three days later, the Nor'Westers arrive with pomp and panoply, Cameron and Alex McDonell mounted and in their "full regimentals." A saluting volley is fired from Fort Gibraltar. An hour later their freight canoes, flags flying, sail grandly past Fort Douglas.

Cameron immediately begins this year's campaign, riding out down the plains "in full uniform with a band of Halfbreeds, Freemen and servants of the NWCo, not less than sixty or seventy." It has the effect he intends — intimidation among Robertson's men. "It is astonishing," remarks Robertson, who resolves to knock Cameron down a peg or two "to remove the dread my men have of him."

Out riding a few days later, Robertson runs into Alexander McDonell, the NWCo trader. They exchange some hot words over last spring but, says Robertson, "parted tolerable good friends considering the subject of our conversation," adding, "When we get among wolves, we must howl." A few days later he is disconcerted when a young HBC clerk rides into the settlement to report that he has been accosted by an NWCo party led by McDonell riding west to Qu'Appelle House. They tried to take one of the clerk's horses and "only desisted when he threatened to shoot." The disturbing element for Robertson is that the Deschamps men were there and took part in the aggression. This contradicts their profuse declarations of friendship. It seems Robertson is not the only one acting strategically.

The next few weeks pass as the building continues and the harvest proceeds. Reports of meat-gathering at Pembina fill Robertson with confidence that there will be winter provision for "any number of people that may come out."

On October 13, a spectacular event breaks the routine — Peguis brings his whole band up to Fort Douglas for a celebration of friendship. A line of 150 canoes appears around the bend north of Point Douglas, led by chiefs and hunters who fire a volley in salute as they approach. The prepared colonists let fly a series of welcoming blasts from their cannon. Behind the men come canoes carrying the women and children. Both parties raise all the flags they have. Robertson writes, "It had a wild but grand appearance, their Bodies painted in various

Colours, their heads decorated — some with branches and others with feathers. Every time we fired the cannon, the woods re-echoed with their wild whoop of joy."

The canoes carrying the women and children sail on to a designated spot where they land and begin raising their lodges. The men land in front of the fort, Peguis in the lead, welcomed by a volley from the colonists. They are led to the main house, where the hall is "rather small but they seated themselves in tolerable good order." Robertson lights a calumet (medicine pipe), puffs it into life and passes it to Peguis, who smokes and passes it to "the next in respectability," and so on round the whole band. "During this ceremony, not a word or even whisper was heard," writes Robertson. Then come the speeches, again begun by the host.

"One of the greatest pleasures in this World is to see those we love and esteem, in particular those who have showed us kindness in adversity . . ." and so on for twenty minutes or so. Robertson's regard and flattery are aimed at discrediting the scoundrels in the other fort as much as to gratify his Saulteaux Anishinaabe friends: "You have bound the English in a tie that can never be dissolved" is balanced with "There is a trader in [our midst] . . . who talks like a warrior . . . but who is only fit to be laughed at" and "[Who] places before you a keg of rum and a little tobacco — How many of your relations have been killed by this Enemy? And how many have starved to death in search of the industrious beaver? . . . They have bequeathed you misery!"

The degree of Hudson's Bay Company hypocrisy in these self-righteous denunciations does not seem to raise a blush from our Colin. He claims the HBC had originally come for beaver, yes, but "the principal object was to enlighten you and teach you religion, not to make you dependent on but [rather] independent of, white men; to show you that real riches were only to be found in the soil, by cultivating it, and placing you in Villages surrounded by your families," but "[the NWCo] forgot their duty to you and their [king] — every good motive was swallowed up in the riches they were amassing." (This man is apparently shameless.) "Every step toward civilization is like a dagger to their hearts." By now he is drinking his own snake oil envisioning a glorious future, "not far distant when I will behold you placed on the banks of some beautiful river surrounded by family and Friends, your little stores filled with provisions to fill the wants of a dreary winter. — Look at the Beaver! The foresight of that industrious animal ought to teach you an example worthy of imitation." He goes on about the heart of a man being where we should judge him, not by the muskrats he traps.

Then, again without a blush, he offers them rum and tobacco and a little ammunition, a little cloth, and blankets for the children.

Peguis pledges his undying friendship — "I am always the same! I never change!" — and duly slags Duncan Cameron — "He is unworthy of our notice. May the stings of a bad conscience punish him for his falsehoods!"

He agrees with Robertson's opinion about "that fiery water. . . . We love it, we are slaves to it! . . . Your council and good advice will in time break the chains that bind us to [it]."

He grieves the departure of Miles McDonell — "I loved the Captain." But "I was loathe to spill the blood of white men. . . . Now I am happy, very happy that you are here again."

Peguis, says Robertson, speaks "in simple language, but the sentiments are full of goodness . . . and he concludes with a smile truly sublime."

If Peguis has fully understood Robertson's nonsense about "civilizing" his people into farming, he just lets it roll by. There is no evidence that either man is anything but genuine in their mutual respect. The celebrations go on for days, Robertson freely distributing the corrupting spirits he so denounces.

The day after these speeches, he gets news of an attack by the Nor'Westers on the HBC post at Qu'Appelle. Unlike Miles McDonell, Robertson is as much an HBC man as he is a Selkirk man, and he immediately calls a "Council of War" with his principal farmer Alex McLean, his young officer John Bourke and Mr. Stett, an HBC trader. If the NWCo is allowed to get away with this unanswered, he will lose face in front of his new Brûlé converts. The gentlemen are unanimous in urging a strike on Gibraltar, the sooner the better, but "nothing can be done tonight — the Indians are intoxicated."

Next day, October 15, Robertson's hand is forced:

> This morning, when I was sitting at breakfast planning how
> I should take over Fort Gibraltar, my servant informed me
> that Messrs. McLean and Bourke were bringing Cameron and
> Seraphin prisoners to the Fort.

McLean and Bourke drag their captive into Robertson's room. Apparently, they have first administered a horsewhipping — or perhaps that happens later, it is not clear. (No one mentions it at this point, but a horsewhip will be hung on the wall to commemorate this moment of sweet revenge.) At any rate, Cameron is appropriately cowed when they bring him in front of Robertson, asking, "What do you intend to do with me?"

"In the first place," answers Robertson, extemporizing, "you must deliver up all the arms you hold that belong to the colony." After a time Cameron agrees, and Robertson, as captain of the "Royal Ossiniboia Militia," orders Alex McLean to take twelve men and "take possession of Fort Gibraltar and hold it until further orders." McLean obeys and "this he accomplished in a masterly manner," records Robertson.

Peguis gets wind that big doings are afoot and unhesitatingly puts action behind his talk, leading a fully armed band of warriors to Robertson's side. But Robertson has done all he wants at this stage, unwilling to start a full-out war with the North West Company until he has spoken to his superiors at York Fort. He decides to let Cameron go tomorrow, "as I haven't the means to send him off to York [as a prisoner]." But he does intend to milk this a bit, writing, "I shall lower his consequence a little, for the safety of the Colony." He ostentatiously sends Cameron back to Gibraltar for the night, to be held under guard.

Next morning he makes another show by sending a boat for Cameron, Seraphin Lamar and a Nor'Wester called Hess, along with the stolen cannons and muskets, to bring them down the Red River to his buildings. "Having called in a number of colonists and Indians to witness," he passes judgment on the prisoners, telling them that he will magnanimously grant them their liberty "under the following mild conditions." The first is that Cameron send off an express communication to Qu'Appelle to end the harassment of the HBC post by the men of the NWCo. The second is that they pledge not to "attempt to seduce, either directly or indirectly," any of his colonists.

"These points being agreed," he writes, "I took Cameron back to his post." He leaves him with more threats of consequences should Cameron break his word.

The transfer of Fort Gibraltar is no sooner complete than Robertson gets another shock — the return of St. Germaine from Jack River informing him of "the arrival of eighty Colonists and Robert Semple, Esquire, Governor in Chief of the Hudson's Bay Company's Territories with a controlling power over the Colony." He is astonished that there is no letter or instruction from Semple himself. "Do they mean to take us by surprise with such a number of families?" he writes. "Gov. Semple ought to have sent a boat ahead. . . . This is really sad blundering."

This is a remarkably frank criticism of a superior to commit to paper in his work journal. It is indicative of Robertson's intolerance for bad management.

He sends more hunters south to gather provisions, with orders for Pritchard to begin repairing Fort Daer and the Pembina houses.

Robertson is aware (he does not say how) that Lord Selkirk is in or on his way to Montreal, intending to travel by inland route to Red River next spring.[2] Robertson decides that he must get the news of the resurgent aggression of the NWCo to the earl and engages Jean-Baptiste Lagimonière to carry it on foot. He includes the news of his capture of Fort Gibraltar and says that Cameron has "given the Indians a mild reprimand for the readiness with which they took up arms to assist us. Peguis told me to take care with Cameron, that he is a bad man." He implores Selkirk to bring an armed force with him.

The McLeans, Alex and Christina, leap on the opportunity to send their own letters to the earl. Christina has not forgiven the officers, and she wants his lordship to know it.

---

2   Lord Selkirk is finally making good on his promise to visit Red River in person, sailing with his wife to Montreal. Lady Selkirk anticipates a long sojourn in Montreal, so has brought along her grand piano and her harp.

C. McLean to the Earl of Selkirk [marked by Selkirk, "received, March 1816"]:

My Lord — I am happy to have it in my power to write your Lordship from Red River Settlement. Indeed it is more than I expected to do in June last, but I must take the liberty of telling you, Lord Selkirk, that he [meaning Selkirk] has himself greatly to blame for everything that happened, for he should have sent more respectable people than the idle Doctor and the Cowherd from Glengarry[3] to be Captain McDonell's Council.

They thought they would do a great deal when they made Captain McDonell give himself up . . . though they had plenty of men that were both able and willing to defend the place till Mr. Robertson would come. But they would not allow [it], indeed they were very anxious to make their escape and did not seem to think very much of what was lost by it.

Fragment of Christina McLean's letter to Selkirk. (Library and Archives Canada, Selkirk Papers, p. 20258)

---

3   This obviously refers to Archie McDonald, but he was actually from Glencoe.

So we would all [have] gone home if providence had not sent Mr. Robertson in our way. . . . But for my part I'm all too fond of revenge to think of ever leaving the Country without having some satisfaction of those rascals that was the cause of my Suffering so much.

She goes on to say that she'll hang on despite having no manservant or maid, but if "the Captain" is not back by next year, "we will all go home for him."

Her husband, Alex, is more concerned with practical matters, asking that "4 men Servants and one maid Servant be engaged for my service . . . as I am unable to work with my hands." Also, "a Still and Cauldron for distilling whisky and other necessaries for forwarding that work."

He asks that Selkirk grant him an Appointment of Respectability. "Indeed I make so bold as to say if more confidence was placed in me from the beginning I would be of material service, pardon my boldness." He finishes with an Alex McLean flourish:

I remain, My Lord,
Your Lordship's
Most faithful and obedient Humble Servant.
A.M. McLean, Captain
Osniboyan Royal Militia

With these missives added to the others, Lagimonière takes off on October 17 on a hike that will go down in history. Avoiding Nor'Wester lookouts by travelling south of Lake Superior, then up to York in Upper Canada and on to Montreal, he will walk 2,900 kilometres and deliver the letters into Lord Selkirk's hands on March 10, 1816, in time for Selkirk to raise a small private army before heading west. Mission accomplished, Jean-Baptiste will come back home. His return trip will be more difficult.[4]

---

4   More details are available from Lynne·Champagne: biographi.ca/en/bio /lagimoniere_jean_baptiste_8E.html.

Rumour has it he is paid £50 for the trip and his family is taken into Fort Douglas for the duration. Colin Robertson records neither of these facts but they seem the least he could do.

A week later another canoe arrives from the north, this one bringing John Rogers, the independent adventurer, with another surprise — he tells Robertson that the approaching emigrant flotilla is short of provisions. Robertson expected them to be bringing at least a full winter's food stocks, but he immediately sends a boatload of rations north to meet them, and sends Pierre Pambrun south to help with the meat-gathering at Pembina. He is feeling the pressure strongly, so he goes riding again, his favourite stress reliever. He calls the still-exquisite stretch of riverbank known as the Image Plain "my private spot." At an Indigenous camp nearby, men report hearing signal guns further down the river last night. The newcomers are close.

Semple arrives ahead of the main group, having passed them on the way. Alex McLean is ready with a volley of salute. The officers greet and fawn over their new commander, and "the Governor is charmed by the appearance of the Country."

Next day the newcomers arrive. It is a red-letter day, and leader Alex Macdonell encourages them in celebrating it:

> I allowed all the people to walk on shore who had a wish to do so, having on their best apparel to show themselves off to the people at the Forks, and I proceeded in the boats to [Government] House under a salute of five rounds of artillery fired upon our arrival.

Semple compresses the rest of the day crisply: "The Colonists arrived, the Colours were hoisted, the guns were fired; at night we laughed and drank and danced." Alex Macdonell is euphoric: "Every person embarked at Thurso . . . were now here in far better health and appearance than when they embarked. . . . The people is full of the Beauty of the River. . . . Nothing is wanted now but to pass a good winter [with enough food]."

Robertson is not celebrating. He broods in his journal over the shortcomings of his colleagues: "This afternoon arrived . . . 120 souls.[5] What appears extraordinary is that Mr. Arch'd McDonald and Mr. Fidler sent them off with scarcely enough to take them to Jack River." For all any of their officers and leaders knew, the whole group might have arrived here to no food! Not to mention any indoor place to sleep. Good heavens, the settlement might still have been occupied by the buccaneers of last June! How would they expect these people to survive the winter? He is appalled and wonders on paper,

> After such blunders and such want of foresight, it is astonishing to me how the Colony withstood the Intrigues of the North West Company.

An odd remark: they certainly did not withstand those intrigues.

Worse, he will hear two days later that the emigrants arrived at York Factory with oatmeal enough to feed 150 people for two years. Fidler told Alex Macdonell it would not be required and suggested he sell it to the HBC.

> Such men and such measures [as these] to oppose the NWCo and establish the territorial right of the Company? No! They may as well try to take hold of the moon with their teeth.

Amen.

---

5   Again, a strange disconnect between this number and those in York Factory. I have no explanation.

CHAPTER 24

THE LAST WINTER

NOVEMBER 7, 1815, TO JANUARY 6, 1816

FORT DOUGLAS, RED RIVER SETTLEMENT NEAR THE FORKS.

Pity the newcomers — they have barely struggled out of their bedrolls nursing party hangovers when they are told by Robertson they will have to move on yet again. Today! It seems too cruel, and indeed the people put up a fight. "The difficulty we had to induce these people to take this simple step for their own good is incredible," reports Robert Semple later in his report to Selkirk. Nonetheless, the ice floes on the river make Robertson's argument for him and they grudgingly start packing up again.

The first group is led by Alex Macdonell with Dr. White and fifty-nine men, women and children. There are many more children than arrived in 1813, most of them between seven and fifteen, but at least a dozen under seven and a few below toddler age, including young Selkirk.[1] For them, this must be a bewildering experience, with much to fear in the dark cold of night. They all climb into the accursed batteaux and submit to the tedium of upstream travel, lashed with wind and rain. The spray is freezing around them as darkness comes on around

---

1   Selkirk McKay lived his full life at the Red River Settlement, dying there in 1878, an elder of his church. His headstone still stands (as MacKay) in the Kildonan Presbyterian Cemetery.

5 p.m. Hypothermia threatens, so they put ashore and build roaring fires to thaw out and cook food. When the steam stops rising from their clothes they climb back into their floating freezers and press on through the night, fearful of being locked in the ice before halfway to their destination.

They slog on through the next day, these magnificent men and women, fending off ice floes until, writes Alex Macdonell, "after dark, when a large piece of ice jammed us so much to the shore that our Boat got injured and we were obliged to put ashore and prepare ourselves on foot to Pembina." They collapse into their bedrolls. They are somewhere south of Scratching River (present-day Morris, Manitoba), about thirty-five kilometres from Fort Daer.

In the morning, they leave their baggage with the boat and walk to Fort Daer. They sleep out one more night, and Alex can't resist having fun at the expense of "the English lads," meaning John Rogers and his servant, "whom I found were not so hardy as the other people, not being able to bear the fatigue . . ."

> Mr. Rogers did not sleep any this night, complained much of the severe cold, and gave the Country a good many round oaths, [grumbling] that when one side was <u>warm</u> the other was like <u>ice</u>, and that he was surprised how the Divil the people from Scotland could sleep and <u>snore</u> at such a rate when <u>he</u> could not keep one single moment from the fire!

Rogers is unaware Macdonell is enjoying his soliloquys. To Alex's faked snores he "would say often, By God, Macdonell, you are a lucky fellow." In the morning Alex asks Rogers how he slept.

> <u>Me sleep? I slept none!</u> was his answer. But by God you Scotch are the people for this country. You live on Barley Meal like Colts upon Clover and sleep in the cold as if you had Feather beds.

That morning, "Messrs. White, Rogers and Pambrun proceed to Pembina and I remain as usual with the heavy baggage," by which he means the settlers. Did the English lads suddenly find their legs, or is there some kind of conveyance?[2] Is his "as usual" a little shot at how these privileged few tore ahead from Jack River, leaving Alex Macdonell to do the drudge work? Alex has spirit — willing and diligent, but not without a quiet streak of cynicism.

The following day they reach Pembina about noon, "pretty much fatigued, particularly the children." They are given a good feed of bison meat and shown to "good houses to lodge in." Macdonell is optimistic about the winter.

There is just one hitch — they can't get the bison meat in from the plains where the animals are being killed. That would require sleds and those in turn require snow, but the snow is slow in coming, and all that meat looks pretty tasty to the wolves and coyotes.

No matter. To go by Mr. Sunshine Macdonell, the next week is a positive idyll, with the weather fine, the people fine, fixing houses, building chimneys, preparing sledges and even bringing in some of the meat on foot.

RED RIVER SETTLEMENT.

Robertson is chafing. He feels let down by the HBC. He compares the poor equipment and lackadaisical habits of the HBC men to the smart, energetic and well-equipped men of the NWCo.

Rations are tight here, too. He admires the way Semple accepts the situation and joins in the short rations without complaint. Robertson calls him "a complete voyageur." "He thinks little about himself but seems extremely anxious about the welfare of those under him."

He gets a letter from the Nor'Wester chief, the other Alexander McDonell, and comments, "He [praises] my 'generous and gentle-manly conduct' when the fellow in his heart hates me cordially."

2   There is a story that some Indigenous hunters offered and gave at least some of the children rides on horseback to Fort Daer, so this may be how the officers escaped, too. I have not seen first-hand evidence for that story.

"We are among wolves and we must howl!" he chants again. He decides to visit Fort Daer.

FORT DAER ON THE PEMBINA RIVER.

Colin Robertson's arrival gives rise to the first inklings of the culture clash that lies ahead. He and Alex McDonell see the world differently, and it is reflected in their journal entries. First, Robertson's:

> As soon as the freemen heard of my arrival they brought in 110 cwt[3] of fresh meat and 700 lbs of dried. Bostino [probably Bostonais Pangman, a prominent Brûlé hunter and sometime Nor'Wester] who was such an enemy to the Colony last year brought nearly half himself. I sent for him and took him by the hand. The little fellow was overcome — "that cowardly Cameron . . . persuaded me that the Colonists were my enemies!"

And so on in a pattern of contrition we now recognize. Bostonais swears allegiance to Robertson and the Red River Settlement now and forever.

> I thanked him as well as the other freemen for their good intentions and gave them a few Gallons of Rum.

Alex Macdonell, on the other hand, who met his first plains Bois-Brûlé not more than two weeks ago, sees it more predictably for a European:

> As I am a stranger I have nothing to say, only that I remark when the <u>rum is in question</u> they all seem to be good fellows but I confess I have no confidence in them. In my opinion, when the rum keg is locked up and the Tobacco Roll sparingly

---

3   Cwt = Hundredweight = 100 pounds (45 kilograms). If this is not a typo, which I think it must be, that is 11,000 lbs/5,000 kilos! It is much more likely 11 cwt.

given, their affection towards us is at an end. . . . Mr. Robertson
and I differ, for with him they are the best fellows in the world.

A few days later, Alex goes out to find the baggage that was left when
his group had to abandon their boats. He exults in being alone, "with
my bedding on my back and my provisions rolled within, consisting of a
Buffalo Tongue." He is the intrepid frontiersman, living off the land. He
finds the baggage and presently a carrying party arrives to take it back.

Snow finally arrives on December 2. Some meat comes in on sleds,
and fish are caught through the ice: "Jack, Whitefish, Goldeye, Sturgeon,
Suckers etc. Not in considerable numbers." These run out and there is
hunger for three days. On December 14 Pat Quin brings in a cart of
meat; it is gone in a day.

On the 16th, two carts of meat arrive, "to the great joy of the people."

FORT DOUGLAS, RED RIVER SETTLEMENT.

Robertson continues to feel very good about Governor Semple, who
is still "cracking jokes" about the paucity of his table fare. Robertson
notes it makes the men eager to please him, and opines expansively,
"When men are sent out to this country by quality rather than
by quantity, the Company's affairs may be expected to prosper."
Evidently Robert Semple is a most charming fellow. Maybe that's
what got him this job.

Robertson's approval of Semple contrasts with his opinion of Peter
Fidler, who he thinks is a malingerer. He "has been extremely unfortunate [in his travels] but whether frequent misfortunes be not a polite
name for mismanagement I leave others to judge," he remarks, doing
nothing of the kind.

His criticism extends to James White for his drunken ways, but
especially for his part with his fellows last June when they gave up
their governor to Duncan Cameron. Nor does Robertson keep his
complaints to himself, as we know from a letter White sends to Fidler
on December 8:

The censures that Mr. Robertson so freely casts upon our conduct last spring are of such a nature that I cannot pass over them in silence.

White blames Alex and Christina McLean: "The person in power seems to be their only minion . . . the defamation of others is a good way of securing his good graces." He grumbles on, "Whatever Mr. Robertson may say against our conduct last spring I value not a pin . . . I am still of opinion that we adopted the very best steps" for saving the people and the settlement.

White is sure that Robertson is prejudicing Semple against them, unaware that the men at York Fort have already done that job. White hopes Semple will also realize that "a sweet word from a sweet mouth of a sweet woman may not at all times be true." As for Robertson, he'd better lighten up on the invective if he doesn't want to find himself facing White in a duel. Clearly, infighting is as bitter as ever it was under Miles McDonell.

On November 29, St. Andrew's Day, Robertson throws a party to celebrate Scotland's patron saint. The grog brings on bravado; some of the men ask Semple's permission to go over and take Cameron's fort from him. Semple asks Robertson how to refuse them without discouraging them. Robertson says the Nor'Westers are no threat at the moment, but the time may come when such action will be necessary.

He then addressed the men, thanked them for their readiness [to fight] and when the Enemy attempted to disturb our repose, he would trust entirely to their courage and fidelity. This satisfied them for the moment.

Later, Robertson walks with Semple by Fort Gibraltar. Semple wishes that Robertson had kept the fort when he had it. Robertson points out that he did not have the manpower or authority to do that. But, he assures the governor, he can take it again whenever Semple gives the word.

Semple sits down to write his first inland report to Selkirk, including his assessment of the events of last June. He is astonished by the

"Treachery and Ingratitude pursued by the Highlanders of last season, it being so directly contrary to the received notions of their Character." He can't imagine anything of the kind from the present group. Nor can he fathom the gross mismanagement by McDonell that allowed victory to this Nor'Wester rabble, this collection of "Half Breeds and Old worn out Canadians," especially when he sees how Robertson "kicked them about in a few days — I may say a few hours." He can only credit it to bad advice from Dr. White and Archie McDonald. McDonell was a fool to take it.

Semple's incurious self-certainty and easy dismissal of his opponents will soon enough prove fatally short-sighted. With every written utterance, he reveals himself another of Selkirk's poor judgments, whose rank, in his own view, endows him with superior insight.

He even takes a few shots at Robertson, the man who saved everyone's bacon and who is saying nothing but good about Semple. He questions the number of paid servants that Robertson has engaged, about seventy he estimates, "with very little benefit . . . to balance so serious an Expenditure." Does he ask Robertson about this, or is this just another of his unexamined conclusions?

Semple's good words are for "[Alex] Macdonell whose conduct has entitled him to the esteem of every officer and the respect and confidence of all the Settlers."

He also likes the millwright. "Samuel Lamont is a quiet, excellent, industrious man. He proposes we shall rebuild the Mill this summer and I shall [contract] with him to that effect."

His report finishes with an extraordinary remark: "Meantime, we will endeavour to derive instruction from the misfortunes, perhaps the errors of the past." In fact he will do no such thing. The hole in his self-awareness seems bottomless.

FORT DAER ON THE PEMBINA.

Alex, meanwhile, continues his sunny optimism. On New Year's Day, 1816, he writes, "The Governor in Chief being here he gave a cask of

Rum to the free Canadians, Settlers and Servants, and a Ball — all seem to be happy."

On January 3, Alex's whole entry is underlined: "I have been sworn this day by the Governor in Chief as High Sheriff of Assiniboia and a member of the Gov'r in Chief's Council. " Assiniboia gets its modern spelling, and Alex is raised to dreamt-of heights — another red-letter day. Let the New Year begin!

RED RIVER SETTLEMENT.

Robertson passes Christmas at Fort Douglas, barely mentioning the day in his journal. On New Year's Eve,

> Dined with Mr. and Mrs. McLean . . . This is certainly one of the most provident and industrious families belonging to the Colony. Mrs. McLean has no servant maid and she has five small children to take care of, and is badly [housed], but she bears all these hardships with an astonishing degree of fortitude.

Christina has made another conquest.

On New Year's Day, he reflects on the past year. He curses the NWCo, though he acknowledges that 1815 belonged to them, uprooting the colony and beating the HBC in the trading field. He counts his victories: "The Great Cameron has fallen. His Fort taken, himself made prisoner and lessened in the Eyes of those men who he treated with utmost insolence and indignity." But he is too canny to believe success will come easily. "[The NWCo will fall] but they will make a desperate struggle before that arrives, so that the years 1816 and 1817 will be an unfortunate era in the History of this Country." Impressive prescience, and an epic understatement.

The very next day, Messrs. Seraphin and Pangman come over from Fort Gibraltar, "according to the custom of the Country," to pay their New Year's respects to Robertson. Bourke and another servant named

Cochrane, still smarting from last spring, jump the guests as they leave. Robertson happens to come outside. "Cochrane had already struck Pangman a severe blow with a stick." A grog-fuelled crowd is converging to join in. "I placed myself between the parties," says Robertson, "and called out to let these men go."

Robertson fears this incident will "raise the suspicion of the mâtives, whom I wished to disunite from the NWCo."

Sure enough, Duncan Cameron quickly seizes on the incident to complain loudly of the violence of the colony men. Robertson points out that it was entirely a result of the Nor'Westers' violence last spring. Cameron piously insists that he is determined to live at peace.

"Only necessity obliged me to take up arms last spring," he pronounces.

Robertson snaps back, "Don't humbug me, Cameron. I know what governs your actions and I'll take it as an insult to my intelligence if you try to persuade me otherwise."

"Oh Mr. Robertson, let us drop this. You are becoming heated."

The year 1816 is off to a shaky start. Planning how to handle the NWCo and Cameron will preoccupy Robertson's mind henceforth.

CHAPTER 25

SEND IN THE CLOWNS

JANUARY 7 TO MARCH 17, 1816

FORT DOUGLAS, RED RIVER SETTLEMENT.

Governor Semple, being governor of all HBC territories, leaves in early January to visit the posts at Brandon House and Qu'Appelle, on the river of that name. Travelling mainly by dogsled, he will be away for some time, leaving Robertson in sole control at Red River.

After his encounter with Cameron, Robertson invites James White, Alex McLean, John Bourke and Semple's clerk, Lawrence Wilkinson, to dinner. His report of the evening demonstrates that he, and therefore presumably anyone, can have all the British gentleman's assumptions of superiority and entitlement without being blind to the reality around him.

He writes that he told them of his scolding of Cameron, and how driving a wedge between the "mâtives" and the NWCo will be the best way to keep the Nor'Westers from attacking, at least until a military force arrives with Selkirk. To this end, they should treat the Bois-Brûlés politely, "as well as the Indians and freemen." If they do, he promises, Cameron will be disarmed. However:

> If on the contrary you continue to treat every person that is
> not an Englishman with severity and contempt and by that
> means drive the mâtives again into the arms of the NWCo, the

Colony is ruined. Fort Douglas can always be defended, but
that is not establishing the settlement.

It is hard to imagine a clearer statement of strategy: make them
your friends or face them as enemies again, a stark choice from a man
who understands and respects the Brûlés better than any European
outside Fort Gibraltar. Alex McLean immediately agrees with him. Dr.
White is silent, but Bourke and Wilkinson just repeat their desire for
revenge. Robertson, "feeling vexed at these remarks," explodes.

"Have you the means of revenging the indignities you suffered last
year?" he demands. "How many men have we able to bear arms? Sixty?
And with sixty men can you protect sixty families, some living three
and four miles from the fort?" No response. He presses, "Against a
hundred mâtives and freemen, with Nor'Wester servants?" The young
men keep a sullen silence, and he hammers the lecture home: "Before
we left Winipic Settlement I laid down a policy which still applies,
and your little sarcastic remarks on my partiality towards Canadians,
Mâtives, Freemen or Indians shall not make me alter it one iota."

Semple's clerk, Lawrence Wilkinson, is the only one stubborn
enough to begin a retort, but Robertson cuts him off. "I changed the
subject," he records. "This young Gentleman is a favourite of Governor
Semple but really, his notions are too high for this country."

With the holiday entertainments behind them, the long winter
evenings begin to wear on their nerves, with highly entertaining
results. They first show up in Robertson's journal on January 10 as a
brief irritation:

> In the evening, a dispute took place between Doctor White
> and Mr. Wilkinson on the merits of their respective countries,
> when Mr. W. pulled the Dr. by the nose for no other reason
> than the Dr.'s refusal to pull a trigger with him.

Disappointingly brief. Fortunately, a small fragment of Dr. White's
journal survives, covering just these events and supplying details. White

is a 28-year-old Scot and Wilkinson is an Englishman in his early twenties. White:

> About 8 PM, as I was reading the Queen's Wake,[1] the conversation between Mr. Wilkinson and me turned on the pronunciation of the English language. He argued that no Scotchman could speak the English so correctly as a man born in England. I told him that . . . I knew many in Scotland who could speak the English as grammatically as any Englishman but that I never knew an Englishman who could speak the Scotch dialect like a Scotchman. Mr. Wilkinson got into a great rage. I told him to say no more upon the subject, that it was not worthwhile to be out of temper about such a trifling thing.
>
> While I was reading Mr. Wilkinson took hold of my nose with his forefinger and thumb saying "take that, and meet me tomorrow at the point." I instantly started up and would certainly have punished him for his insolence, had Mr. Bourke not interfered. I told him that if he ever did the like again, that he would suffer most severely for it. . . . He [talked back] and I at last gave his nose a squeeze, saying that we were now equal.

At this point Robertson comes in from an adjoining room and scolds Wilkinson, who goes grumpily off to bed.

Come morning it appears Wilkinson has been stewing all the night through. Robertson reports, "Just as I was sitting down to breakfast I was informed that Mr. Wilkinson was walking before the house with two drawn swords, calling the Doctor to accept of one and defend himself."

James White again:

> Mr. Wilkinson approached me with two naked swords vociferating in a great rage that I had threatened to kick him. Fixing one of the swords in the ground he said "Take that!" Mr. Robertson

---

1   Published in 1812 and still available, this is romantic poetry by James Hogg, poet, novelist and biographer of Sir Walter Scott.

came to the door [and] told him to go in and put by the swords, that he was a fool for behaving in that manner. Mr. Wilkinson told Mr. Robertson that he was a great fool himself and offered him one of the swords. Messrs. R. and B. took the swords from Wilk. Wilk still continued making use of insolent expressions to R. At last Mr. R. took hold of Wilkinson and told him that if he did not be quiet, that he would put him in the river. I then went up to Wilkinson and struck him on the mouth with my fist.

Whoa, that's unsporting! Robertson flies into a rage, says White, and "seeing him in that state, I ran away and he pursued, making Blackguard expressions against me."

Robertson: "If I had been able to overtake the Doctor, who by this time had made his escape, I should certainly have done something that I would have regretted."

As to Lawrence Wilkinson, "I wish to god that Governor Semple had taken Wilkinson with him," sighs Robertson.

FORT DAER ON THE PEMBINA.

A hundred kilometres to the south, matters are somewhat more pressing. The snow has melted, disabling the sleds, and again meat is not coming in. Alex Macdonell decides to lead as many as can travel out to the hunting grounds where they will have plenty of food for themselves while helping to supply the fort. Twenty-five men (and women? — he does not say) walk 110 kilometres into the plains, where they build huts and set about hunting. It seems a terrible risk when they know there are Dakota war parties about. Alex coolly notes, "I have 12 muskets with a proportion of ammunition so that in case they would come we should make a tolerable defence." Twelve muskets for twenty-five people suggests that some of the party are women.

At one point, Alex and Duncan McNaughton trek twenty-five kilometres to deliver aid to an injured hunter. On returning they find themselves "travelling through [a bison herd] all day, perhaps 5000 more or less." The weather draws the bison closer to camp and he records, "Great slaughter among them by the Hunters."

FORT DOUGLAS.

That clip on the jaw from Dr. White hardly slows Lawrence Wilkinson down. Just a week later, with the thaw continuing, he decides to go on a solo Sunday hunting expedition. When he has not returned by late afternoon, Robertson dispatches men to look for him. Alex McLean soon finds him, exhausted, about a kilometre or two north of the fort. He had been lost in the woods since noon and had finally stumbled on the river and was struggling to get back.

What woods along the Red River are extensive enough to get so lost in? At first glance, none. Robertson solves this mystery by following Wilkinson's footprints for two full hours:

> He had kept walking in a circle not more than six hundred yards in circumference. . . . He crossed his own track frequently and sometimes followed it until he got completely bewildered. Had the weather been severe he would certainly have froze to death.
>
> When this young gentleman had recovered a little he . . . talked of the great distance he had walked when he was not above a mile from the Fort. An Englishman wherever he goes must always think himself superior to the strangers he visits.

Clowns to the left of him, jokers to the right . . .

Robertson worries about Fort Daer with the weather so warm and Dakota war parties about. He hears from a couple of Nor'Westers "the unpleasant news of thirty-one Saulteaux having been killed at Turtle River by a war party of the Sioux." His anxiety increases.

White treats Duncan Cameron for illness and comments, "I hope he'll suffer yet for all his atrocious actions."

Cameron complains of much scalding when he voids his urine. He told me that he caught gonorrhea from LeRoy's wife — By whom she was affected I could not learn.

White is also treating James Moore, a colony servant. Tapeworm has troubled Moore for some years past. Last year he passed one that was eighteen feet long. "From his symptoms, I am inclined to think that the worms have again begun to form."

Colin Robertson is still dealing with rumours that are spreading alarm through the nervous colony. "One says [Cameron] is squaring wood for a Bastion. Another says that a band of half-breeds were seen leaving his Fort. Another says that Cameron told an Indian and this Indian told McNulty's wife and this wife told Mr. Bourke and Mr. Bourke told Mr. Wilkinson that he, Cameron, was determined to revenge what he had suffered from the Irishmen last fall."[2]

Robertson suspects that all rumours originate with Cameron himself, so he goes to Gibraltar and tells him to desist immediately. Cameron protests his innocence, of course, saying that he's going off to Qu'Appelle anyway.

With Cameron gone, Robertson feels safe in going to Fort Daer.

FORT DAER.

Robertson is "quite charmed with the industry of the newcomers who have made seven ploughs for sale beyond what they need for themselves. . . . They are highly delighted with the country."

Then there is the NWCo — Cameron has been "at his dirty work again," warning their hunters to watch out for Robertson, that he still has it in for them for last spring.

He is not at all happy that Alex Macdonell has been allowed by John Pritchard, nominal chief at Fort Daer, to take his settlers so far from the fort's protection and sends for him to come in, which Macdonell does,

---

2 This apparently refers to the horsewhipping McLean and Bourke had administered.

pulling five sleds of meat. Robertson orders him to bring the settlers back to Fort Daer, out of harm's way. Privately, Macdonell disagrees: "It is my opinion they should remain for a month longer." The settlers have stated they are not willing to come in until there is a better prospect of laying in more provisions, "and their plans meet my hearty concurrence," writes Macdonell, so he does not pass on Robertson's order. He is nobody's toady, though underestimating the Dakota threat is a reckless gamble.

Macdonell hears, without saying where, that the NWCo is preparing to "strike a Blow" come spring. He orders the muskets cleaned and put in order.

FORT DOUGLAS, RED RIVER SETTLEMENT.

Robertson finds that in his absence, "Mrs. McLean had another baby on February 7. Mother and son are doing well. The youngster is to be christened Miles."

He hears that the Nor'Wester named Hess has been circulating reports among the Indigenous hunters that "not only Halfbreeds, but Crees and Assiniboines are coming to war on us in the spring. Hess would not presume to excite alarm if Cameron did not sanction it."

Governor Semple was supposed to be back at Red River by now, but Robertson gets word from Brandon House that Semple is still in Qu'Appelle, and the rumour machine goes into high gear again: Wilkinson tells whoever will listen that he is sure something has happened to Semple since he is never tardy; another, says Robertson, "comes with a face as long as my arm to say the Blacksmith at Gibraltar is making grape shot." He explains (again) that the Nor'Westers don't have the manpower, they don't have the loyalty of the Bois-Brûlés, and the First Nations are in favour of the colony, "but with some men, all reason is lost."

At last he records some good news: Wilkinson has gone to Fort Daer. "He proposed this trip and I readily agreed to it. Sent two men with him."

On March 4, Robertson is visiting a Brûlé cabin near Gibraltar when Seraphin comes in and asks if he is aware that Bourke and three other men have been prowling about his fort, alarming his people.

"No, Lamar, you must be mistaken for at night you see double; rest assured it was not my people."

"Pardon me Mr. Robertson, I can swear to Mr. Bourke's person and walk."

It would seem the Nor'Westers are as nervous of the colonists as vice versa.

A few days later, he takes a walk near Gibraltar, where he sees "the great Captain strutting about in his regimentals, the first time he has worn the Red Coat since the taking of Gibraltar." So Cameron has returned, and resumed his old swagger. This seems to put Robertson suddenly on his guard. Then, more alarming news: "Mr. Frazer, a Nor'Wester," arrives at Gibraltar with four men from Qu'Appelle, and on March 12, six more arrive from Brandon with three dogsleds of provisions.

To his journal he proposes a bold move: "What would be the consequence of taking Gibraltar?" He would dearly love to go through their correspondence and the letters that will soon arrive on their express from the west. "What does these diabolical men mean?" (Grammatical lapse is a sure sign of stress in Robertson.)

Robertson is more agitated by the day — more men are arriving at the opposition's fort. "It is alarming — we have only eleven men here! Our numbers being so diminished has relieved the alarms of our opponents. . . . Sent off Monsieur Nolan [to Fort Daer] to tell Macdonell and Pritchard . . . to keep a watchful eye on Frazer and Hess in Pembina."

On the 15th he restates his anxiety about the fast-approaching NWCo Winter Express and the orders and plans it may be carrying: "Are they to bring bands of savages upon us? They shall not be the first [to strike] at The Forks."

Two days later, Robertson makes good on this last statement. In the morning he reconnoitres things at Fort Gibraltar, then returns to call a meeting of the militia officers, McLean, Holt and Bourke. "I informed

SEND IN THE CLOWNS

them that I intended to take Cameron's fort this evening. My officers approved of my plan (Mr. Wilkinson excepted)."

> I then assembled [eleven] men. . . . At half past six I had them under arms and just as I was marching off, Mr. Wilkinson threw himself into the ranks. . . . I communicated to Messrs. McLean and Bourke the plan of attack — that I should lead the van and enter Cameron's Hall; that Mr. McLean should attack the men's house on the right and Mr. Bourke that on the left. As we approached, the dogs gave the alarm. I then quickened my pace and came up to the small wicket in the gate just as the guard was attempting to shut it. This I forced; my faithful servant followed me and in five minutes the Fort was ours.

Cameron is again his prisoner, along with his letters and plans. What now?

CHAPTER 26

ROBERTSON ASCENDANT

MARCH 17 TO APRIL 15, 1816

FORT GIBRALTAR AT THE FORKS.

R obertson's victory is so swift, bloodless and complete, it seems to surprise him as much as the Nor'Westers. He exults that though the Nor'Westers outnumbered them two to one, they had no time to get to their weapons and the "cool, determined courage of both officers and men was truly pleasing," especially McLean's troop in taking the men's quarters. Though happily non-violent, it was a near thing, thanks to Bourke and his Irish temper. Robertson had gone straight into the main hall and was disarming Cameron and others when

> Bourke arrived and presented a pistol to the head of Siveright
> and I believe would have shot him had I not been present.
> Perhaps Mr. Bourke thought he had not surrendered.

Or maybe Bourke just badly wanted to shoot somebody; it had felt so good to horsewhip Cameron last fall.

. Robertson leaves Gibraltar in McLean's charge and goes back to Fort Douglas, where he dashes off a letter to Macdonell in Fort Daer and Semple at Brandon House. He dispatches them by fast dogsled.

FORT DAER ON THE PEMBINA RIVER.

Alex Macdonell returns from a salt-gathering expedition just as Robertson's letter arrives. It describes the fort's capture but contains no specific instructions for him, so Alex again acts on his own initiative. He decides to arrest key members of the Nor'Wester contingent at Pembina. With McLeod, the HBC trader, Dr. White and John Pritchard, he surprises Frazer, Hess and Bostonais Pangman and makes them prisoners. His justification is that they have been plotting an attack on Fort Daer, using "all the Half Breeds and others they could muster." The next day, he sends them north to Fort Douglas, under guard, with a letter of explanation for Robertson and strong advice to keep them imprisoned with Cameron.

AT FORT GIBRALTAR.

Robertson is eagerly reading Cameron's correspondence, beginning with a half-finished letter he finds on Cameron's desk that was interrupted as the invaders burst in. It is addressed to a friend at Fond du Lac, an NWCo post (now Superior, Wisconsin). Cameron writes that the settlers who fled Red River last June had been determined to go all the way back to Britain, when "a Wellington in Words, Colin Robertson"[1] arrived and led them back to Red River, where they would "cover themselves with glory."

He goes on to describe his own capture last fall, transforming it into stage melodrama: Ambush, pistols presented to heads, transport to Robertson's fort where they were grossly abused. McLean took an armed party to Fort Gibraltar, got "drunk as a beast" and allowed his men to "commit every kind of excess." The final indignity was to be taken back and made a prisoner "in my own house."

Cameron takes credit for convincing Robertson to give back the fort, "but not until all the Arms in our Fort was dastardly carried away."

---

[1] A reference to the victor of Waterloo who is now the hero of the hour in Britain.

He relates the New Year's Day attack on Seraphin Lamar and Bostonais Pangman, and wishes his correspondent could send

> some of your Pilleurs[2] who are fond of mischief and plunder [to] come and pay a hostile visit to these Sons of Gun — they might make a very good booty if they went cunningly to work, not that I would wish them to Butcher anyone, God forbid.

Another letter is from the hand of Cuthbert Grant, and has a more alarming message:

> The Half Breeds of Fort des [Prairies] and English River are all to be here in the spring and it is to be hoped we will come off with flying colours and never see any of them again in the Colonizing way in Red River.

Fort des Prairies and this English River are far to the west, so the implication is that Bois-Brûlés from across the Northwest are being rallied to attack the settlement.

The NWCo express canoe arrives from the west and is duly intercepted by Robertson's men; the mail is brought to Fort Douglas. In the Nor'Wester Siveright's presence, Robertson reads a letter intended for Cameron from Alex McDonell of the NWCo at Qu'Appelle:

> There is a storm brewing . . . over the rascals, meaning the Colony. Little do they know the situation they are placed in; last spring will be a joke compared to what this will be.

"Now, Siveright," says Robertson, "what think you of this language? I must know how this 'storm' is to attack this unfortunate settlement."

Siveright leaves him "very much chagrined at the discoveries I have made."

---

2 "Pillagers," the nickname for certain Chippewa Anishinaabe bands around Fond du Lac.

Robertson turns some of his Fort Gibraltar prisoners loose ("they all has large families") and begins the process of occupying their fort. He gives us a nice description of it:

> It is certainly in an excellent state of defence. It has two Bastions at the [opposite corners] of the Square, and the Square is formed with Out-Palisades eighteen feet in height and those are proof against musketry. This is not only a strong place but very comfortable lodgings such as I have not been accustomed to for some time past.

Next day he "arranges an apartment for Mr. McLean's family."

On Saturday, March 23, the fourteen prisoners taken by Alex Macdonell at Pembina arrive at The Forks. Robertson is not happy to see all these Brûlés under guard. It makes him look like their enemy, the last thing he wants. He is caught between the necessity of releasing them and the need to credit Alex Macdonell for his initiative.

This would seem an ideal opportunity to make clear to Alex the difference between the Nor'Westers and the free Brûlés who merely work on contract. Yet somehow the distinction will be lost on Macdonell and he will feel only unjust reproach from Robertson. Despite how clearly he expresses it in his journal, Robertson will never be able to communicate his strategy effectively to the "gentlemen" of the colony — except possibly Alex McLean and Christina.

BRANDON HOUSE, 200 KM WEST OF THE FORKS.

Robert Semple reads Robertson's belligerent letter to McDonell, then sends it on, but not before rewriting it to make himself the conqueror rather than Robertson, a revealing bit of pettiness. He sends another note to Qu'Appelle: "Remember what I now say to you — Should you or your Indian or Black Breed Allies attempt any violence against the Hudson's Bay Co. at Qu'Appelle or elsewhere the consequences to yourselves will be terrible." "Black Breed Allies," as a term for the Bois-Bûlés, is strong language, even by 1816 standards.

THE FORKS.

Robertson has regularized a quasi-military guard of fifteen men, putting them under the command of Alex McLean and outfitting them in regimentals.

Semple finally returns to Fort Douglas and a relieved Robertson notes that he "approves of everything I have done; the intercepted letters he thinks of the highest importance." Semple is also complimentary about the "Guard" and the strong state of Gibraltar.

When Robertson suggests they send Cameron to York Fort along with the incriminating mail from the express, Semple waffles. Even when Robertson explains how awkward it will be to have Cameron a prisoner when all his "Freemen and mâtives" begin arriving in the spring, Semple only agrees to "think about it."

Next day, Semple decides to hold on to the NWCo mail in Red River. Instead of taking action, Semple compiles a list of charges against Cameron, continuing Miles McDonell's fiction, or delusion, that the issue here is the rule of law.

Briefly, the charges are:

1. Seducing the servants and Settlers of Lord Selkirk
2. Assembling . . . Vagabonds . . . to destroy Colony
3. Causing the deaths of colonists
4. Burning a mill, buildings and sundry houses etc.
5. Wantonly destroying cattle and stealing horses
6. Encouraging Indian tribes to make war on British Subjects
7. Intending to repeat these actions again in 1816

Again, in his choice of the word "vagabonds," he dismisses the highly able and most dangerous people in his territory.

From Qu'Appelle, the HBC trader James Sutherland writes that the Nor'Westers at Qu'Appelle are spreading it about that the colony will be attacked this spring by "150 Halfbreeds from all quarters." According to Sutherland, one fellow is recruiting at Île-à-la-Crosse, another one along the Saskatchewan, and Cuthbert Grant is to be Generalissimo of the whole. The "Halfbreed flag" is flying over the North West fort at Qu'Appelle. Fortunately they seem to have given up trying to "employ Indians" to destroy the colony.

Peguis and four of his hunters visit Fort Douglas and are pleased with developments. Peguis takes it on himself to lecture other First Nations people at The Forks on the merits of the colony and the deceitful ways of Duncan Cameron. "This Indian will be of great service to us," remarks Robertson.

On April 3, Robertson writes in his journal,

> On this day last year, Mr. Cameron and his men stole the Colonial Artillery and by this time three fourths of the Colonists had espoused his cause; what a change!

Next day, he talks to Semple about the folly of putting the 1815 people on their own farm lots. Semple is all for it, but Robertson thinks it's too dangerous, preferring that they raise their first year's crops on Point Douglas, under the protection of the fort. Spread out along several kilometres of riverbank, they are too vulnerable.

On Robertson's birthday, April 5, the guard salutes him with a volley and Semple and the officers all gather for dinner, and "pass a very pleasant evening." It will be one of the last.

As the snow melts, a great prairie fire sweeps toward the colony from over the western horizon. Robertson orders some controlled burning around the settlement to keep it at bay.

FORT DAER, PEMBINA.

Watching smoke and flames from the wildfire in the distance, Alex

Macdonell notes that with the approach of spring, the people are "with the idea of getting down to their farms."

On April 8 he starts for The Forks. The people will follow by boat when the river opens.

FORT DOUGLAS.

On April 12, two weeks after his return, Semple declares the taking of Gibraltar "a measure not only justified but imperiously demanded by the conduct and avowed hostilities of our implacable Opponents." Of the captured NWCo correspondence, he says, "a more complete disclosure of plans of deliberate villainy has never yet met my eye . . . Pillage Burning and Murder planned."

Semple writes an order to Pierre Pambrun, a veteran of the War of 1812 and Robertson's second-in-command: "Have received intelligence that the Agents of the NWCo intend to [ambush] our boats from Qu'Appelle. You will proceed as soon as possible with [a body of men] to Brandon House," and with Fidler decide how best to protect the boats. "It is my wish that you carefully avoid every act of hostility until fully justified by the conduct of our enemies."

On April 20, as he is walking with the governor, the newly returned Alex Macdonell writes, "All of a sudden, like a shot, the River gave a general crush, and the whole moved with a rumbling noise [and] crushed everything that came in its way." The Red River is open for navigation.

For the next week, Alex Macdonell and Semple are engaged setting fishing nets and enclosing the proposed garden plot against rabbits, deer and livestock. Wilkinson plans out the garden beds while Rogers plows the ground. Apparently, gardens are not beneath the efforts of gentlemen. Nor is gathering frogs for bait. When it rains, the plains are alive with them.

By mid-April, Semple is still going through the impounded documents from Fort Gibraltar, where he finds clear evidence of NWCo scheming a year ago:

- John Smyth's letter to Cameron, asking to go with the deserting group.
- A letter in Cameron's writing from April 3, 1815: "I have authorized the settlers to take possession of the Field Pieces and to bring them over here."
- A letter from January 1815 desiring Hess to "excite the Indians."
- Another letter from Cameron to Hess, cautioning him "to prove cunning and secret" while spreading rumours that Lord Selkirk intends to send no more supplies to support the settlers, and to make a list of all the freemen, "but take good care that the English find nothing out."

And so on. If there were a court within a thousand kilometres, Cameron's goose would be cooked. Of course, there is not.

Even as matters are marching toward another life-or-death showdown for the settlement, colony politics are preoccupying the officers. About this time, Ener Holt, the man who accidentally shot Bourke in the Hernum and Cloircle, writes a letter from Fort Douglas to John Pritchard at Fort Daer. From it we can gather the general feeling among the officers toward Colin Robertson ("Mr. Lofty"), whose barbs about last June still sting.

My Dear Sir,

. . . Mr. Lofty once in my presence injured your character but this I would not admit of, and you of course must submit to be tried by a court martial where you no doubt will be honourably acquitted and Mr. Lofty replaced to answer for himself.

He tells Pritchard that he, Holt, has been given command of the schooner *Cuchullin*, which is to be equipped with a cannon, "Man of War style," and stationed at the mouth of the Red River to intercept the NWCo canoes. "I will be in my proper glory, and shall not fail to give the Scoundrels a dabbing if I can." He reports the dispatch of men to protect the boats coming from Qu'Appelle, led by "Mr. Lofty's Pleo of perfection, Mr. Pambrun."

He can apparently take for granted that Pritchard shares his opinions. This behind-the-back undermining of Robertson's authority does not bode well for the trying times approaching.

CHAPTER 27

WITH FRIENDS LIKE THESE . . .

APRIL 22 TO MAY 10, 1816

FORT GIBRALTAR AT THE FORKS.

Robertson still broods in his room at the captured fort. He frets in his journal about Duncan Cameron, still confined to quarters in Fort Gibraltar, but allowed to entertain visitors. Some of those visitors, Indigenous men, are becoming inconvenient, asking for Cameron to be set free. Robertson does not want to disrespect them, but he has no intention of freeing his prisoner. He writes the governor, still in Fort Douglas, that it is imperative they send Cameron away, to Jack River and beyond.

"My motives are simply this," he explains, "nothing is more annoying to the feelings of an Indian than to see a prisoner. Death they prefer to confinement." And Cameron has been "making the pitiful man," playing on their phobia.

On the other hand he does want Bostonais Pangman to be freed, to avoid offending the Bois-Brûlés. Semple does not act on either of these.

Another prairie fire is tearing through the plains in the distance. "They burn with great brilliancy, giving the impression of a large town in flames."

There is a general chill in the governor's attitude toward him lately, and Robertson thinks he knows why: Alex Macdonell. "Ever since that

Gentleman's Arrival, I have perceived a coldness towards my plans for establishing or defending the Colony." Worse, it seems to extend to his allies among the leadership. Factions are forming. "This will be attended with bad consequences." Why Alex would take sides against Robertson is not yet clear.

On April 26, he notes that the settlers are complaining about the behaviour of the officers. So are those Indigenous people, Brûlé and First Nations, who have reason to deal with them.

> One Gentleman turns up his nose and says, "filthy creatures, how they smell." Another observes, "Damn that Canadian, he has always his pipe in his mouth . . . we will punish the fellows now that we have the physical force to settle the business."
>
> This is talking as if we had a company of soldiers at our back, without ever considering the means we have to oppose the measures of our opponents and the resources they possess.

Robertson mulls over a number of changes he would make, ending with the only one he will effect, namely, to dismantle Gibraltar's stout palisade and take the pickets down the river to erect around Fort Douglas, which is still without one.

He decides that he will put his proposals to Semple, and "if he be still averse to follow my plans I will surely request liberty to leave the Colony."

In all this, even Robertson never advises Semple to withdraw the Pemmican Proclamation, the grievance that rankles the Brûlés at least as much as their threats disturb him. Although he has respect for and some rapport with the Bois-Brûlés, Robertson seems not to understand much better than Miles McDonell the central role in their livelihood and culture played by the buffalo and their freedom to hunt them and live on their meat. For the buffalo, they will go to war. It is a crucial, not to say fatal, misunderstanding.

He writes to the governor once more and once more he is rebuffed. It is starting to be too much — "I am afraid he is badly advised. He ought to go to Cumberland House, where he could aid Mr. Bird to repair the disasters the Athabasca Expedition has suffered."[1] When Robertson actually suggests this to Semple, the governor replies that he would have gone, but "Mr. Macdonell informed [me] that the Colonists would lose their confidence in the Country were [I] to leave the Colony at this Juncture."

"Then," asks Robertson, "will you allow me to go?"

"No, Mr. Robertson, your name is everything at this crisis."

"My name, Governor Semple, will not mean much if my plans are ignored."

Semple complains that he does not have the means to defend the fort without Robertson.

"But Sir, with the slender means of defence you have, I learn that you intend to place the Colonists on their lands?"

"Mr. Macdonell says they will insist on it."

"They may, Governor, but I would advise them not to, and if this failed I would use a little authority to enforce my advice when it is for their own welfare."

The governor replies "evasively," leaving Robertson "in doubt how to act."

Robertson's plan to have the new settlers farm communally under the fort's protection seems an excellent one, but as we saw two years ago, Highlanders are not easily put off and obtaining their own land is the sole reason they've come.

Alex Macdonell's journal, meanwhile, is consumed with the minutiae of spring. Anyone who passes a winter on the prairie is hard-pressed not to become giddy at its retreat, and Alex is not immune:

> Remarkable fine weather for seed time . . . more fish caught now than we are able to consume . . . more ducks and geese than can be kept, millions of them passing every moment in the day.
>
> Took a ride out to Frog Plain. The Grass springs up delightfully and the face of the country begins to look beautiful. In

---

[1] Over the winter, his brigade in Athabasca has suffered starvation and death. Attending to it is probably why the option of leaving appeals to Robertson.

the evening a heavy shower made the whole country look green, Frogs leaping with joy in millions around us.

The next day, April 28, Macdonell reports "a little dispute between Mr. Semple and Mr. Robertson respecting the Settlers' lands." It is not "little" in Robertson's telling:

He meets with the governor and Alex Macdonell to drive home the inadvisability of putting the colonists on their land. Alex smiles a bit smugly, irritating the testy Robertson, who growls that Macdonell is inexperienced and doesn't realize the consequences of what he's suggesting.

"Upon my word," says Alex, "I don't think the colonists could be convinced to settle anywhere but on their own lands."

"Not if you don't insist, they won't."

Robertson changes the subject to the treatment of the Indigenous peoples, who he maintains must be treated more kindly.

The governor sniffs, "I see no good that can come from coaxing." Alex adds a hearty "Certainly not!" and Robertson grinds his teeth some more.

"Coaxing, as you call it, is our only choice. If we drive the mâtives into the arms of the North West, we are at their mercy again. If on the other hand we can survive this summer, the colony is established. No sacrifice, not even 'coaxing' should be too great if it ensures survival." The other two don't reply to this.

Later that afternoon the great mass of settlers arrive at The Forks from Pembina and the subject is put aside. Each family has brought a month's provisions, to the leaders' relief.

A couple of days later, a delegation of colonists meets with Robertson, and he uses the meeting to explain why they should delay their understandable eagerness to claim their own homesteads. He says they listen attentively, and by the time the meeting breaks up, all agree, "except old Murray."

Pleased with himself, he finishes up some work and then goes over to see Semple and "communicate the happy change I had effected." But someone gets there ahead of him (old Murray?) because to his shock, the governor greets him with, "Mr. Robertson, Cameron could not have done more to ruin the Colony than you have done this morning. Explain yourself, Sir. You have been exciting fears in the minds of the settlers."

Stunned, Robertson replies, "No, Sir. I told them the truth. The Colonists are in danger if they are put upon their lands."

He can't bring himself to describe the rest of the conversation, merely recording, "After a . . . disagreeable altercation I left the Gentleman. I cannot remain in the Colony after this."

He describes his proposal: how the settlers could have been issued deeds to specific lots and "when the present storm was blown over" have the plowing they did on the earl's farm returned on theirs by the governor's plowmen. "None of the Emigrants could or would have objected against this. But the little success I have obtained over our opponents has excited a degree of contempt for the Enemy that to me is very alarming.

"I am indeed sick of this business. I mean to resign my position; things are going wrong and my temper is getting ruffled."

Who can blame him? With hindsight we can see his plan as an obvious solution. But Semple feels no need for defence, so sees it as alarmist overreaction. So on May 3,

> This morning, in a letter to Governor Semple, resigned my position. The Governor would not accept it.

This throws him into crisis:

> I strongly suspect that Mr. _____ is at the bottom of all this misunderstanding with Governor Semple. I am really at a loss how to act — if I leave this Colony and anything happens, blame may be attached to me; if I remain my plans will not be followed. What am I to do? Oh jealousy, you are the cause of many evils.

The blank presumably refers to Alex Macdonell. Jealousy from Macdonell over Robertson's influence with the governor — is this the root of all these conflicting messages from Fort Douglas? It certainly fits. Macdonell seems always to oppose Robertson without ever proposing an alternative strategy. It is not the strategy but the man that is his problem. Petty jealousy is a powerful — not to say powerfully dangerous — emotion.

Angry as he is, Robertson's loyalty to the settlement wins the day:

> I am really anxious to see this Settlement prosper. . . . Yes I must stay until this storm is blown over.

Seraphin Lamar shows up and tells Robertson that Alexander McDonell of the NWCo "wished an interview with me at Brandon House to settle all differences amicably — Stop Mr. McDonell! I know you!" Robertson is not about to be lured 200 kilometres from his fort to expose himself to capture by McDonell.

Semple agrees, but is deeply offended that the invitation was extended to Robertson rather than himself, and tells the Nor'Wester so in a letter: "I myself am on the spot and must alone be answerable both to friends and enemies." Another touchy rank-proud Englishman. Menacingly, or so he hopes, Semple adds, "I also, should I be compelled to it, have my schemes of farther and still farther retaliation, the shock of which should be felt from Athabasca to Montreal."

Sheer bravado, and McDonell will know it. He invited Robertson because it is Robertson he fears, and perhaps wants to arrest. Arresting the Grand and Most Excellent High Governor of the Hudson's Bay Territories is a bit steep, even for him.

This same day, May 3, "our" Alex Macdonell's mind is in a very different place:

> The Settlers have all gone to their lands, delighted with the prospects of being comfortable and I am not less so, having had them in charge from Britain until now, during which time they have suffered some inconvenience, tho' I cannot call it hardship.

An arresting statement, given that he is referring to months of travel by heaving ship and open boat, followed by winter in makeshift hovels, always cold and often hungry. No hardship at all.

On the day they are taken to their land, each family celebrates by planting a bushel of potatoes. They are a motivated group, but this is too early for prairie planting.

On May 4 Alex comments, "a great many Indians at the NWCo trading House encamped; all the free Canadians are also come from the plains. It is found necessary to strengthen the Guard."

And next day, "Piquash [Peguis], the Indian Chief arrived this morning together with his Brother . . . and they seemed to be very well disposed towards us."

Later: "Mr. Semple went into a Canoe and up the river for the first time in his life, to the other Fort." Responsible for the entire HBC Northern Department though he has never in his life been in a canoe. What were Selkirk and the London committee thinking?

Over at Occupied Fort Gibraltar, Peguis's visit is noted by Robertson: "Peegues the Indian Chief arrived this morning. A few [First Nations men] were prevailed upon by Cameron to come ask his liberty. Our Indians quarrelled with them, and had I not been present, something serious would have happened, our Indians being the most numerous."

Adding to his vexation and stress are Rogers and Holt, who have taken up residence at Gibraltar. They are too friendly with Cameron (and his liquor) on one side and too surly with Indigenous men on the other. He appeals to Semple to call them back to Fort Douglas, but Semple breezily replies that "Mr. Macdonell does not like them." So Robertson "must put up with them at the risk of offending men I wish to bring to our interest."

On May 8, he gets another sharp note from Semple. He has made the admittedly odd choice of entertaining Cameron to dinner. "I am told this gave offence to Governor Semple. Why does he not remove this man?" Then he adds, somewhat confusingly, "When we are among wolves, we must howl."

When Robertson happens to offend Rogers, Holt takes his friend's side and they both scold Robertson for showing more attention to

"Canadians" than to "Gentlemen." Robertson reminds them who is in charge and tells them, essentially, that they can like it or lump it — that is, return to Fort Douglas. Then he confides to his journal, "I feel for poor Rogers — his error proceeds from the head, not the heart." This is a generosity of spirit that he clearly can't communicate to Rogers, for the next day, "I this morning received a challenge from Mr. Rogers, which I treated with all the contempt it deserved." The exact grievance is not spelled out.

That afternoon, when Governor Semple, showing himself less and less suited for leadership, actually takes Rogers's part over his best officer's, he and Robertson "have words." Robertson decides he has to fight this boob, Rogers. He takes it wholly seriously, "resigning my situation," and spending much of the night putting his affairs in order, should the dice not roll his way.

Anticlimactically, he hears nothing from Rogers the next day until

> Holt waited on me this evening with a letter from Mr. Rogers postponing the affair until a future period. Holt was inclined to be insolent; I kicked him out of my room.
> How I am tormented by inexperienced people!

This is only aggravated by Semple's lack of support.

Robertson now shifts gears, in the way only he can among this lot, keeping his eye on the goal instead of overweening amour propre.

> We had a grand assemblage of Indians today at Gibraltar. Peegues and [Anishinaabe Chief] The Premier were the chiefs. In their harangues they blamed Cameron.

An outline survives of one speech. It is annotated "Handwriting of Mr. Shaw," a Nor'Wester, and seems to have been spoken in the presence of Duncan Cameron. The round brackets are in the original:

> Premier Speech to Governor Semple —
> Father I thank you for having come on our lands. These people here (pointing to Mr. Cameron), after having spoiled

our land, made us Pitiful. We who come far. I was never accustomed to clothe myself with skins. I have still a Son at Lac la Pluie whom they [the NWCo] keep in slavery . . . (Facing Mr. Cameron, proceeds thus) You who wished to call me Your Father, and when I saw you appear with your Regimental Dress I was not pleased, and foresaw it would not end well. You see the consequence of it today — I never approved your measures. You took against these people (the English).

Semple at one point addresses the Indigenous chiefs, with his characteristic charm. Robertson characterizes it as "excellent." He goes on, "I have met with few men in my life whose knowledge of human nature exceeds that of Governor Semple, but . . ." and here Robertson puts his finger on Semple's greatest weakness: not vanity, not ignorance, but indecisiveness, lack of resolve, or as Robertson puts it, "wavering in line of conduct which he himself has laid down."

Unfortunately, in contrast to Semple's "knowledge of human nature," Robertson seems to have a knack for alienating his colleagues and superiors,[2] despite his convincing and occasionally generous voice on paper.

While Robertson stews and puts the threat posed by the North West Company at the centre of his efforts, most of Alex Macdonell's entries during this time record crops sown, the weather (a cold May),[3] the repair of the schooner and the wonderful quality of Red River butter.

We who know what is coming may be reminded of the dancers in the ballroom of the Titanic as it steams obliviously into the ice field, with Robertson the boy in the crow's nest shouting warnings into the wind.

---

2   In later years, HBC Governor George Simpson, himself an irascible martinet, will loathe Robertson and characterize him as a "Romantic" who "fancies himself the hero of every Romance that passes through his hands."

3   Eighteen sixteen is famously The Year Without a Summer, due to the 1815 eruption of Mount Tambora in present-day Indonesia: en.wikipedia.org/wiki/Year_Without _a_Summer.

CHAPTER 28

COILED SPRING

MAY 11 TO JUNE 14, 1816

BRANDON HOUSE HBC POST, 200 KM WEST OF THE FORKS.

A round this time, Peter Fidler welcomes a boat from Fort Qu'Appelle carrying fifty-one bags of pemmican. In a letter, James Sutherland, chief trader at Qu'Appelle, tells him that these are interim provisions for The Forks in case his main convoy does not reach them in time, "for without provisions our people will be starved out and it is as yet uncertain what obstacles we may meet with."

Sutherland says he has several more boatloads of pemmican ready to depart, but the river is so shallow they will have to proceed slowly, and "a great number of Halfbreeds are collected here and I daresay will attack us."

The coming month will determine the fate of the Red River Settlement. No one now doubts that an attack is coming. How big, when and with what combatants is still a question. Reports and rumours abound. Cuthbert Grant is raising a Bois-Brûlé militia force, bringing men into posts across the prairies to hear rousing speeches on the threat to livelihood and freedom posed by the colonists. No one present can or will contradict these claims, and the Pemmican Proclamation seems to bear them out, so resentment blooms into hate across fur-trade country. Brûlé men who have barely heard of this tiny experiment are now convinced it must be obliterated, strictly on the word of the North West Company and its magnetic agent, Grant.

RED RIVER SETTLEMENT.

At The Forks, only Colin Robertson seems to grasp the magnitude of the threat. Against Brûlé skill, determination and rage, he knows, all the colony can hope to do is prepare a defence and hold out until the attackers exhaust themselves or Lord Selkirk arrives with an armed force. Robertson is confident they could do that, if only he could pierce the complacency of his fellow officers, and particularly the impenetrable smugness of Governor Robert Semple.

But he can't, and for Robertson, it's over. He's done all he can. Now, he can't wait to scrape the Red River gumbo off his boots. He dines with Semple and reports all their "little differences" settled. Robertson is to leave on Saturday, taking Cameron with him to Jack River. From there he will strike out for Cumberland House and his Athabasca brigade. Semple, for his part, has agreed to combine the two forts into one: "This will bid defiance to our opponents," Robertson reports hopefully, and then he suddenly interrupts this matter-of-fact journal entry with a cry from the heart:

> Oh that the Settlers were within the palisades of Fort Douglas
> — then all would be right!

He checks himself and records that Alex Macdonell called after his dinner with the governor to express dismay at Robertson's leaving at this juncture, as "everyone so looked up to me." This is an unfathomable statement from the man who has undermined him at every turn. "Is this man sincere in what he professes?" he asks the universe.

Then, typically if not predictably, Semple reverses himself, nullifies Robertson's resignation and requires him to stay. Robertson's only reaction is "All's well that ends well." Sarcasm? He unpacks his trunk.

He now ruminates daily — hourly — on what the Nor'Westers may be planning. The answer comes on May 16, proving Sutherland at Qu'Appelle right in his intuition. A horseman rides in with the news that McDonell and the Nor'Westers have ambushed the pemmican flotilla and seized everything but the boat that had been sent ahead with fifty-one bags. They have also taken the boatmen, including officers, hostage.

Robertson sends for Alex Macdonell to propose immediate retaliation. He suspects Duncan Cameron is behind this, hoping to be released in exchange for the provisions and men. Robertson wants to do the opposite — send him off out of NWCo reach. For once Macdonell agrees.

The pemmican is key to Robertson's plan to weather a siege in Fort Douglas. He is relieved when the fifty-one bags arrive on a boat from Brandon. They provide a little breathing room.

Next morning, Semple comes to see him, "embarrassed and very undecided how to act." Robertson reassures Semple he is going nowhere until this is solved. Semple, relieved, confirms that Duncan Cameron will be transported north under guard. Robertson moves into action.

Fearing that the seizure of the pemmican is the precursor to an attack, he orders the freemen and Indigenous families who are camped near the fort to move across the river. He fears that attackers would use their lodges for cover and "in returning the fire accidents might happen to the natives, which I wish to avoid."

Hearing that Cameron, in preparation for being taken away, has given his personal pistols to Rogers, who has promised to return them in London, Robertson goes to Rogers and takes them for himself, along with Cameron's sword.

Cameron is put into a boat with an armed detail and sent north to await the ship for Britain. He will not be back.

Robertson's appropriation of Cameron's private property offends Semple, and he sends Bourke over to bring the pistols to him. Robertson declines, citing his need for self-defence until affairs "assume a tranquil appearance." After which point he will deliver both sword and pistols to Lord Selkirk, not Mr. Semple. He makes it sound firm but reasonable.

Alex Macdonell calls this response "unpleasant" toward Semple and his sensibilities. Robertson's apparent lack of tact, especially when he is being righteous, must be hard to bear.

By May 20 it is clear the Robertson-Semple relationship has frayed beyond repair. Both men profess "hurt" at the other's attitude. In Robertson's journal entry for that day, we hear his inner monologue clearly and can imagine him tossing in his bed as the words spin round and round in his head.

The Governor talks of his feelings and the sacrifices he has made.

Did Gov. Semple come out to this Country on a mission the remuneration of which was to be estimated by the extent of his services? No!

Did he bring an Expedition from Canada of considerable magnitude through the Enemy's Country without receiving any assistance from the Hon'ble HBC's officers? No!

Did Governor Semple find a Settlement destroyed on his arrival in this Country and the Settlers on their way to England? No!

Did Governor Semple take back these few Settlers and re-establish them on the lands they had been driven from only two months before? No!

Did he with a handful of men twice take possession of the Enemy's Fort and thwart the plans of our opponent? No!

Did he provide for the subsistence of nearly two hundred souls in an Enemy's Country without an ounce of English Provisions? No!

Governor Semple found all this done by me whom only a few days ago he told, "that Cameron could not have done more to destroy the Colony than I had done."

All this was accomplished by one who was only obliged to lead the Expedition from Montreal and then return to England to his friends and connexions. It is he who has made sacrifices and great ones.

Wrote Governor Semple in the evening.

Colin Robertson's midnight rant. (Library and Archives Canada, Selkirk Papers, p. 17529)

Exhausting. Of course, none of what he lists means that Robertson is always right, but he is certainly justified in feeling that they make him and his advice deserving of respect. Semple writes back without addressing the points in Robertson's letter. "How cautious this Gentleman writes," says Robertson, "and how evasive."

Fidler writes, happy to report that all the captured Qu'Appelle men have been released except Pierre Pambrun and Mr. Bird's son.

He adds, "Bostonais seems to have been a principal instigator in seizing our Provisions at Qu'Appelle." This is a blow to Robertson's strategy; he'd hoped Bostonais Pangman, the buffalo hunter, had crossed over to his side. Either he was deceiving himself, or arrest by Macdonell and Bostonais's subsequent detention undid all Robertson's work.

He visualizes the campaign the Nor'Westers will employ. Alexander McDonell will

> form a strong camp near the Colony and . . . commence the
> business of [subversion] again. His Black Allies will harass
> the Colonists; some he will take prisoner, these he will treat

well — this will excite dissatisfaction. Alarming reports are circulated and at last a free passage is offered to Canada to relieve them from the terrors of this barbarous Country.

Everything that has happened before supports this scenario, but the "Gentlemen at Fort Douglas" remain unconvinced.

Indeed, our Alex Macdonell has been focussing on his people, barely perturbed by Robertson's alarms. They are happy with the country but understandably disturbed by the Nor'Westers' threats. Some men want to go out and recover the pemmican by force, but Alex advises them to "do their duty and take care of their families."

Robertson fires John Bourke as storekeeper, following complaints about Bourke's practices. "Accusations came tumbling in by the dozen," writes Robertson, "which time would not permit me to investigate, but I really believe [Bourke] does not stand A-1 in point of honesty." Bourke, says Macdonell, is not happy at all.

On May 23, all the movable property in Gibraltar is shifted over to Fort Douglas — henceforth Gibraltar will be simply a "military post." Next day is spent "training my men to defend their respective posts when attacked — the poor fellows are willing in the cause."

On May 25, the recently released captives from Qu'Appelle arrive at The Forks. They describe the NWCo ambush:

> The boats were descending a shallow rapid [on the Souris River] when two of the craft were stove in. While our people were repairing this damage, fifty of the Halfbreeds, Canadians and freemen sprang from the bushes and seized the arms of the men.

This story of ambush infuriates the ordinary settlers. Alex Macdonell reports that they are eager now to attack the North West post at Portage la Prairie to reclaim the pemmican. The proposal gets as far as forty men volunteering to go under Robertson's command before further "mature consideration" leads to postponement until they get more information on the target fort.

According to Robertson, who has been involved from the start, the action was postponed because after agreeing to everything, the vacillating Mr. Semple decided he must "hear from above" before proceeding.[1] Robertson is predictably exasperated: "I wish Governor Semple had thought of this before the men were put under arms. This Gentleman . . . has shown of late a great want of decision. . . . He is misled by the false representation of his officers."

Whatever the process, their mature consideration probably saved many lives, both their own and Nor'Westers'.

These aggravations, distracting as they are, don't blind Robertson to progress in the colony. One day he rides down the full length of the colony and is "charmed and highly pleased" with what he sees the people have accomplished. He runs into Governor Semple, who is feeling the same way. They speak amiably and Robertson observes,

> When I am alone with Governor Semple everything is right; he pays attention, and I think considerable deference to my opinions. When absent it is quite the reverse; he attaches too much consequence to the officers under him.

On June 2, Robertson has to intervene with Alex Macdonell on behalf of a colonist. Robertson had promised the widow McLean a calf — why, he doesn't say — and Macdonell is refusing to honour it. Robertson knows this will mean trouble, as "this family is much respected."

"I am really sick of contending with people of no experience," he complains, not for the first time.

Sure enough, when the news spreads among the people, Robertson is besieged with requests that promises he made to each of them be put into writing. "This I have complied with," he sighs, "They are of a trifling nature." Trifling or not, they push him over the edge: "I

---

1   I am not sure what "above" means here. It usually means the boss at York Factory, but Semple is the supreme governor now, so who or what is he waiting on?

am now determined to leave this place. I am harassed and tormented between the old Colonists, Mr. Macdonell and the Governor who [sides with Macdonell]."

It is King George's birthday, and he summons the guard to mark it. "They fired three volleys. Gave them a glass — took an extra one myself, not only for the King, but to drown my own cares."

Alex Macdonell marks this day, too, writing, "the Officers dined together, Mr. Robertson excepted." He notes, "Messrs. Holte and Rogers very <u>drunk</u>."

A sobering letter arrives from Brandon House. Peter Fidler writes to Semple:

> The [first of June], about 48 Halfbreeds with a few Canadians all on horseback entered our yard with guns presented. They then shut the gates to prevent any of us from going out.

They wrecked the place, breaking down doors, threatening people and "plundering." The men hid their powder and ball ammunition, but the invaders found it "and they carried it away in great triumph." Only the furs were left in the Brandon House storerooms. Then they forced everyone out of the fort under threat of burning it down.

They talk of driving the colonists from Red River, he warns, and advises Semple to post a watch at some distance to warn him "when the ½ breeds arrive [at Red River]." He counts fifty-two men.

On June 9, Alex Macdonell writes, "Mr. Robertson preparing to go away."

This time he truly is, at what seems the moment he is most needed. It has been an exceptionally trying few days, even for this place. That extra dram he needed on the king's birthday was only the beginning.

Three days later, Peguis complained to him of the treatment his people were receiving at Fort Douglas. Of all the people to misuse and alienate, these should be the last.

The day after that the colonists, hearing Robertson intended to leave, came and beseeched him to stay until "the present troubles are over." When he won't agree, a number, including widow McLean's family, say they will leave with him. "This places me in a very awkward situation with the Governor."

On June 10, he almost relents again. An Indigenous messenger arrives from Brandon House with the news that "the NWCo are coming in force, say eighty halfbreeds and sixty Canadians and will be here in a few days." He writes Semple that his "duty to Lord Selkirk" forces him to stay until this storm is over. He urges consolidating their defence by combining the forts into one. Semple sends back his agreement, so Robertson, at Fort Gibraltar, heads over to Fort Douglas to discuss details, "leaving Mr. McLean in charge."

At Fort Douglas, the two men agree to pull down the palisade at Gibraltar and re-erect it around their own fort. John Bourke and a party set out to begin the work of dismantling, but Robertson neglects to send notice over to McLean — a mistake.

Some time later, as Semple and Robertson are still discussing details in Semple's room, Bourke arrives in a red fury. Bursting in with a cocked pistol, he puts it to Robertson's chest and shouts, "You scoundrel! You nearly had me murdered!"

Taken aback, both men are speechless. Feigning a calm he does not feel, Robertson turns to the governor. "Sir, Mr. Bourke is fortunate — this is the first time I have ever left the Fort without being armed."

At this Robertson gets up and walks out. Bourke follows him, still waving the pistol and demanding Robertson fight a duel with him. "I answered that a cowardly assassin was not entitled to that privilege." He then delivers an ultimatum to Semple: either Bourke leaves tomorrow or I do.

He then goes back to Gibraltar and gets the story from McLean — Bourke had appeared with his party and begun "to break down the House." McLean ordered him to stop until Robertson returned, at which point Bourke said he cared not a damn for Mr. Robertson and went on "pulling at the planks." McLean and others took him bodily and threw him out.

Sixty men[2] immediately go to Semple and demand that Bourke be discharged. When he declines they "pile their arms alongside the House." Robertson's fifteen-member guard is about to do the same, but he stops them. Miserable, he writes the governor to send someone to take over the fort because he is determined "to remain no longer." Semple makes no reply.

In Alex Macdonell's journal he reports Robertson's request to "quit the river" and Semple's objection. He does not connect Robertson's wish to leave with the lack of support he gets from himself and Semple. Whose fault is this? Are they wooden-headed, or is Robertson too impatient and imperious to explain, to plead his case rather than demand it? These are not stupid men, just inexperienced and proud.

On June 11, departure day, Semple comes across to take over Fort Gibraltar. Robertson is having a terrible day. He is moving from one room to another to avoid some angry colonists who are determined to leave with him. When Semple finds him Robertson says, "O Dear me, Governor Semple, what part of my conduct warrants this treatment?"

"I have suspended Bourke from his duty," replies the governor.

"Is this all, after the outrage he has committed?"

"But Mr. Robertson, you wrote me yesterday that you would stay on Lord Selkirk's account."

"Would you have me [dine] with a man that attempted to assassinate me?"

Semple has no answer, so moves on. "Well, do not take Widow McLean's family with you."

"No Sir, don't you see that I wish to avoid them?"

"I would do anything to reconcile them to [stay]."

Robertson sends for the widow and her three sons, waiting for him on the riverbank. When they come, the governor, seeming "much affected," promises to make things right for them. They relent, and go to unload their baggage.

---

2   Sixty! This is reported by Robertson. It cannot include settlers or he would have said it. This must be HBC and RRS servants, plus the men who have come here from Qu'Appelle after the ambush.

At the dock, Semple takes Robertson's hand and pleads, "Don't leave me Mr. Robertson, I entreat you, on Lord Selkirk's account. Think seriously what you are about to do." But this time Robertson cannot bring himself to put duty before personal pride. By his own account so overcome that he can't speak, he steps into his boat. His men cast off.

As he comes opposite Fort Douglas, he says, "Peegues and the Red Lake Chief came to the Boat and entreated me to remain, but my faithful Swede pushed off the boat saying, 'No, if you remain they will kill you.'" They row on.

Neither Semple nor Macdonell is happy but they are perhaps relieved. "All the officers quarrelled with him," writes Alex, "myself excepted, so that he left no person to regret his departure except Mr. McLean whom had always been on good and intimate terms."

Down the river at a spot called, appropriately, Reflection Bay, Robertson awakes next day full of second thoughts, "my spirits much depressed."

> I thus reason with myself — Shall I return and be obliged to suffer further indignities from these unexperienced men? If they are unanimous and prudent, the NWCo will never attack them in their Fort. But the contempt with which they treat the enemy is what alarms me the most. After taking all these things into consideration, I ordered my men to return back.

And he does, dispatching two men on horses to Semple's fort. He warns his men he might return and, "they all seem willing to return with me. It is astonishing to see their attachment to the Colony."

AT FORT DOUGLAS.

Alex Macdonell notes Robertson's letter, "signifying his desire to return if it was agreeable." Then next day he records proudly, "[The Governor] wrote Mr. Robertson that . . . he might do as he pleased, but that he had appointed me in Charge of the Colony in all cases during his absence until the Earl of Selkirk's pleasure be known." The self-satisfaction in this report suggests that jealousy has indeed been behind his opposition to Robertson.

REFLECTION BAY.

Robertson gets Semple's reply, "thanking me for my offer, but seeing no good that could result from my presence." He is hurt:

> I must confess I feel grieved and disappointed with the answer — how could I even dream of such an answer after what passed between us the day we parted. This adds one more to the many proofs this Gentleman is governed by the opinions of others.

He then lists the characteristics of these "others":

> Macdonell — the best of the bunch but inexperienced.
> Rogers — addicted to liquor, intolerant of anyone not English.
> Holt — a man of no principle.
> White — no talent for the intrigues of our opponent.
> Pritchard — his volatile disposition makes him unfit.
> Bourke — courageous but without honest principle.
> McLean — if only his judgement were equal to his courage.

Only Pierre Pambrun and the HBC man John McLeod are judged worthy, but they are off taking Cameron to Jack River. He can't understand how men as inferior as these turn a man of Semple's judgment against him. "He knew my views and made me acquainted with his — indeed we unbosomed ourselves to each other without reserve."

With that, Robertson and company sail off north, leaving the colony to its fate. But the colony does not leave Robertson; two days later he writes, "What will be the fate of the Colony is a thought never absent from my mind. Our opponents are certainly bent on its destruction, but . . ."

On he goes, chewing over all the possibilities. He finally comforts himself that Semple's fort is impregnable and has provisions for a month, and the NWCo cannot afford its business being delayed that long. "I am strongly of the opinion that some arrangement will take place favourable to the Colony." So it might have, had he stayed or had Semple the good judgment to listen to him. As it is, he has probably just saved his own life, but not in a way he could know at this point.

On the positive side, now that they are on the lake in a breeze, "we have no moschettos tonight."

THE FORKS.

Unaware that they have sealed their own doom, the Children of Empire proceed with unwarranted fearlessness. If they'd had a Doomsday Clock in 1816, its hands would be seconds from midnight.

PART IV

ROBERT SEMPLE

CHAPTER 29

"THIS DAY I SHALL
REMEMBER"

JUNE 19, 1816

FORT DOUGLAS, RED RIVER SETTLEMENT.

A s the Doomsday Clock closes on midnight, Alex Macdonell strikes the hours:

On June 15,

> Putting up the Bastion this day. . . . No sign of the half Breeds, but it is feared they may appear before we can have up the Stockades.

June 16,

> Fine warm weather. The crops look remarkably well. Rode this morning to see the Settlers and prepared them to join us in the Fort.

June 17,

> At 5 O'clock this evening, four riders were seen in the plains, going toward the Frog Plain, in consequence of which Messrs. Bourke and Holte with some men were sent in pursuit, but night coming on they could not trace them.

Mustuch,[1] an Indian, arrived from the Brandon House and stated that the NWCo half Breeds and Canadians would take five days before they could be here. . . . This evening it was thought advisable to call the Settlers into the Fort in consequence of a surmise that the enemy was near at hand. It was necessary now to put ourselves in as good a state of defence as circumstances could admit of, though the Stockades could not be put up for four or five days.

Our ordnance and small arms are in pretty good condition to defend, but the misfortune of an Open Fort with numerous women and children is a matter of serious consideration, but our men are all faithful and it is hoped we have nothing to fear.

Did not put off any part of my clothes for seven nights, but constantly on watch, a duty for every person concerned with the Colony.

June 18,

Busy all this day making entrenchments round the Fort and putting up the Stockades, confused with women and children.

Next day, June 19, Alex gives us the only spontaneous and immediate report of the day that anyone will ever see.[2] He begins his journal entry with the understatement of his life:

1   Elsewhere spelled Moustouche or Moustuche Bat[t]ineau or Botino. He is a Brûlé, not First Nations, on good terms with the HBC. He warns that fifty to seventy men are on their way to Red River.

2   What follows is the day as seen by the settlers. For the Métis point of view, I recommend Jean Teillet's book, *The North-West Is Our Mother* (Patrick Crean Editions, 2019). Teillet makes a genuine attempt at a fair and balanced telling from the Métis standpoint, though, like every one of us, including me, she has to choose which so-called facts and claims to accept, reject or emphasize. I do not fully agree with her choices, but I do respect the points she makes. Accommodation must be made if genuine reconciliation is ever to be achieved.

This day I shall remember while I live —

About 4 O'Clock in the afternoon, a great many horsemen were seen in the plains about two miles from this Fort. Having no doubt they were the North West Company half Breeds and Canadians, the men were got under arms. Some of the settlers were working upon their farms . . .

The Governor called all Volunteers in order that he might ascertain what these riders wanted, at the same time expressing his anxiety about the settlers that were absent. He went off with about 26 of our best men [including] six Officers and left me in charge of the Fort.

Others will put the first sighting at 5 or 6 p.m., but it makes little difference, sunset being at about 8:10 p.m. solar time.

Alex Macdonell's journal on the night of Seven Oaks.
(Library and Archives Canada, Selkirk Papers, pp. 18051–52)

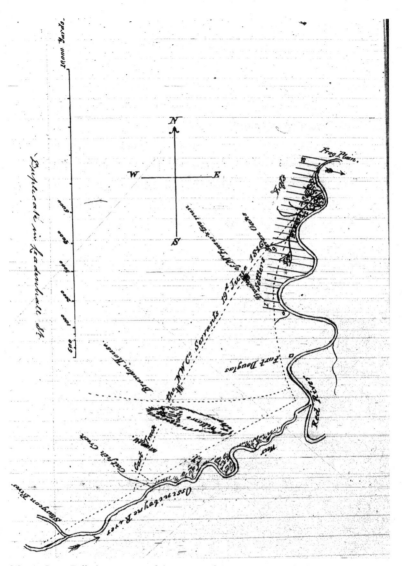

Map 9. Peter Fidler's 1817 map of the events of June 19, 1816. (Library and Archives Canada, Selkirk Papers, p. 3910)

The passing group is comprised of sixty to eighty armed and mounted fighters, accompanied by two carts carrying bags of pemmican and other supplies. The horsemen, under the command of Cuthbert Grant, have ridden from the North West post at Portage la Prairie, just as all the warnings predicted. Their supplies were sent down the

Assiniboine by boat. At the mouth of Catfish Creek (now Omand's Creek), they met and transferred the supplies to the cart. Now they are making their way to Frog Plain at the northern boundary of the settlement, where they will set up camp. The plan is for the armed party to move down after dark to surround Fort Douglas and either take it in a surprise attack tomorrow or besiege it as long as necessary to starve the occupants into submission, shooting or capturing anyone who comes out until they surrender. It is a straightforward plan that would almost certainly have worked if they had been able to pull off the surprise, especially since the fort's wall is incomplete, making it unable to withstand a siege.

They are intending to use rising ground to shield them from the settlers' sight, but marshy conditions have forced them too close to the fort. They are in fact much less than two miles away.

(Notions advanced in later years that they are merely trying to get pemmican around the settlement's blockade guns have no merit. No one at the time denies the attack plan, and they have only enough pemmican — no more than twenty bags,[3] and most reports say less — to feed themselves for the time they have allowed for their plan to succeed. The myth of running the blockade will be invented years in the future.)

In the event, according to much sworn testimony on both sides, John Farquharson will say:[4]

> I was on watch . . . when I saw a party of horsemen with a few Carts crossing the plain towards the Settlement. They were nearly opposite Fort Douglas at a considerable distance, so it was only when they crossed over a rise that we could distinctly make them out, whereupon we immediately alerted the Governor that the Halfbreeds were coming.

---

3   *Report on the Disturbances in the Indian Territories*, also known as the Coltman Report, p. 166. See Chapter 32 for more information.

4   This and other quotes are taken from sworn affidavits. It is probable that some were originally given in Gaelic.

Governor Semple, Alex Macdonell, John Rogers, John Pritchard and John Bourke go to the roof of a barn and study the riders through a "glass." The riders are crossing left to right, about three kilometres or less from the fort, and all agree they are armed with spears and muskets.

Scrambling down from the roof, Semple immediately calls for twenty men to collect their arms and join him. He is going to confront the riders to "find out what they are." All snatch up muskets. Alex McLean straps on his sword. In addition to his double-barrelled "fowling piece" (shotgun), Semple sticks two pistols into the long green sash around his waist. Some men, at least, fix bayonets to their barrels. Other men — there are between forty and fifty present — volunteer to join the sortie party, but Semple cuts that short. Everyone else must stay to defend the fort. Alex Macdonell says he "begged [Semple] to allow me to go with the men and for him to stay at the Fort. . . . But he maintained that there was no danger. . . . I requested he bring the 3 pounder Field piece. This he would not wait for."

In a few minutes, Semple, twenty men, and six officers including Holt, Rogers, Bourke, Pritchard, Wilkinson and Dr. White, as well as Alex McLean, strike out from Fort Douglas to confront the enemy, not a trace of a plan between them except to "see what they are about" and to make sure the few settlers out working their fields are safe.

Semple seems to be doing his best to confirm Colin Robertson's opinion of him: indecisive, ill-advised and at the mercy of the wind. What is in his head? Given the alarms, rumours and reports of the past weeks, he knows there are only two possibilities: the Nor'Westers intend to sneak their contraband pemmican around him onto the Red River and thence to Lake Winnipeg and out of Assiniboia; or they are planning an attack on the colony.

How does his present action address either? Is he intending to challenge sixty or seventy armed plainsmen and confiscate their pemmican with a few feebly armed clerks, farmers and labourers? Ditto for protecting his colonists. Does he think his band of weekend warriors will deter or delay any plan of attack?

Or do we take him at his word, that he really just wants to know what they are about? If so, why the posse and why on foot? This simply cannot end with him triumphant.

One has to conclude that he believes his status as a colonial governor, bestowed by a boardroom of perfumed gents in London, plus his class rank as a wealthy, educated gentleman, will be sufficient to awe these rubes into submission.

Could Robertson's assessment possibly have been more correct? Which prompts the question: What would Colin Robertson do? His plan to weather a siege would not survive an open fort. We will never know.

SETTLERS' FARMS, NORTH OF FORT DOUGLAS.

Alex McBeath (now McBeth) is working in the potato cellar on his lot, "the third beyond Alexander McLean's,"[5] when his son comes suddenly comes in and says "the Halfbreeds and North West" are coming. Whereupon, according to his deposition,

> I went to the door and saw a large party of horsemen and carts crossing the plains and these horsemen coming down to my Lot in consequence of having seen my fire. The horsemen came up and asked me where Mr. Macdonell the Sheriff was on which my son answered he is gone to the Frog Plain and being asked whether he was certain, he answered "Yes, he is gone for fish," whereupon they rode off and I, my Wife and Son escaped towards the Fort and were joined by William Sutherland, his Wife and some of their children.

Whether his son believes what he says or is simply trying to misdirect the questioner, he certainly gives his family time to escape.

---

5   Approximately where St. John's Cathedral now stands.

Settlers farther north are not so lucky. William Bannerman, seventeen, and his 15-year-old brother, Alex, are planting turnips on their father's lot,

> about half a mile from Frog Plain, when about 5 in the after-
> noon the alarm was given that the halfbreeds were coming.
> I saw three men on horseback, so I hastened to get down to
> the Fort for protection, along with my brother and Alexander
> Murray and his Wife but had not gone far when I saw five men
> on horseback coming in pursuit from Frog Plain. They soon
> overtook us. . . . As they caught us, Alexander Murray's wife
> [Elizabeth, 54] fell down from fear. Some were painted like
> Indians in red and black and all were armed with Guns, long
> spears, Pistols and Knives. One spoke pretty good English. I
> said they had no right to stop us but he replied that there were
> 200 halfbreeds and Indians in the Plains and that we would
> be killed if we tried to reach the Fort, so we must go with
> them to Frog Plain. They asked if Mr. Colin Robertson was in
> the Fort. Someone said he had left for York Factory ten days
> before. Then we were obliged to go as their prisoners to Frog
> Plain. There, we were put into the tent of a Freeman named
> Bellegarde and watched by a halfbreed.

Alexander Sutherland's encounter is even more hair-raising. The 26-year-old's misgivings about working his lot that day, "about the 12th or 13th from Fort Douglas[6] or about a mile and a half south of Frog Plain," were put to rest earlier in the day

> when Messrs. Wilkinson and Holt came riding in from the
> plains and stopped to tell me they did not believe that the
> Halfbreeds were coming that day. They then rode off toward
> the Fort.
>
> Less than ¾ hour after they left, I was working my pota-
> toes when I was taken by surprise by five Halfbreeds, one (Alex

---

6   Actually Lot 10, according to Fidler's list.

Fraser) coming directly up from the riverbank while the others came from the west . . . I threw my hoe into the bush and made to escape when Fraser called, "Kill that damned rascal on the spot! I saw him throw his gun into the bush." Several immediately presented their spears to my body to do so, but another replied, "No no, don't kill him — it wasn't a gun, just a hoe." Their faces were horridly painted like Indians going to war, black with streaks of red.

Fraser demanded what had become of Mr. Colin Robertson. I said he was gone to York Factory. Fraser replied, "You're telling a damned lie now." He threatened that if I didn't tell the truth I would be put to instant Death. I repeated what I had said, and Fraser said they would keep me until they had got hold of the Gentlemen at the Fort, when they would find out my damned lies and punish me.

I asked one of them who spoke English what was his name and he said, "My name is an Indian and you do not know me." Then they took me to the cart track and brought me to Frog Plain. On the way we met another party of Halfbreeds armed with Spears, Swords and Guns and painted as the others. . . . They said that if they could catch Robertson, they would skin him alive and make dried meat of his flesh. My repeated answer that he had gone to York Factory made them angry all over again. At last I told them to kill me at once if that would make them happy, but stop continually poking my breast with spears. Several were preparing to take me at my word and would have killed me but for the one who spoke English [who stopped them].

They take him to their encampment at Frog Plain, "where I was put into Lavendure's tent where I found Alexander Murray and his wife, also prisoners."

Meanwhile, Semple and company, striding purposefully northward, encounter the McBeath and Sutherland families, running for the fort.

According to McBeath, a veteran of the 73rd Regiment of Foot (later the Black Watch),

> On observing that the Governor had twenty to thirty men with him, I remarked that the North West Co. were very numerous and that he would do well to take two field pieces with him and keep his back to the River to avoid being surrounded and I offered if I could have a gun to go out with him, to which the Governor replied, "No no there is no occasion. I am only going to speak to them," whereupon I went on to the Fort with my Wife and Sutherland and his family. We were over-taken on the way by [John] Bourke whom the Governor had ordered to go back for one of the Great Guns. . . . We all entered the fort together.

The governor seems to come partially to his senses after hearing the veteran's advice. He sends Bourke back for a cannon and as many more men as Macdonell thinks he can spare. The troop settles down to await Bourke's return, but after an unspecified interval (during which no one reports any conversation on strategy or tactics) Semple orders them forward again. We can only surmise that he truly does not expect matters to go beyond words.

What is going through the minds of these men, hurrying along a dusty cart track with their heavy muskets, sweating in the heat of late afternoon? Many must know just how far their fighting skills fall short of those of mounted buffalo hunters. Later reports say that some have as little as two rounds of ammunition, others ten. Likely, they just see themselves as a symbolic show of force in support of their governor, who has their complete and thoroughly undeserved trust.

When a gunshot explodes in their midst, everyone ducks, some spinning about to find the ambush or the target. But there is none — it is merely Ener Holt, whose tension has expressed itself through his trigger finger, accidentally firing into the air. No harm done, except to nerves. Semple snaps at him, in the words of Michael Hayden, "very much displeased and told Mr. Holt that he should be more careful or he might kill somebody." On they go.

(Take a moment here to imagine bumbling Lawrence Wilkinson, probably the most terrified one of the bunch. He must be thanking fate that it was Holt and not he who disgraced himself.)

They reach Lot No. 7, about three to four kilometres from Fort Douglas. A copse of trees blocks the view ahead and when they round it, *there they are*, about sixty of them, directly ahead, many minutes and miles closer than expected.

A sobering sight: mounted warriors, some in warpaint, many carrying spears or lances in addition to muskets and pistols. Nonetheless, stalwarts that they are, the colony men move toward the advancing force, led by Semple. At this point, according to Michael Hayden, Michael Kilkenny mutters, "We shall all be shot. . . . If you will give me leave, (speaking to the Governor) I will take down Cuthbert Grant, their leader." Governor Semple reacts angrily, "I want no firing at all!" Hayden, it must be said, has a flexible memory for the truth, but John Pritchard reports something similar, though in his account the offer is made by James Bruin and Semple rounds on whole the group, snarling, "'Who could be such a rascal as to make such a proposition?' . . . Mr. Semple was very much displeased indeed."

As the groups converge, the Nor'Westers, mainly Bois-Brûlés with some "Canadians" and even two or three First Nations men, divide into two columns, one going to the left of Semple's party, one to the right. When they stop, they form a half-moon around the colonists, who stand about in no particular order and try to look stern while, unless human nature has changed radically in the last two centuries, fairly jumping out of their skins.[7]

They are cooked. Outnumbered, outgunned and, as fighters, hopelessly outclassed. The outcome is clear before it begins. The only sane strategy is to give the Nor'Westers no possible excuse to get into it. Here is where Semple's leadership and negotiating skills face their true

---

7 This spot is marked by a cairn at Rupertsland and Main Street, as near the battlefield as any of its sponsors could estimate in 1891.

test, devoid of any spin added by Colin Robertson or Alex Macdonell. Any rational person would now shift into honest-broker mode: "Hey gents, no need to get belligerent here. We just want to know what you want. Let's talk. Mr. Grant, sir! Can we parley?"

Alas, Semple's rationality takes a leave of absence when entitlement and haughty self-regard are at stake.

A "Canadian" named François Boucher (Bouché) leaves the ranks and canters forward toward Robert Semple.

Why Boucher? He will say later that his friends urged him, saying he "spoke a little English" so he should "see what they wanted that they came after us." But their leader is Cuthbert Grant and his first language is English, making him the obvious spokesman. Had it been Grant, something of a "gentleman" in manners, Semple's response may have been tempered, but instead it is this . . . this . . . this *bumpkin*, riding forward like an equal.

Their exchange is reported by at least two colonists who agree in their recollections (which does not equate to its being accurate):

> Boucher: What do you want?
> Semple: What do you want?
> Boucher: We want our fort!
> Semple: Go to your fort, then.
> Boucher: You damned scoundrel! You have destroyed our fort!

To which Semple, with stunningly disastrous judgment, responds, "You damned rascal! You dare tell me so?" and grabs Boucher's bridle. Or his gun. Or both in succession. He calls on his followers to take Boucher prisoner. His first negotiating opportunity and he throws it aside without hesitation. This has the distressing ring of truth. Semple's pomposity is his, and therefore everyone's, undoing.

Fairness demands we hear Boucher's somewhat different memory of the event:

> I rode up quietly and before I got close to Governor Semple I
> asked what they wanted that they pursued us. I told him we

were afraid he meant us harm. Some other words passed. He laid hold of my bridle and he then laid hold of my gun. I told him I had not come out to fight. He called out to some of his people to take that rascal prisoner. Some of them came up to me with guns and bayonets in a threatening manner and I called out to them, "Prenez Garde!" At this time my people came up. Seeing our people advance they cried out, "We are all dead men! My god we are all dead men!" Governor Semple called out, "You damned rascals, this is no time to be afraid!"

Not quite the same ring of truth, but take your choice.[8] At any rate, the take-him-prisoner part is commonly agreed. Boucher's sensible response is to leap off his horse before anybody can lay hands on him and run back to his lines. But then —

BANG!

The crack of a musket. It is *on*!

---

8   This is taken from sworn testimony at a trial in Upper Canada in 1818. In another telling by Boucher it is he who says, "You are all dead men."

CHAPTER 30

GUNFIGHT

JUNE 19 TO JULY 6, 1816

FORT DOUGLAS, RED RIVER SETTLEMENT.

Bourke stands panting, having raced back for a cannon on the governor's orders, and more men. Macdonell gives him a cannon with a cart to carry it, but will spare no man except the carter, Hugh McLean. They leave immediately, Bourke riding the horse, McLean in the cart.

When they reach the spot where Bourke had left the party and find no one waiting, they crack on in hot pursuit. At last Semple and party come into sight, and — hellzapoppin! In Bourke's restrained language, he "saw that the party of horsemen had surrounded the Governor and [I] distinguished the flash of guns firing. Fearing that we might be killed we thought it prudent to carry the cannon back to the fort. . . . Part way back I met and joined about 10 men from the Fort, sending the cannon on without me," and turned back.

Once more into the breach . . .

Nobody will ever pinpoint who fired that first shot, but consensus, such as it is, says it came from the colonists' side. Only Michael Hayden will insist otherwise, but his testimony will be demolished by a skillful lawyer.

The next shot, however, is well documented. It comes from the horsemen's side, hits Ener Holt, master and commander of the colonial navy, and kills him dead. Close on its echo comes another, and Semple himself goes down, shot in the knee.[1] Michael Hayden is nearby on his right. Semple, says Hayden,

> immediately cried out to his men, "Do what you can to take care of yourselves," but instead of seeking their own safety, [they] crowded round the Governor to ascertain what injury he had received, and while they were thus collected in a small Body in the Centre, the [horsemen] fired a general volley amongst them, by which a greater part were killed on the spot. The persons who remained standing took off their hats and called for mercy[2] but in vain.

In another statement he says that some in the cluster around Semple fired at the horsemen until the volley decimated them.[3]

Hayden goes on,

> I was lying just a little to the right of the main party with Michael Kilkenny, George Sutherland and Donald McKay, who being at a distance did not close round the Governor but fought singly to defend themselves. I was on my knees reloading when Kilkenny called out to me to look around and scarcely a man was left not killed or wounded. After a few words we both endeavoured to escape, followed by Sutherland and McKay and also Mr. White the Surgeon. We were pursued by about six halfbreeds who kept firing and killed Mr. White

---

1   Later, Cuthbert Grant will tell Pritchard that he fired the shot that wounded Semple, but this is not established. There are many claims for this distinction.

2   Cuthbert Grant will later claim they were not calling for mercy but cheering, thinking they had won, a claim that makes absolutely no sense, common or otherwise, and that no one else ever suggests. (Coltman Report, p. 206)

3   Michael Hayden's deposition, July 20, 1817. (Coltman Report, p. 206)

at the last of the group.[4] Kilkenny and Sutherland outran us and swam across the River. McKay and I found a batteau in which we escaped.

John Pritchard, who had once declared that "fifty English were equal to two hundred halfbreeds,"[5] is now rapidly recalculating. He testifies,

I saw Sinclair and Bruin fall wounded or killed, and Mr. McLean a little in front defending himself but by a second shot I saw him fall. At this time I saw Captain Rogers getting up again. I called to him, Rogers for God's sake give yourself up, give yourself up. Capt. Rogers ran towards them calling out in English and broken French that he surrendered and praying for them to spare his life. Thomas McKay, a half breed, shot him through the head and another half breed ripped his belly open with a knife, using the most horrid imprecations.

When I saw Mr. Rogers fall I expected to share his fate. As there was a Canadian among those who surrounded me, I said "Lavigne! You are a Frenchman, you are a man, you are a Christian — for God's sake save my life! I give myself up. I am your prisoner." McKay, who was among this party said, you little toad what do you do here? I fully expected again that I would lose my life. I again appealed to Lavigne and he joined me in entreating them to spare me. . . . They struck at me with their guns; Lavigne caught some of the blows and joined me in entreating for my safety. . . . One Primeau wished to shoot

4   Nor'Wester descriptions have James White turning on the riders with his musket and being shot in self-defence. That an alcoholic sawbones would still be carrying a heavy gun, let alone have the sang-froid to stop and turn on someone trying to ride him down, does not pass the sniff test. Neither do colonist reports embroidering his death with descriptions of spearings and hackings a little too graphic and detailed to be noticed by men fleeing for their lives. On the other hand, Hayden's barebones description conforms to the Rule of the Hindmost (the devil takes him) and by that, seems most likely.

5   Coltman report, deposition of Francois Eno dit Delorme, an interpreter, p. 159.

me. He said I had formerly killed his brother. I begged him to recollect my former kindness to him at Qu'Appelle. At length they spared me, telling me I was a little dog and had not long to live, that he [Primeau? McKay?] would find me when he came back.[6]

I then went to Frog Plain, taken by Boucher. I was again threatened by one of the party and saved by Boucher who conducted me safe to Frog Plain. There I [later] saw Cuthbert Grant.

Back on the battlefield matters are already settled, not quite before they began but very shortly thereafter. The only colonial combatants remaining active are Bourke and his companions, running toward the sound of gunfire.

Bourke:

We started toward the place where the Governor was. We observed that the Horsemen who had surrounded him were now dispersed and scattered over the plains. We did not see the Governor or any of the men. I hesitated and then some of the hostile party cried out in English, "Come on, come on, here is the Governor. Won't you come and obey him." I advanced a little further when the same person cried out, "Give up your arms!" Apprehending that the Governor and his party had been destroyed and believing that it was the wish of the murderers to get me also into their hands I turned back to the ten men with me and we made all haste to escape. As we fled, I received a shot in my thigh and Duncan McNaughton was killed.

So the gunfire ends with a bullet in the back of a fleeing settler. The bloody field is quiet, except, presumably, for the moans of the

6   His reminders of kindness go back to when he was a clerk for the NWCo. His prior knowledge of these men undoubtedly saved his life.

wounded. These are quickly ended by summary execution, as members of Grant's party go from man to man, killing any who show signs of life. Semple is shot through the back of the head. Then they loot the bodies, take their clothes and, bizarrely, slash and mutilate the corpses. This is where battle, if there had been a battle, turns to massacre, the only descriptor it will carry in English for the next 150 years. The mutilation will be used to demonize the Bois-Brûlés for generations. By no means all of the horsemen take part in this, and unsurprisingly, no one will ever admit to it.

If the Brûlés removed their single fatality,[7] there are twenty corpses littered across the prairie. In addition to Semple and Holt, there is John Rogers, gentleman adventurer and racist bigot; and James White, whose most violent act, despite his weakness for alcohol, seems to have been his unsportsmanlike poke at the annoying Wilkinson. That poor sad sack, too, has now redeemed his honour with his life. Alex McLean, who survived so much over the past four years, has now died with his sword in his one good hand, leaving Christina and their children without a breadwinner.

The only officer to survive, apart from Alex Macdonell back at the fort, is John Bourke, wounded in the leg.

The rest of the dead, described simply as Servants, are less familiar, though we have run across Duncan McNaughton several times. Both he and James Bruin, who was prevented from sniping Cuthbert Grant, have been with the colony since the very beginning, never the object of any complaint. There is no evidence or reason to believe either one ever caused harm to a native-born person.

Revulsion in the face of callous slaughter is inevitable, and the settlers' descendants will indulge in generations of self-righteous rage that continues into our time. And certainly it was brutal to commit and remains painful to describe. But murder and looting on the battle-field are standard procedure in plains battles at this time and in warfare everywhere for all time before it. Not that this makes those committed

---

7 A man named Batoche (Coltman Report, p. 233). If that is not irony, I don't know what is.

at Seven Oaks any prettier, or less abhorrent. But neither were they unique or exceptional.

FORT DOUGLAS.

One can only imagine the reaction here. The dismay, the horror, the *panic*. Their fort has open walls and the buildings are a poor defence. No one has left us a description of that night, but we can guess. Some must have considered or even counselled fleeing across the river, perhaps giving the women and children into the reliable protection of the Anishinaabe or other First Nations. What about escaping in boats, south, up the river to Pembina and Fort Daer, away from the Nor'Westers? No time, no ready boats, no escape; how would they feed themselves, or defend themselves if caught? Really, their only option is to get everyone inside and prepare for attack.

Though there are less than six hours of total darkness, this night must seem endless, punctuated by staggered arrivals of survivors bringing blood-curdling tales to stoke fear. "John Forbes and Beth Beaton [a man] came from places they'd been hiding, as well as Michael Hayden, George Sutherland, Donald McKay and Michael Kilkenny, who had escaped across the river," reports John Farquharson, the day's watchman.

It is safe to say that no one over the age of ten will get a wink of sleep, and for excellent reason.

Alex Macdonell continues the journal entry quoted in the previous chapter. Again, this is the only account actually written on the day. After a brief but accurate description of events, he writes,

> I can only say that the Hudson's Bay Company lost one of the best men it ever had at the head of its affairs and his friends a most sincere and affectionate son and Brother. His father lives in the neighbourhood of Glasgow.
>
> I consider his loss to the Colony of the greatest consequence. . . . As for the other Gentlemen, they were all well

disposed men whose attachment to the Colony could not be surpassed.

Grief, in its rawest form. And no time to mourn.

At Frog Plain, Pritchard's struggle to survive continues. His claims of having his life threatened repeatedly are backed up by his fellow prisoner, the feisty Alex Sutherland, who will testify,

> Later that night, Half breeds and others of the North West Company returned with Mr. Pritchard and Anthony McDonald. Their lives were repeatedly threatened in the course of the evening, and some wanted to destroy all the prisoners. We were all saved at different times by Freemen's wives, Indian women, and especially the wife of Lavendure. And if Cuthbert Grant had not been there, the rest would certainly have followed through on their threats; [they] said that in preventing our murder, Mr. Grant was deviating from his orders. The man mentioned above who would not tell his name told me, "It was lucky for you that I was there or you would be dead now." He added that, "I have done well since I saw you — I killed five myself."
>
> Later that night we were offered food and Fraser told me, "While you are here you shall have something to eat and drink, which is more than we will allow them in the Fort. They may have provisions but it will be our fault if they get a drop of water out of the river." I heard them discussing how they would reduce the Fort by starvation, by shooting any person who ventured out for water or anything else. They would set the houses on fire by throwing arrows with lighted torchwood onto the roofs — I heard this from Grant and Fraser in particular. Fraser said, "Look what we've already done today and judge what we may do."

Pritchard reports Fraser making a remark that illustrates the cutting power of the casual racial slur:

Fraser added in French, "Mr. Robertson said that we were Blacks, and he shall see that our hearts will not belie the colour of our Bodies."

These people were greatly disappointed in not meeting with Mr. Robertson who (as they told me) they would have taken alive and after flaying him, they would have cut his body into small bits and boiled it for the dogs.

Evidently Colin Robertson did not win anything like the hearts and minds he thought he was winning. He misread the situation almost as badly as Semple.

Pritchard speaks to Grant at some length:

Cuthbert Grant told me they had not expected to meet us on the plains but that their intention was to have surprised the Colony and they would have hunted the Colonists like buffalo. They had [intended] to have got round unperceived at night, surrounded the Fort and shot everyone who left it, but being seen, their scheme was frustrated.

Grant said he spoke to Mr. Semple after he was wounded and that Mr. Semple asked him to get him taken to the Fort as he was not mortally wounded. Grant said . . . that he would send some persons to convey him there and left him in the care of a Canadian, but almost directly after an Indian[8] came up and shot him in the breast and killed him on the spot.

Several men are mentioned as the possible executioners of Robert Semple. The "Indian" mentioned by Grant (later named as Machicobaou)[9] is one. Another candidate is the young man reported by Alex Sutherland:

---

8   This "Indian" who takes the heat off the Brûlés for cold-blooded murder is cited several times, but it is only Brûlés who are seen wearing or carrying Semple's belongings. And the shot in the breast simply did not happen.

9   Coltman Report, p. 184.

I saw Cotonahaye, son of Bellegarde the Freeman, with the Governor's Pistol, Sword and double barrelled Gun and white neck Handkerchief. He presented them to his father.

The interpreter Nolin says he was told it was one of the Deschamps, a family Robertson had been sure he'd won to the settlement's defence.

Grant tells Pritchard they are going to attack the fort later tonight and at the first shot of resistance will kill every man, woman and child in it. Pritchard "begged him in his deceased father's name[10] to have compassion on the helpless women and children and spare them whatever they might do to the men." Grant, he says, concedes, after much entreaty, just so long as all property is given up and the settlers all leave the river. Pritchard agrees to act as go-between.

Around the campfires at Frog Plain, and simultaneously back at Fort Douglas, even in these first raw hours after the event the adversaries are forging their separate narratives about this day, stories that will be set in stone for generations: on one side the grotesque fiction of honourable victory in heroic confrontation; on the other the dubious notion of blameless victims of a savage massacre with no responsibility for the confrontation or its escalation. These contradictory narratives will haunt their descendants even to the present day.

But back to the moment . . . It is still dark when Pritchard starts back:

When I was allowed to leave the plain it was late at night and Mr. Grant accompanied me as my protector, almost to the spot on which I had seen my dearest friends fall by the hands of merciless Savages.

On my arrival at the Fort, what a scene of distress presented itself. The Widows, Children and relatives of the Slain in the

---

10 Grant's father, a Scot also named Cuthbert Grant, was a respected clerk and partner of the North West Company. Pritchard would know him by long reputation.

Horrors of despair were lamenting the dead and trembling for
the Safety of the Survivors.

Come the grim dawn, Peguis and his people will put themselves
between the two camps. Pierre St. Germaine, one of Robertson's lieu-
tenants, testifies,

> Next morning, Piguisse and the Blackman went out with two
> carts and brought back the bodies of Governor Semple, Mr.
> Wilkinson, Mr. Rogers, Mr. McLean, Mr. Holt, Mr. White
> the doctor and some of the servants of the Hudson's Bay
> Company. Some of the bodies were entirely naked and the rest
> nearly so. They were mangled with numerous wounds from
> Guns, Spears or Knives and covered with blood, their legs and
> arms fractured, their faces much disfigured with wounds.

Alex Macdonell resumes his sad recording of events:

> [June 20] I have got the <u>dead Bodies</u> collected with the
> assistance of Indians, and interred the Officers near the
> Government House. No person can describe the mangled
> state of the Bodies and from the excessive heat of the
> weather, they were soon in a putrefied state, so that I had
> no time to get coffins made for them, the Governor and Mr.
> McLean excepted.
>
> The Governor had a ball through the knee, another through
> the arm which was entirely Broke, and the third through the
> neck, fired as I suppose from behind when he was laying down
> on the field.

So, no bullet through the breast. The significance of this is that
it brings every other detail into question. It is best not to invest too
heavily in any specific claim.

For whatever reason, many bodies are left where they fell, as the
young captive/hostage Alexander Sutherland reports.

Next day I was allowed to go to Fort Douglas and on the way saw the bodies of the slain, nearly naked with limbs and skulls fractured, covered with blood and wounds . . . I went back later in the afternoon with others to bury them and saw many of the Indians, especially Piguiss, a Saulteaux Chief, crying like children.

Over the following weeks, anyone who passes the killing ground will report these bodies, poorly buried, half exposed, torn apart by animals.[11]

Alex Macdonell continues his June 20 journal entry, quite remarkably given the stress he must be feeling. He relates Pritchard's message from Cuthbert Grant and others, threatening to murder the hostages at Frog Plain immediately if the fort is not surrendered and the people taken away, out of Red River. He says he told Pritchard that he would do neither, since he still had sufficient force to defend the fort. ("Though," he confesses, "I feared they might murder their prisoners.")

He says he was undermined by Pritchard, who went among the settlers repeating Grant's ultimatum. The settler men, fearing for their women and children, refused to support Macdonell's defiance, despite having promised to just hours before:

Seeing myself in this situation, without assistance, provisions for no more than 5 days, no officers in which I could put the least confidence, the best of the men killed, the Settlers would not defend — so that under all these circumstances together with being in an open Fort, I considered the best way to save the effusion of more blood [was] to give up the Fort.

In the course of the day I entered into an agreement with the Commanders, saying that I should quit the river under certain conditions.

11 Court testimony of Pierre Pambrun, at York, Upper Canada: "the limbs of the prisoners were out of the ground, and many of their bodies in a mangled condition."

Poor Alex Macdonell. He was never to have been the man making these momentous decisions. It is difficult to imagine that even Colin Robertson could or would have held out under these conditions. Despite what he had hoped for in April and May, Fort Douglas never reached a state of readiness adequate to resist this level of aggression. He would have been forced to act as Alex does now. Once again the people will have to sacrifice their work, livestock and tools and flee to the protection of the HBC.

Naturally, the mercantile details between the two fur trade rivals must be attended to, and in a most businesslike way since, whatever other complexion might be put on the details of this event, it is first and last a North West Company operation: the ultimate aim is continued commerce, which requires no appearance of illegality in regard the rival's trade goods or other property. On June 21, Alex writes that he is busy all day, listing the HBC goods being taken into NWCo custody.[12]

At last, on June 22, 150 people in eight boats, they push off about noon, "all well except Mr. Bourke who had a flesh wound by a ball through the thigh," writes Macdonell. Then later, "Slept this night about nine miles above Netley Creek." They have minimal provisions and whatever possessions they can carry, as well as the colony records. As a condition of their surrender, Pritchard says, "[Cuthbert] Grant had promised us an escort to protect us against two other parties of halfbreeds whom he said we should meet. . . . But in the end we went without an escort."

THE RED RIVER, NEAR LAKE WINNIPEG.

Indeed, next day they do meet another bully-gang on its way to assist in the obliteration of the colony, led by Nor'Wester Archibald McLeod, and comprising "9 canoes and a Batteau, with 130 men and two pieces

---

12 Pierre St. Germaine's deposition ends with a six-page, double-column inventory of the goods at Fort Douglas, signed by himself, John Stett (HBC) and Cuthbert Grant. Everything from "1 schooner" to "12 swedges" (a tool for making grooves in horseshoes).

of artillery and 8 of the partners with him." Chief among the partners is Alexander McKenzie, known as The Emperor, a heavy hitter in the North West Company. Without the safe passage promised by Grant, the settlers are ordered ashore, threatened and intimidated. Their luggage is broken open and searched for the incriminating NWCo letters that Robertson intercepted (see Chapter 26). Alex Macdonell proudly records,

> I had taken the precaution to secure the intercepted letters before I had left The Forks, having delivered them to one of the Girls, who had them round her middle, and when the boats were searched she took a walk upon the shore, by which means I had them safe.

He doesn't identify this gutsy young woman.

Pritchard, Bourke and several others are arrested and taken off by the Nor'Westers to Fort William. The rest are released, once again refugees, homeless, landless and on the run, this time with a crushing burden of grief to carry as well.

The trip up the lake is another ordeal of patience, struggle, contrary winds, drenching squalls, separation and reunion — a typical lake journey — but at least it is July. They reach Winnipic Settlement and safety, on July 6.

No one else dies.

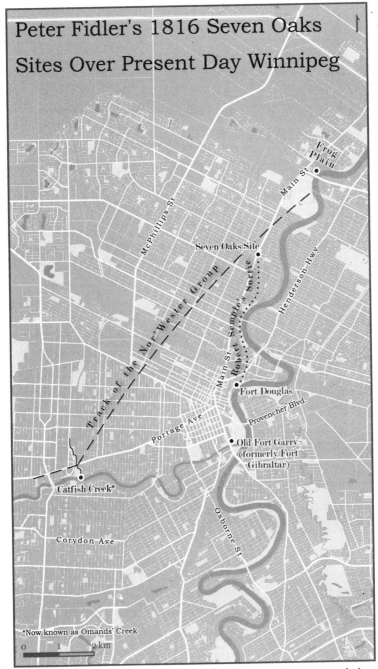

Peter Fidler's 1816 Seven Oaks Sites Over Present Day Winnipeg

Frog Plain

Main St.

McPhillips St.

Seven Oaks Site

Henderson Hwy

Track of the Nor'Wester Group

Main St.

Robert Semple's Sortie

Fort Douglas

Provencher Blvd.

Portage Ave.

Old Fort Garry (formerly Fort Gibraltar)

Catfish Creek*

Osborne St.

Corydon Ave.

*Now known as Omands' Creek

0   1   2 km

Map 10. The events and places of June 19, 1816, as they would appear in today's Winnipeg.

CHAPTER 31

EXILE. AGAIN.

JULY 7 TO OCTOBER 6, 1816

WINNIPIC SETTLEMENT, ON PLAYGREEN LAKE.

It is high summer when the refugees get out of their boats to begin the rehabilitation and expansion of the shantytown that sheltered some of them last June. It is a great pity that no record exists of their conversation in the boats and around the night fires. Beyond the sense of tragedy, how do they feel about Red River after two successive years of being ejected? We can't know but we get a clue from Alex Macdonell's first journal entry upon arrival:

> I intend to send two boats to York Factory for English Provisions and some goods for the winter, if I can prevail upon the Settlers to remain, which I hope will be the case. Very anxious about the fate of the Earl of Selkirk.

That "if" suggests that the Highlanders are of two minds about whether further struggle is worth the price. Alex, for his part, sticks fast to the cause. His determination to re-establish the colony as soon as possible is remarkable.

He believes Lord Selkirk is on his way to Red River, and that he may have a force of soldiers with him. This is probably his strongest motivation to hang on, but it is also his greatest source of anxiety, after the welfare of the people. Has the earl been ambushed or waylaid? When might he arrive? Will he come north when he finds Fort Douglas in Nor'Wester hands?

On July 9, Macdonell sends Pierre St. Germaine with sixteen bags of pemmican to await Selkirk at the mouth of the Winnipeg River. He stews every day about the earl's fate, convinced the Nor'Westers will "try every means to take his life." Sometimes, "I think he will not venture to come this season." Other times, "the hardship of not being able to communicate with him is unsupportable." And if he doesn't arrive, for any reason — "I am certain that without military force, these Settlers will never return to Red River and let people say what they please, it is the only thing which can establish a permanent Peace." Meanwhile he must keep up a brave face and "not let the people travel down to the Bay, for if they should go home, the whole object is lost."

(In fact, Selkirk set out from Montreal on June 18. As to force, he is accompanied by around one hundred armed veterans of the disbanded De Meuron and De Watteville regiments, who agreed to escort him in return for his offer of land in the western territory. Selkirk will learn of Seven Oaks on July 24 at Sault Ste. Marie.)

The people are back on a restricted diet, mainly lake fish, supplemented with some game and the eternal oatmeal.

YORK FACTORY, ON HUDSON BAY.

Colin Robertson reaches York Fort two days after the colonists' arrival at Winipic Settlement, totally unaware of what has transpired. He intends to take the August ship back to England and his other life; he has for some reason abandoned his original intention to go northwest to Cumberland House. He describes his arrival at York Factory — HBC headquarters, Northern Department — with typical Robertson acerbity:

> Neither York Fort nor its inhabitants strike a stranger either
> as a place remarkable for hospitality or politeness. When you

arrive at the beach (for there is no wharf) you cannot step on shore without the risk of getting entangled in the mud. There you may remain, although the top of the bank is covered with officers and men looking down on you with their heads on one side, like so many Turkeys perched on a tree. These Gentlemen will not even condescend to inform you of the best track to where they are assembled in solemn silence.

"We are murdered here by moschottos," he complains in one of his many spellings of that most hateful of insects.

He is not surprised to find Duncan Cameron here, also awaiting the ship, but he is dismayed by the freedom Cameron has been granted and the degree to which he has beguiled his guards into becoming hosts. It particularly irks him that Cameron dines with the officers.

He grumbles about this and everything else for three days, when his complacent self-certainty is suddenly shattered: "The Colonial boat returned with the melancholy[1] intelligence of the death of Governor Semple and the destruction of the Colony. It seems we have [also] lost five officers and fourteen men. What dreadful calamity!"

Suddenly he is in full logorrhea mode, writing furiously on the North West Company's crimes, quoting captured letters and remembered conversations and events. Writing is his process. Pages fly from under his pen until he makes a dramatic decision: "I have resolved to go and meet the Settlers and endeavour to prevail on them to remain at Winipic Settlement until the arrival of Lord Selkirk, who . . . is accompanied by a body of troops and is endeavouring to force his way to Red River."[2]

---

1 "Melancholy" is the universal adjective people of the period use when they hear about Seven Oaks. It is used by Selkirk, by HBC men, by sailors, by lawyers and judges in Upper Canada. Clearly, it is a word that held more power in 1816 than it would later.

2 He ends this marathon rant, which includes a verbatim copy of an entire letter and long excerpts from others, with a mournful "Eleven o'clock PM. A violent head ache. O Life, what art thou!" What human heart in any age would not instantly recognize this lamentation and the emotional exhaustion behind it?

To call him a man of action does not do his vigorous response justice. Red River is definitely not his problem anymore. It could even be said to be none of his business. Yet without hesitation, just three days after his deliverance from the purgatory of river and portage, he is ready to leap back into the roiling waters to weather weeks of more discomfort, danger and the torment of "moschottos." His fevered writing fills the time it takes to load two boats with "provisions, ammunition, two Field pieces and other arms for the defence of the Colonists." The moment they are ready, he is off.

After a couple of days of struggling through the shallow waters of summer, he abandons the heavy batteaux for a light canoe with two Indigenous paddlers, taking "two blankets, two shirts and three days provisions," and leaving even his personal servant behind, but his impatience demands it.

His wry gift for observation is not dulled by grief or the rigours of the voyage. One night he comments, "We supped on ducks, a number of which were killed coming along. The Indians cooked them well. However, I was not inclined to investigate their process of cooking." He follows this with a long passage of praise and admiration for his paddlers and the people they come from (unnamed but probably the people known as Woodland Cree).

A couple of days later they are "eat up with muschattos."

By July 25 he is in Jack River. Thirteen days for the upstream trip!

"Arrived here about 12 o'clock, found Mrs. McLean with her small family and a few more of the Colonists. It was a melancholy meeting."

Next day he presses on to Winipic Settlement, where he finds "the unfortunate Colonists." The conversation is painful, he says, and when a number of them ask his advice on what to do, he tells them to sit tight and wait for news from Canada. There are neither ships nor provisions at York Fort, he warns them. They are better off here.

He records what he is told about Seven Oaks. It is fascinating to watch a calamitous and chaotic event start to take shape as memory, story and eventually myth. Alex McLean has already been elevated to hero status, as Robertson records:

The Enemy wished to make a prisoner of Mr. McLean but this Brave Gentleman, having received a shot in his right hand and the left being already disabled from last Spring, refused to be taken prisoner and with the most heroic courage raised his carbine on his wounded arms and Bayoneted two horses in attempting to run at the enemy when he received his mortal wound.

We can only hope that this is the story his children were told to make them proud of their courageous, if not quite this suicidal, dad. The bare eyewitness account by John Pritchard ("I saw Mr. McLean a little in front defending himself but by a second shot I saw him fall") conveys no less courage, but it lacks in the retelling.

It seems clear that the immediate author of the whole disaster is Robert Semple, but since admitting that would taint all of them, and blacken the name of a man they admired and mourn, the survivors must find treachery. Pritchard, not here to defend himself, is given a craven role, not backed by any eyewitness:

> Mr. Pritchard threw himself alongside one of the dead bodies where he lay until the affair was over. . . . When [men] came to finish the wounded, Pritchard started up and . . . requested an interview with their Chief Grant. The ruin of the Colony was the price demanded and yielded to by Pritchard for preservation of his life.

Pritchard, they tell him, engineered the surrender by terrifying the settlers, even though the servants wanted to fight on. Robertson winds up with,

> This I believe to be a correct account of the melancholy affair. . . . It was given me by Mr. Macdonell, M. Kilkenny, G. Sutherland and I. Forbes [all servants], the three former escaped after the Death of Governor Semple.

Of course Alex Macdonell was nowhere near the fight and Kilkenny and Sutherland had their fast-receding backs to it, so no one here actually saw what happened to either Alex McLean or John Pritchard.

Mr. Bird of the HBC wants very much for Robertson to take on defence of the colony once it is re-established. Robertson asks for a force of forty HBC men. "This force, properly applied would effectively prevent our opponents from committing their depredations," he says. "This, Mr. Bird could not assent to."

This makes Robertson's mind up to go back to England rather than continue with the settlers. Next day, August 7, Alex Macdonell writes,

> I have received a letter from Mr. Bird, saying that the plan which had been proposed for the defence of our property has been given up, that Mr. Robertson objected to it, and I am much disappointed.

Nevertheless, two days later, Alex reports, "Settled with the Settlers today to remain in the country and to winter at Jack River."

Robertson shows no resentment toward Alex Macdonell, and even comes to his defence.

> It was intimated by some of the servants that Mr. Macdonell could have made a better defence after the death of Governor Semple. . . . Mr. MacD had a heavy charge — so many women and children — and is a perfect stranger in the country. All these things will tend much to justify his conduct in delivering up the Fort.

Later he finds himself echoing the complaints of many before him. He says of the Highlanders, "They are certainly a very headstrong people. I could manage a thousand Canadian families with more ease than I could ten from the Highlands of Scotland." Many would consider that an accolade.

As for my great-great-grandfather, Sam Lamont's taste for frontier adventure has come to an end. When the boats are made ready to take Britain-bound colonists to meet the ship at York, he is among them.

The flotilla, under the joint leadership of Robertson and Macdonell, sets off downstream for York Factory on August 12. Robertson arrives at York on the 29th, ahead of the colony boats. His first reaction is deep disappointment: "No ship! How fare my friends on the other side of the Atlantic? It is now two years and three months since I sailed from England and not one line from friend or relative! I both hope and fear."

With that brief wail, he forces himself to return to business, analyzing and musing on the possibilities of improving the route and developing the country between here and Lake Winnipeg. This man's mind never stops churning, nor his hand a-scribbling.

Macdonell arrives and notes without comment that there is no ship.

Both men weather the next three weeks as the whole fort becomes more and more edgy with the stubborn emptiness on the horizon. At stake are supplies and trade goods for the winter. Without them, a year's trading will be all but lost, never mind the hardships of scarce food. It is nerve-racking for all concerned. "Nothing but long faces to be seen upon account of the ship's non-arrival," writes Macdonell on September 15. He is anxious to be going before ice locks the rivers. He can snowshoe out, but without many dogs he can't haul winter provisions.

Poor Mrs. McLean and her five children will have to stay at York over the winter if the ship does not come.

Sam Lamont's mental state must parallel Robertson's; both can almost taste the food, the familiarity, the warmth, the *comfort* of home. And yet, each day it gets further out of reach. Finally, on September 20, neither Macdonell nor Lamont can wait any longer. Writes Alex, "All my baggage for inland is packed up and nothing more remains but to proceed with the first tide tomorrow morning."

When morning comes: "I have engaged Samuel Lamont to go inland . . . and just as we are stepping into the Boat, [a boy arrives] saying that the ship from England has hove in sight, to the great joy of everyone here . . . I have now lost the prospect of Samuel Lamont and James MacIntosh."

And Sam scampers away to deliverance. Apparently the ship had been lost along the coast for the past two weeks, trying to find York.

Although delighted to see the ship, Colin Robertson is once again crushed by disappointment. The mail packet arrives, but "No Letter either from the Committee or my friends. What can all this mean?"

It is almost too much to bear, even for this paragon of reason over passion.

Alex has one more duty toward Christina McLean, which goes about as well as we might expect:

> Made out an order for Mrs. McLean for fifty pounds sterling, upon her landing in England, to fit herself and her children out before she could appear before his Lordship, but she refused it as she did not receive one hundred pounds, and Mr. Robertson was also displeased on the same account . . . I left the order with Mr. Bird.

And with that, Alex Macdonell is shot of the family McLean, which one hopes is some consolation for the loss of Lamont, his only millwright, his best axeman and an employee about whom a bad word was never committed to paper. (Well, there was that time he told John Bourke to take a hike, but that hardly counts — everyone told John Bourke to take a hike.)

On October 2, the passengers board the *Prince*, but the tension is far from over. Two days are lost fitting a new rudder, and when they finally do cast off, contrary winds trap them in the anchorage for two more days. Finally, on October 6, Robertson can record,

> Sailed from Five Fathom Hole about 10 o'clock AM with a fine Southerly wind. God grant us a pleasant voyage.

Laughter off. It's the gods, sensing yet another opportunity to crush the spirits of mere mortals.

EPILOGUE

OCTOBER 1816, AND BEYOND

ABOARD THE HBC SHIP PRINCE OF WALES.

T he dream of a winter homecoming lasts exactly one week. On October 13, Colin Robertson writes,

> Last night we fondly indulged the hope of entering Hudson's Strait this morning, but what was our disappointment when we found the entrance blocked with tremendous mountains of ice. To add to our uneasiness the new ice was fast forming around the ship, so much that it required a heavy press of sail to force a passage.

Shortly thereafter they fall in with another HBC ship, the *Emerald*, and together the two vessels make for James Bay and safe haven for the winter. It is a voyage as grim as any described in this book, striking its most desperate note on October 23 and 24, when Robertson and most of the passengers have transferred to a small single-masted HBC schooner. Robertson:

> October 23, God knows where . . .

October 24, 1817? 1816 [*sic*] — Last night was one of the most
dreadful nights I ever passed . . .

A declaration to be respected from the pen of Colin Robertson,
made evident by his confusion over the year. Without going into
detail it involves an open deck hatch that lets in icy seawater. Christina
McLean and five of her children are among the wretches getting
drenched. Little Miles is just a year old. Robertson writes that the next
day, Christina, despite "great fortitude," is much indisposed.

They wash up at last at Moose Factory, on the southern shore of
James Bay, where they "spend the winter," three words that hold a life-
time's worth of boredom, inconvenience and terrible food. The winter
is one of the coldest in recent memory and, come spring, north winds
force the slow-melting ice into James Bay, blocking it far into summer.
There is unrest, complaint and even a short mutiny by the *Prince*'s crew
before they finally escape on August 24, 1817. Colin Robertson is not
aboard; he has departed for Montreal by land. Sam Lamont will reach
his Islay home in October: a year to get to Red River, a year to get back.

At this point my great-great-grandad leaves the Great Experiment
on the Red forever, but he is not quits with Canada. Sam will marry
Catherine Shaw in 1822 and produce six children. In the 1830s the
Clearances will reach Islay, sparking wholesale migration to Canada,
which Sam, Catherine and the children join. This time they will find a
homestead in peaceful Simcoe County, in what is now Ontario. Both
will live into their late seventies and see their daughter Mary give birth
to their grandson Donald Livingstone, my grandfather, leading eventually to the writing of this book.

Duncan Cameron is on board the *Prince* and is taken to London to
answer for his sins. After all this he is released without trial and after
that . . . frankly, I don't care.[1]

Mrs. McLean and all the little McLeans — Hugh, Donald, John,
Mary and Miles — are on board and will be until November 7 when

---

1 For those who may, here is the brief answer in the *Dictionary of Canadian
   Biography*: biographi.ca/en/bio/cameron_duncan_7E.html.

the *Prince* finally drops anchor in the Thames. Christina immediately begins her assault on Selkirk and the HBC for a pension which, given Miles McDonell's assurances during the siege of 1815, to wit —

> and confirmed to them the reward I formerly held out — of a pension to any that should be disabled or maimed defending the property, etc.

— would seem to be automatic, since her Alex lost the use of his hand defending the property, then got himself shot and hacked to pieces. It is not. The London office rejects her claim to a pension but grants her a small stipend pending Selkirk's return. This and the generosity of friends allow her to linger in London for two years, until the earl gets back. When he does, Selkirk won't see her and his representatives remain firm — no compensation. Using the argument that the promised pension was for servants of the earl, not settlers who were presumably fighting in their own interest, and the not unreasonable claim that they have already been fairly generous, they offer her a good-will payment of £20 a year. Finally stalemated if not defeated — it is hard to imagine Christina McLean defeated — she accepts and retires to Scotland and obscurity. A remarkable woman.

In Montreal, Colin Robertson is arrested and charged for the capture of Fort Gibraltar, spends the winter of 1817 in a Montreal prison and is acquitted in the spring. He goes back to Athabasca, is re-arrested and hauled again back to Lower Canada, but this time flees to England. There he finds that his business has failed, so he returns to Canada and the HBC, where he works until a stroke disables him in the 1830s. He retires to Montreal, is elected to the Legislative Assembly, and dies in 1842 after being thrown from a sleigh.[2] Montreal traffic — lethal even then.

Several people will be charged and stand trial for their roles in the dramatic events of 1815 and 1816. No one will ever be found guilty, simply

---

2 George Woodcock's article on Colin Robertson, *Dictionary of Canadian Biography*: biographi.ca/en/bio/robertson_colin_7E.html.

because of the near impossibility of mounting a fair trial so far from the alleged crimes in both distance and time. Whatever its shortcomings in the early nineteenth century, colonial justice does have standards and these prosecutions don't meet them. Physical evidence is non-existent, witnesses have to be brought great distances and supported for months, and the justices seem unsure that they even have jurisdiction over the "Indian Country" beyond Canada's borders. This holds for both sides of the conflict: Colin Robertson is acquitted as already mentioned, and several NWCo associates, accused in the theft of cannons and destruction of the settlement in 1815, go free.

Cuthbert Grant is taken to Montreal, but must first stand trial for another, unrelated murder, of which he is acquitted. He is then duly charged with theft, pillage and murder at Seven Oaks, for which he probably would also have been cleared for the reasons stated above, but he takes no chances — he jumps bail and flees back to Red River in 1818. It is tempting to see this as a craven act or even a tacit admission of guilt, but it is much more likely to have been advised by agents of both fur-trading companies, who want a political solution in Red River to safeguard profits. Grant is seen, reasonably, as the leader most likely to be able to take the Bois-Brûlés in a peaceful direction and to bind them to the Company if he is so inclined. To ensure that he is, the HBC eventually hires him at a salary of £200 per year, and gives him the title Warden of the Plains.

Grant succeeds brilliantly in this role, and nothing in his long, distinguished tenure as founding leader of the Métis Nation and Warden of the Plains suggests that the slaughter at Seven Oaks was ever part of his plan, and the good he does for his people and for civil society in the west goes a long way toward atonement for that terrible day. Nonetheless he bears a large portion of responsibility for it, for which he is never "exonerated," as his twentieth-century admirers will claim. "Excused" might be a better word.

The writing is already on the wall for the North West Company, and eventually its partners realize that their best bet for continued riches off the literal backs of rodents and the figurative backs of their trappers is to throw in with the Hudson's Bay Company and recreate its monopoly. This they do in 1821 and grow fat for another century.

Lord Selkirk hears of the shootout at Seven Oaks while resting at Sault Ste. Marie as he makes his way west in the summer of 1816. He immediately sets out with his hired soldiers for the NWCo headquarters at Fort William. His escort surprises and overpowers the fort's guards, and Selkirk takes possession. He sends messages on to Alex Macdonell and "the people" in their refuge on Playgreen Lake, then settles in for the winter, gathering evidence from the fort's files on Nor'Wester "crimes." In December he dispatches some soldiers for Red River, where they take back Fort Douglas without violence and prepare for his arrival, which comes at last on June 21, 1817.

It is a very busy summer, because the governor of Lower Canada has sent a commission, in the person of Colonel William Coltman, to inquire into the affairs of both companies and the events leading to Seven Oaks. Coltman takes his job seriously and his ultimate report is an impressive example of exhaustive investigation and inquiry, but it is also a political document rather than a judicial one. Its intent is to play down any clear blame on either side, but especially the North West Company, of which Coltman himself is a shareholder. Commerce is the goal, and conciliation the method.

The settlers finally arrive back in Red River on July 19, 1817, at least thirty-five men along with wives and children — probably around a hundred in total. They are immediately smitten with their lord. Selkirk reciprocates by granting them free title to their farms (instead of making them pay for land which is his only by act of imagination). Apart from this, according to Selkirk biographer J.M. Bumsted, he "spent precious little time with them," and "displayed little interest either in establishing a rapport or in serving as a leader."[3]

What he is keen on, to his credit I suppose, is getting local First Nations to formally agree to the colony's existence on their traditional lands and establishing a description and price for the exact tracts he wants to settle. He invites five prominent chiefs to Fort Douglas, and as

---

3   Bumsted, p. 352.

far as I can tell they spend one day in negotiations, after which they all apply their pictograph signatures to a document laying out the terms verbally and graphically. With this treaty, the first to be signed west of the Great Lakes, a portion of the Red and Assiniboine River valleys has been magically transformed into private property, European style.

This is not one of the treaties commonly cited today. They were signed in the 1870s and later and superseded the Selkirk Treaty. The Selkirk Treaty does not define First Nations land, which is still assumed to be the whole territory, but the limits of settler jurisdiction. In that sense it is opposite from the treaties in force today, at least as the later ones have been interpreted in the decades since. Still, it is a land treaty,[4] and it begins the process of transferring the land from its historical and Indigenous owners to the invading settlers.

Western British North America has its first permanent agricultural colony, its first settler colonists and, in the De Meurons, its first quasi-military force to defend both (now memorialized as "Desmeurons" on a St. Boniface street). Now it has its first treaty. Three years later, with the arrival of Reverend John West and triumphalist Christianity, the malignancy is complete, from the Indigenous point of view.

Selkirk delights in the good health and energy he reports from all this outdoor activity in 1816 and 1817. Nonetheless, his chronic tuberculosis returns in 1818 and, despite moving to the south of France for its restorative climate, he dies on April 8, 1820, aged forty-eight.

The existence of a European settlement at the forks of the Red and Assiniboine Rivers will never again be threatened, but neither will it flourish exactly as intended. A few more drafts of Scots settlers will bring the settlement's population to about 200 in 1821, and that will only grow to about 1,000 twenty-five years later, largely by natural increase and the steady influx of retiring Hudson's Bay Company employees. It will remain the principal — in some senses only — European agricultural settlement west of Lake Superior until after the creation of Manitoba in 1870. A few small farms will be tended

---

4   The full treaty and map that supports it can be seen here: gov.mb.ca/chc/archives /hbca/spotlight/selkirk_treaty.html.

around HBC forts to supply fresh vegetables, but Red River is unique as a purely agricultural settlement.

By far the greatest change after 1820 is the influx of Bois-Brûlés, now using the term "Métis" more and more, and their Anglophone cousins, at that time still called "half-breeds," who settle in their own communities along the two rivers. By the 1840s they will outnumber Europeans six to one, causing one historian to remark, "Selkirk's child was healthier than ever he could have expected, though very different from his original vision."[5]

Neither culture — settler or mixed heritage — is homogeneous, except in their mutual antipathy. The settlers never forgive or forget Seven Oaks, and certainly never recognize their role in bringing it about; and no one of mixed ethnicity seems ever to regret it. Still, the sheer size of the country and the interdependence of everyone living in it keeps the resentment non-violent and formal relations civil, for the most part.

After 1835, the HBC takes over the administration of Assiniboia from the Selkirk estate and, true to form, their main concern is the maintenance of their monopoly. This rankles all factions in Red River, but mainly the Métis, who strain against any outsider imposing rules on them. The end of the North West Company has meant the end of the regular connection with Canada. This only reinforces their sense of themselves as a unique nation, which indeed they are: a nation with its own language, Michif; its own territory, though shared; and its own economy, built around fur trading and the buffalo hunt.

The harvesting of buffalo by First Nations and Métis is the most significant contributor to the internal economy, feeding Indigenous peoples, fur traders and settlers alike during hard years of agricultural shortfalls. For the Métis, it is also much more: it defines and expresses their identity as a people.

Their twice-yearly hunt, involving hundreds of people of all ages in great columns of Red River carts screeching across the prairie for weeks on end, is without doubt the most spectacular annual event on the

---

5   Gerald Friesen, *The Canadian Prairies: A History* (Toronto: University of Toronto Press, 1988).

plains in the decades from 1820 to 1870. It has been described in many books about the place and period, but the original, from which all others blossom, is in Alexander Ross's history, published in 1856.[6] Ross describes the 1840 hunt (whose capital and labour value he estimates at a jaw-dropping £24,000) first-hand and in lurid detail. It involves 1,200 Red River carts, 620 hunters and 1,000 women and children. They are gone from the settlement for two months. Meat is the paramount object of the hunt in the early years, but hides become important as time goes on, especially for trade with Americans.

The buffalo hunt and Métis culture define the Red River Settlement after 1830 far more than the clutch of sodbusters clinging to the banks of the Red, but theirs is a glory doomed from the start. Helped along by obscene commercial slaughter in the U.S., the once-abundant supply of buffalo is gradually exhausted, and by the 1860s the hunt is failing regularly. When Canada "buys" Rupertsland from the Hudson's Bay Company in 1869, the fate of Indigenous people, Métis and First Nations, is sealed. The government of John A. Macdonald is not interested in buffalo; it is interested in creating an agricultural hinterland, settled by millions of farmers who will buy equipment and supplies from central Canada and sell grain, especially wheat, to the world. To achieve this they will mimic the techniques of the Scottish Clearances, only this time, instead of Highlanders, the displaced will be the First Nations and Métis. The results for the displaced will be no less "melancholy."

In the case of the settlers of 1813–16, while they were unquestionably the vanguard of all that has happened since, they were not knowingly part of the problem. With the notable exception of Selkirk and his close associates, they had no designs on extending empire or acquiring it. They came more as economic refugees than adventurers, to a land they were told was available for farming. They had no reason to feel that their tiny plots on it could discommode anyone, nor did they,

---

6   Alexander Ross, *The Red River Settlement: Its Rise, Progress, and Present State* (London: Smith Elder and Co., 1856), pp. 242–65. This book is freely available on Google Books.

then or for the next two generations. Nevertheless, they started it and set the pattern, and that must be acknowledged.

By his own lights, even Lord Selkirk behaved honourably enough toward the First Nations peoples of Assiniboia. The same cannot be said for his treatment, mainly through his agents, of the Bois-Brûlés. In resisting the North West Company, Selkirk and his officers dismissed and contemned the unique history and way of life of the people of mixed heritage, and by doing so repeatedly brought on themselves and their relatively blameless servants and settlers the hostility that would culminate in the disaster of Seven Oaks. For that, and the generations of bitterness, recrimination and oppression that followed, Thomas Douglas, Earl of Selkirk and ultimate authority in the Red River Settlement, must bear his share of historical guilt.

A NOTE ON SOURCES

Most of this book was written directly from material in the Selkirk Papers, held in Library and Archives Canada, with a microfilm copy in the Archives of Manitoba. The chief sources were the journals of Miles McDonell (today, Macdonell), Archibald McDonald, Alexander Macdonell, Peter Fidler and Colin Robertson, with fragments from James White. There were also reports and letters to and from Lord Selkirk, William Auld, Robert Semple and others. The Selkirk Papers are numbered in the order received, from 1 to over 20,000. While it would have been cumbersome to have annotated all these extracts, I have kept a complete record of specific page numbers for all quotes and paraphrased passages and can provide these on request.

Where I have quoted from non-settler sources without citation, these too are in the Selkirk Papers and would have been available to Selkirk's officers, for example, letters to and from Duncan Cameron and others of the North West Company, taken with Colin Robertson's capture of Fort Gibraltar. I tried as much as possible to stay within the settlers' world and experience.

For passenger lists and ships' logs, as well as quotes from Hudson's Bay Post journals, I have made use of the Hudson's Bay Company archives, part of the Archives of Manitoba.

For biographies of most characters, I have relied upon the magnificently useful online edition of the *Dictionary of Canadian Biography*: biographi.ca/en.

Where I have unavoidably left the settlers' world and time, I have cited my sources, such as in references to depositions taken by William Bachelor Coltman for his Royal Commission Report of 1818. This report is available and downloadable from Library and Archives Canada as:

> William B. Coltman, Report on the Disturbances in the Indian
> Territories (Lower Canada, 1818)

The few examples of trial testimony in Upper Canada are also in the Selkirk Papers.

For the history and background of the Métis Nation, I have relied upon Jean Teillet's book:

> Jean Teillet, *The North-West Is Our Mother: The Story of Louis
> Riel's People, the Métis Nation* (Toronto: HarperCollins
> Canada, Patrick Crean Editions, 2019)

For details in the life of Cuthbert Grant, I recommend the above as well as

> Margaret A. MacLeod and W.L. Morton, *Cuthbert Grant of
> Grantown* (Toronto: McClelland & Stewart, 1963)

For the life of Chief Peguis, including the excerpt from Lieutenant Chappell's book:

> Donna G. Sutherland, *Peguis: A Noble Friend* (St. Andrews, MB:
> Chief Peguis Heritage Park, 2003)

For the background and activities of Lord Selkirk, there are several books available, the most complete of which is:

J.M. Bumsted, *Lord Selkirk: A Life* (Winnipeg: University of
Manitoba Press, 2008)

For the Scottish Clearances, there are many sources on the internet
and several books. I mainly relied on this classic:

John Prebble, *The Highland Clearances* (London: Secker and
Warburg, 1963)

For the visceral experience of those times I recommend Donald
McLeod's first-person recollections, originally written in 1841 and reis-
sued in 1892:

Donald McLeod, *Gloomy Memories in the Highlands of Scotland*
(Glasgow: Archibald Sinclair, 1892)

There is one rich source I elected not to use, partly because it is
hard to say whether the officers at Red River would have seen it and
partly because it takes us too far out of the narrow field of view of the
settlers that is the premise of this work. I cite it here as it supports my
contention that Duncan Cameron was a conscious and conscienceless
manipulator and provocateur in his unscrupulous recruitment of Bois-
Brûlé men in the attacks of 1815, at least, to the point of counselling
murder. It is a deposition "voluntarily given by [Joseph or] Baptiste
Boudré, alias Musqua, in the Indian language at Edmonton House
January 2nd, 1816, before . . . James Bird, Chief factor and Interpreter
of the Indian Language."

Boudré was a canoeman at an unnamed northern post of the NWCo
when he was sent by his employer with "a feather in his cap [and] a large
glass of Rum . . . with other HalfBreeds, to Red River to defend the
property of the NWCo which was menaced by Miles McDonell." Once
there, they were received "with unusual attention" by Duncan Cameron,
who put them with other "Halfbreeds, Canadians and deserters from
Lord Selkirk's Settlement," totalling "upwards of one hundred." Cameron
ordered "the Halfbreeds, who amounted to forty-one, to go with Mr.

Grant at their head, form a camp [at Frog Plain] and endeavour to seize the person of the Captain [McDonell] or at least prevent him from making his escape." Boudré goes on to describe the events in Chapters 17, 18 and 19 in which he took part, including the attack that that wounded Alex McLean and James Warren, and the attempted seizure of Archie McDonald, in which he came close to murdering McDonald. All orders, he says, came from Nor'Westers, and he obeyed them because he (along with the others) was promised a reward by Cameron. He cites several examples of friction between the Bois-Brûlés and Cameron, all to do with the rewards they'd been promised. After the expulsion of the settlers and the burning of the settlement buildings, Boudré and others accompanied Cameron to Fort William, where each was presented with a feather and a suit of clothes, with a promise to call on them again if needed. "And that was all the extra payment [we] received for [our] exertions in expelling the Settlers." This may explain why he was so ready to testify against Cameron, whom he clearly identifies as the prime mover in all these events.

ACKNOWLEDGEMENTS

The "lonely and solitary business of writing" inevitably involves a large number of people, without whom no worthwhile book can be written. First are those who read parts or all of my manuscript as it evolved, in alphabetical order: Andy Blicq, Cheryl Anderson, Brad Caslor, Richard Condie, Lin Gibson, Wendy Lill, Lisa Marr-Laing, Ed Reed, Michael Scott and David Springbett. All made thoughtful comments and suggestions, many of which I followed at the time and more whose value I only recognized later.

David Carr and Merit Jensen Carr gave invaluable support, as did Heather MacAndrew and Lin Gibson in introducing me to ECW Press, my first choice when that time came.

My daughter, Michaelin Lower, produced the original maps, a proud collaboration with a gratifying result.

The staffs of the Archives of Manitoba, the Hudson's Bay Company Archives and the Provincial Library of Manitoba are an indispensable resource, too often under-supported by the governments they serve.

No one told me how much a good publisher contributes, not just to a book's publication but to the creative process. Jack David saw something and took a chance on a first-time writer, despite the rawness of the manuscript. His wisdom put me together with editor

Lesley Erickson, whose firm but reassuring guidance transformed that rawness into a readable story.

Managing and Production Editor Sammy Chin has the perfect combination of confident authority and friendly diplomacy required to shepherd an anxious author through the arcane machinery of a publishing house. Through her, my gratitude and respect extend to the many able professionals whose work she coordinates.

Finally, far from the least of my debts is the one I owe the love of my life, Elise Swerhone, my partner and collaborator whose indomitable toughness, unwavering encouragement and gentle affections continue, after four-plus decades, to teach me the true meaning and many layers of love.

APPENDIX

List of passengers who sailed from Stromness on the *Prince of Wales*, June 19, 1813.

Sources for this are: the *Prince of Wales* passenger manifest in the HBC archives; lists prepared by Lucille H. Campey in her book *The Silver Chief* (Toronto: Natural Heritage Books/Dundurn Press, 2003); and lists prepared by George H. Bryce in *The Romantic Settlement of Lord Selkirk's Colonists* (Toronto: Musson Books, 1909).

Those with asterisks after their names were on the trek from Churchill to York Factory, April 1814, and the first group to go south to The Forks. These identify forty-three of the fifty who made the trek.

NAME	AGE	OCCUPATION	FROM
George Campbell	25	Farmer	Archurgle parish, Creech
Helen, his wife	20	--	Archurgle
Bell, his daughter	1	--	Archurgle
Betty McKay, Alex'r Gunn's niece (Pedlar)	24	--	--
John Sutherland	50	Weaver	Kildonan (Died Sept. 2, 1813)
Catherine, his wife*	46	--	Kildonan

NAME	AGE	OCCUPATION	FROM
George, his son*	18	Weaver	Kildonan
Donald, his son	16	--	Kildonan
Alexander, his son	9	--	Kildonan
Jannet, his daughter*	14	--	Kildonan
Angus McKay*	23	Shoemaker	Kildonan
Jean, his wife*	20	--	Kildonan
Alexander Gunn*	49	Weaver	Kildonan
Christine, his wife	47	--	Kildonan (Died Sept. 20, 1813)
William, son*	21	--	Kildonan
Donald Bannerman	50	--	Badflinch Kildonan (Died Sept. 24, 1813)
Christine, his wife	44	--	--
William, his son*	18	--	--
Donald, his son (mute and epileptic)	8	--	--
Christine, his daughter*	16	--	--
George McDonald	46	Labourer	Dalvait (Died Sept. 1, 1813)
Jannet, his wife	50 or 57	--	--
Betty, his daughter	17	--	--
Catherine, his daughter	23	--	--
Barbara McBeath, widow	55	--	Borobal
Charles, her son	15	--	--
Henry, her son	16	Shoemaker	--
Andrew McBeath*	19	--	--
Jannet, his wife*	17	--	--
William Sutherland	24	Labourer	Borobal
Margaret, his wife	16	--	--
Christian, his sister	26	--	--
Donald Gunn	65	Shoemaker	Borobal
Jannet, his wife	52	--	--
George, his son*	14	--	--
Esther, his daughter*	24	--	--

NAME	AGE	OCCUPATION	FROM
Catherine, his daughter	20	--	-- (Died Aug. 29, 1813)
Christian, his daughter	10	--	--
Angus Gunn	22	Shoemaker	--
Jannet, his wife	24	--	--
Robert Sutherland, brother of William S.	19	Labourer	Borobal
Elizabeth Frazer*	30	--	--
Angus Sutherland	20	Shoemaker	Auchraich
Elizabeth, his mother	40	--	--
Betty, his sister	18	--	-- (Died Oct. 26, 1813, of consumption)
Donald Stewart	38	--	Balecheulish, Appin (Died Aug. 20, 1813)
Catherine, his wife	35	--	--
Margaret, his daughter	8	--	--
Mary, his daughter	4	--	--
Ann, his daughter	1	--	--
John Smith	50	Labourer	Asbus parish, Kildonan
Mary, his wife	48	--	--
John, his son	10	--	--
Jean, his daughter*	14	--	--
Mary, his daughter	5	--	--
Alexander Gunn (Pedlar)	46	Tailor	Ascaig, Kildonan
Elizabeth McKay, his niece*	19	--	--
Neil Smith	17	--	--
George Bannerman*	22	Labourer	Kildonan
Jno. Bruce	30	--	Aultsmoral, Kildonan
Alex'r Sutherland*	24	--	Balnavaliach, Kildonan
William, his brother	20	--	(Died)
Betty, his sister	22	--	--

NAME	AGE	OCCUPATION	FROM
Haman Sutherland*	20	--	Kenacoil
Barbara, his sister*	22	--	--
James McKay*	19	--	--
Ann, his sister* (a.k.a. Anäis, Anna)	22	--	--
Jno. Matheson	23	Weaver	Aultbreakachy
Robert Gunn*	22	--	Kildonan
Mary, his sister	20	--	
Hugh Bannerman*	19	Labourer	Dalhamy, Kildonan
Elizabeth, his sister*	21	--	--
Mary Bannerman*	24	--	--
Alex Bannerman*	21	Shoemaker	--
Christine, his sister*	19	--	--
Jno. Bannerman	24	Shoemaker	Duible (Died Jan. 1814)
Isabella, his sister*	20 (or 16)	--	--
Jno. McPherson*	20 (or 16)	Labourer	Gailable
Catherine, his sister*	24	--	--
Hector McLeod*	17	--	--
George Sutherland*	18	Shoemaker	Borobal
Adam, his brother*	16	Labourer	--
Jno. Murray*	21	Shoemaker	Siesgill
Alexander, his brother*	19	Shoemaker	--
Helen Kennedy	--	--	Sligo, Ireland
James McDonald*	21	Blacksmith	--
Hugh McDonald*	22	Carpenter	--
Samuel Lamont*	22	Millwright	Bowmore, Islay
Alex'r Matheson*	22	Dealer in honey?	Keanved, Kildonan
Jno. Matheson*	22	Labourer	--
Jno. McIntyre*	23	Tailor	-- (Joined HBC July 1814)
Edward Sheil	--	--	Ballyshannon, Ireland
Jno. or Jos. Kerrigan	--	Tailor	Ballyshannon, Ireland

NAME	AGE	OCCUPATION	FROM
Christian Gunn	--	--	--
P. Laserre	--	Surgeon	-- (Died Aug. 16, 1813)

Miles McDonell's list of "deserters," settlers who left the Red River Colony with the NWCo on or before June 18, 1815 (Selkirk Papers, p. 1542).

"DESERTERS" AND FAMILY	
Neil McKinnon, wife Margery and 4 children	6
John Cooper, wife Mary and child	3
Angus McDonald, wife Mary and 3 children	5
John Walsh, wife Elinor and 2 children	4
Miles Livingston, wife Jennet and 2 children	4
James Smyth, wife and 3 children	5
Hector McDonald, wife Peggy and 3 children	5
Hector McEachron [sic], wife Betty and 2 children	4
George Campbell, wife Helen and 2 children	4
George Sutherland, mother Catherine and 3 siblings	5
Angus McKay, wife Jean and child	3
Alex'r Gunn, wife and child	3
William Bannerman, wife Anne, mother Christian	3
Jennet McDonald, Betty Grey and Jean Grey	3
Andrew McBeth, wife Jennet, mother Barbara and child	4
William Sutherland, wife Margaret and child	3
Donald Gunn, wife Jennet and 3 children	5
Angus Gunn, wife Jannet and child	3
Robert Sullivan, wife Bell and aunt Elizabeth Fraser	3
Angus Sutherland and mother Elizabeth	2
Alex'r Gunn, nieces Elizabeth and Betty McKay	3
George Bannerman and wife Christy	2
Haman Sutherland	1
James McKay and wife Christy	2
John Matheson (Aultbreakachy) and wife Barbara	2
Robert Gunn, piper	1

"DESERTERS" AND FAMILY	
Hugh Bannerman and sister Isby	2
Alex'r Bannerman and wife Mary	2
John McPherson	1
Hector McLeod	1
John Murray and brother Alex'r	2
Alex'r Matheson	1
John Matheson and wife Mary	2
John Early	1
John Basset and wife	2
Thomas Seymour	1
Isaac Greenfield, John Graham, John Bates, single men	3
John Boggs, Daniel Sullivan, Thos. Martin, single men	3
Laikey Fallon, Roger Foy, Michael Marley, single men	3
John Freeman, Donald McKinnon, Donald McDonald, single men	3
Hugh Swords, James Golden, John Funy(?), single men	3
Edw'd Shiels, Phip. Leyden, Alex'r McLellan, single men	3
William Wallace, Jos. Cathus, Pat Swords, single men	3
Jas. McDonell, Pat Quin, Michael Hyland, single men	3
John Underwood, Peter Dunn, Michael Cryan, single men	3
Austin Joyce, Jas. Pinkman, Jos. Kenny, single men	3
Total	133

Lucille Campey produced a list of those who remained loyal and went north to Playgreen Lake with Archibald McDonald, Peter Fidler and James White in July of 1815 to establish Winipic Settlement. It may not be complete, but it is the closest we have.

SETTLERS	
Alex'r and Christina McLean and family	6
John Pritchard and family	3
Pat McNaulty and family	4
Widow Stewart and family	4
Widow McLean	1
Mrs. Jordan	1

Miss Kennedy	1
John Smith and family	6
Alex'r Sutherland and sister	2
George and Adam Sutherland	2
John Bruce	1
Donald Livingstone and family	3
John McVicar and family	3
Alex'r McLean and family	4
Martin Jordan and family	2
Servants	
A. McLean	1
Duncan McNaughton	1
Samuel Lamont	1
Michael Kilbride	1
Pat Clabby	1
Pat Corrigan (Corcoran?)	1
John Fowler	1
Neil Muhler	1
Peter Dhal	1
Peter Isaacson	1
Hugh McLean	1
Donald McMillan	1
James McIntosh	1
Archibald Curry	1
Colin Campbell	1
Donald McLean	1
John Scarth	1
Price Holte	1
Magnus Spence	1
Andrew Spence	1
John Bourke	1
James White	1
John McLean	1
Total	46

John Rogers's list of passengers who disembarked from the *Prince of Wales*,
August 26, 1815.

NAME	AGE	OCCUPATION
James Sutherland	47	Weaver
Mary (Polson), his wife	48	--
James, his son	12	--
Janet, his daughter	16	--
Catherine, his daughter	14	--
Isabella, his daughter	13	--
William Sutherland	54	Weaver
Isabella, his wife	50	--
Jeremiah, his son	15	--
Ebenezer, his son	11	--
Donald, his son	7	--
Helen, his daughter	12	--
Widow Mathewson	60	--
John, her son	18	Labourer, Schoolmaster
Helen, her daughter	21	--
Angus Mathewson	30	Tailor
Christian Mathewson	18	--
Alex'r Murray	52	Shoemaker (brought out a pair of millstones)
Elizabeth, his wife	54	--
James, his son	16	--
Donald, his son	13	--
Catherine, his daughter	27	--
Christian, his daughter	25	--
Isabella, his daughter	18	--
George McKay	50	Weaver
Isabella (Mathewson), his wife	50	--
Roderick, his son	19	--
Robert, his son	11	--
Roberty, his daughter (Married Donald McKay, Aug. 31, York Factory)	16	--
Donald McKay	31	Labourer

NAME	AGE	OCCUPATION
John McKay, his son	1	--
Catherine Bruce)	33	--
Barbara Gunn	50	--
Wm. Bannerman, her husband	55	--
William B., her son	16	Shoemaker
Alex'r B., her son	14	--
Donald B., her son	8	--
George B., her son	7	--
Ann B., her daughter	19	--
Widow Gunn	40	--
Alex'r McKay, her son	16	--
Adam McK., her son	13	--
Robert McK., her son	12	--
Christian McK., her daughter	19	--
John Bannerman	55	Labourer
Catherine (McKay), his wife	28	--
Alex'r B., his son	1	--
Alex'r McBeth	55	Labourer (brought out a pair of millstones)
Christian (Gunn), his wife	50	--
George McBeth, his son	16	--
Roderick, his son	12	--
Robert, his son	10	--
Adam, his son	6	--
Morrison, his son	4	--
Margaret, his daughter	18	--
Molly, his daughter	18	--
Christian, his daughter	14	--
Alex'r Mathewson	34	Shoemaker
Ann, his wife	34	--
Hugh, his son	10	--
Angus, his son	6	--
John, his son	1	--
Catherine, his daughter	2	--
Alex'r Polson	36	Wheelwright

NAME	AGE	OCCUPATION
Catherine (Matheson), his wife	30	--
Hugh, his son	10	--
John, his son	5	--
Donald, his son	1	--
Ann, his daughter	7	--
William McKay (brought out a pair of millstones)	44	Shoemaker
Barbera (Sutherland), his wife (will give birth to Selkirk on the inland journey)	35	--
Betty McKay, his daughter	10	--
Dorothy, his daughter	4	--
Janet, his daughter	2	--
Joseph Adams	25	--
Mary Adams	23	--
Reginald Green (Sergeant of the Passengers)	21	Miner
George Adams	19	Labourer
Henry Hilliard	19	Labourer
Edward Simmons	20	Labourer
Christian Bannerman (Married Robert McKay, Sept. 4, York Factory)	22	--
Jane Mathewson	22	--
Alexander Sutherland (Sergeant of the Passengers)	25	--
John McDonald (Sergeant of the Passengers)	22	Saddler

List of colony casualties at Seven Oaks, June 19, 1816, as recorded by Alexander Macdonell, July 15, 1816. Nationalities in the original.

KILLED	NATIONALITIES
Robert Semple	Scottish
John Rogers	English
L. O. Wilkinson	English
James White	Scottish
Alexander McLean	Scottish
Ener Holte	Danish — geographically Norwegian
Duncan McNaughton	Scottish
Duncan Macdonell	Scottish
James Moore Sr.	Scottish
James Moore Jr.	Scottish
George Mackenzie	Scottish
Henry Sinclair	Scottish
James Bruin	Scottish
Donald Sutherland	Scottish
John Mehin	Irish
Bryon Gilligan	Irish
James Gardner	Irish
Patt Maroony	Irish
Daniel Donovan	Irish
Adam Sutherland	Scottish
Reginald Green	Irish
WOUNDED	NATIONALITIES
John Bourke	Irish

The names of the men and two of the women who were back in Red River when Lord Selkirk visited in 1817. This list was compiled by George Bryce from the signatures on a petition presented to the earl, so does not include family members.

Donald Livingston, George McBeath, Angus Matheson,

Alex. Sutherland, George Ross, Alexander Murray,

James Murray, John Farquharson, John McLean,

John Bannerman, George McKay, Alexander Polson,

Hugh Polson, Robert McBeath, Alexander McLean,

George Adams, Martin Jordon, Robert McKay,

Wm. McKay, Alex. Matheson, John McBeath,

John Sutherland, Alex. McBeath, Christian Gunn (widow),

Alex. McKay, William Sutherland, Alex. Sutherland Sr.,

James Sutherland, James Sutherland Jr., William Bannerman,

Donald McKay, John Flett, John Bruce,

William Bannerman Jr., Roderick McKay, Ebenezer Sutherland,

Donald Bannerman Jr., Hugh McLean, George Bannerman,

Donald Sutherland, Beth Beathen (male), John Matheson,

George Sutherland, Margaret McLean (widow), Robert MacKay.

INDEX

Note: Pages in italics indicate illustrative material.